THE AUTHOR

ADRIAN HASTINGS was born in 1920 in Kuala Lumpur, Malaya where his father practised law. He was educated at Douai, and at Oxford where he read history. He studied theology in Rome and was ordained in 1955. Father Hastings has worked in Africa since 1958 and belongs now to the diocese of Masaka, Uganda. At present he is working in Tanzania, the East African hierarchy having given him the task of setting out the objectives of Vatican II, which he does by preparing and publishing a fortnightly bulletin called *Post-Vatican II*. In Uganda he has done parish work and has taught in a minor seminary; he was a Visiting Lecturer at Lovanium University, Leopoldville, in the Congo, and has travelled widely in Kenya, South Africa and Basutoland; he is also a staff-member of the *African Ecclesiastical Review*. His previous books include *Prophet and Witness in Jerusalem* (London, 1958), *One and Apostolic* (London, 1963) and *The World Mission of the Church* (London, 1964). He has also contributed articles to *African Ecclesiastical Review*, *New Blackfriars*, *Downside Review*, *The Tablet*, *The Clergy Review*, *The Month*, etc. He is a member of the Joint Anglican-Roman Catholic Commission on Ecumenical Dialogue that had its first meeting at Gazzada in 1966.

Church and Mission
in Modern Africa

Church and Mission
in Modern Africa

by
ADRIAN HASTINGS

FORDHAM UNIVERSITY PRESS

FORDHAM UNIVERSITY PRESS
Bronx, New York 10458

First published 1967

Nihil obstat: TH. VAN ASTEN, W.F.

Imprimatur: ✠ MARK MIHAYO
Archbishop of Tabora
15 March 1967

Library of Congress Catalog Card No.: 67–30321

Printed in Great Britain by
William Clowes and Sons, Limited, London and Beccles

In Memory of

JOSEPH KIWANUKA
Bishop of Masaka
and
Archbishop of Rubaga

23 February 1966

Contents

Preface

THIS BOOK has been written in a variety of moods, under many different roofs, in several countries, and over more than two years of changing personal work and also of a quickly changing Africa. It reflects this. One cannot be for ever revising one's judgments of an earlier month. Chapters take on a character and resist further tampering. They must now stand together though one reflects more the author's mood in England on leave in 1965, another a Ugandan minor seminary in 1964, a third a country parish in southern Buddu early this year or again the way things look today from central Tanzania.

The least I can do is to recall with great gratitude those whose hospitality enabled me to write in peace under their roofs: first my sister Susan in Sheen, and my sisters-in-law in Oxford and Flackwell Heath, all three always so welcoming, the Dominican Nuns at Headington, Canon Diamond in Cambridge, the rectors of Bukalasa, Katigondo and Kipalapala, and last, but very dear, Mgr Kukera and the fathers at Bigada.

With so many people have I talked over this point or that, it would be impossible to mention them singly. But to three who have read all or most of the book in typescript I must express my special thanks: Canon John Taylor, Father van Amelsvoort W.F., and—as ever—my mother who has not only read and re-read but typed and re-typed many parts of it. Naturally for what is finally written I alone can be held responsible.

A number of sections were first written for a special purpose or have already appeared in print. Much of Chapter I was originally a paper read to a Newman Association History week-end in September 1965. Most of Chapter II was published in *New Blackfriars*, August 1965. Section 4 of Chapter III was written for an Ad Lucem group, printed as a leaflet by the Africa Centre, Hinsley House, and then reprinted in *AFER*, October 1966. Sections 5 and 6 of the same chapter appeared in the *Dublin Review*, Spring 1966, and Section 2 in *New Blackfriars*, December 1966. Chapter IV was written as a paper for an African Studies week-end at George Square, Edinburgh in November 1965 and printed in *New Blackfriars*, March 1966. The second section of Chapter VI was in *AFER* for April 1966, while Chapter VII was written for *Teaching All Nations* of April 1965, reprinted in *AFER* and then as a leaflet by the Africa Centre. All have undergone a greater or lesser measure of reshaping since their first appearance, but I remain indebted to the editors of these various reviews for permission to republish here.

ADRIAN HASTINGS

Kipalapala,
18 November 1966

Introduction

I OFFER in the following pages a tentative personal assessment of a vast reality: the Catholic Church in modern Africa and the missionary effort that goes with it. It is, of course, wildly rash to attempt any such thing. The subject is so enormous, the work so diverse that no one can possibly be expert, or near-expert, in the whole. The individual's experience is inevitably limited to certain areas, and even to certain aspects of Church life. Nevertheless it seems so vitally important today to attempt an assessment of this kind, inadequate as it must remain, that I resolved to face the risks involved.

A book of this kind has nothing in common, in its way of tackling ecclesiastical problems, with a text from an ecumenical council. While it is the function of bishops and of others in authority to come to final balanced decisions, it is for theologians and Church writers to discover and examine problems, put forward arguments, propose remedies. Without this sort of thing, effective episcopal decisions cannot follow. Wise decision, whether papal or conciliar, must come out from extensive discussion, and discussion involves the clash of a variety of viewpoints. It would not be desirable that readers should agree with all that follows. On the contrary, many of the matters touched upon surely need further investigation. That is the whole point. A critical assessment of Church work, especially mission work, is needed. Not nearly enough is done to study situations objectively before we attempt to deal with them; nor to evaluate customary methods of work. What the Church often needs is some sort of "Royal Commission Report"—something of the type of the Anglican *Paul Report* on "The Deployment and Payment of the Clergy". Cardinal Rugambwa has written that "Patient field work, frank discussion of problems and their possible solutions, and bold experiments are as necessary in Africa as anywhere else"[1]: there are no words we could more profitably take to heart.

[1] In introduction to Mgr Mullin's *The Catholic Church in Modern Africa*, Geoffrey Chapman, 1965.

The growing science of religious sociology could help us here, but as yet it seems hardly to have been applied to Africa. I cannot help feeling that lack of vigorous thinking of this kind on missionary problems greatly impeded the work of the bishops in Rome. The first drafts for the decree on missionary activity were manifestly inadequate and had to be rejected, and even the final document on the whole seems a fine summary of accepted positions rather than a chart to guide us through a revolutionary situation. Its theology is rich, but it hardly begins to grapple with some of the missionary Church's most pressing practical problems.

Most books on the Church in Africa have been either detailed studies of a particular subject—"Twenty-five years among the Yao", or the history of a particular congregation or famous missionary figure—or they have been travel books, describing a journey, with interviews here and there, illuminating conversations with an archbishop, a politician, a taxi driver, a page on this problem or that, a stress on the obvious contrasts. This sort of thing has its value, but once it gets beyond the platitudinous it can really offer no sort of ground for a judgment: one cannot know whether the selection illustrates what is normal or what is exceptional. But to go further and attempt a real assessment, a generalization, is to face even greater hazards. Limited knowledge and the variety of situations guarantee that no generalization will ever be more than partially true, and will admit of many exceptions; and whenever one makes a general statement, one can be sure that there will be people to jump (often quite properly) to their feet and cry that this is not true of their diocese, of their tribe. Years ago Roland Allen wrote of a "difficulty which besets anyone who would write of missionary methods in general terms: it is not easy for him to find any expressions which are universally true, or any rules which have no exception. The result is that the moment he makes any statement some individual arises to cry out that that statement is not true, because in his experience it is not true in his district. . . ."

Like Roland Allen I can only ask such readers "to pay heed rather to the essential principles than to the particular details".[2] Father James O'Connell, a lecturer in Ibadan University, Nigeria, recently published a penetrating, brief analysis of the Church's

[2] *The Spontaneous Expansion of the Church*, World Dominion Press, 4th ed., 1960, p. 4.

chief needs in that, the greatest of West African countries.[3] My own experience is chiefly East African. The very close agreement of his conclusions with many of the central themes of the present book helps me to feel that the general picture is much the same everywhere, despite important local diversities.

Where my generalizations remain one-sided or the weight of the argument wrongly placed it is for others to show it. The Council has called for scientific research into mission problems,[4] let us not delay to offer it. The African Church today is facing an utterly unprecedented crisis of re-orientation, being hit at one and the same time by three different hurricanes of change. The first is the social and political revolution of Africa—where the Church had geared herself to tackle a pre-medieval society, she is now faced with quickly growing elements of a fully twentieth-century one; the second is the rapidity of Church expansion; the third, the revolution in the universal Church represented by the Vatican Council. To come without shipwreck through such a storm we need not only hard work but quick and correct thinking and the courage to change. Opportunities still wide open to the Church today in Africa may be lost soon for centuries, just as the opportunity she had thirty years ago in China is today only bitter history:

> There is a tide in the affairs of men
> Which taken at the flood leads on to fortune;
> Omitted, all the voyage of their life
> Is bound in shadows and in miseries.
> On such a full sea are we now afloat.

In the ways of the Holy Spirit the Church too has her special moments within the complex flow of human history. They can be fully grasped or—under the pressure of narrow-mindedness, legalism, the identification by Church members of the ecclesiastical world they are accustomed to with the ways of God as such, fear of the out-going—they can be omitted.

Africa is far from wholly modernized. On the contrary. Her societies are mostly poor, unstable, growing still more in numbers than in skills. And there remain considerable communities who

[3] "The Church and Modernisation in Africa", *AFER*, October 1963, pp. 326–37; cf. also "Will the Success of the Church Continue in Africa?", *AFER*, April 1966, pp. 134–45.
[4] Decree on Missionary Activity, n. 29.

have hardly begun to be affected by any of the social and mental changes of our age, who still live in the same tribal world that their ancestors have known for centuries, and the Church has to cater for them as well. With particularly limited resources, she has to be concerned with a strikingly wide range of situations, and consequently requires a very special flexibility of approach. Yet it is just this, perhaps more than anything else, that she has hitherto lacked.

I have tried to tackle this vast subject, not only at the practical level of identifiable immediate needs within a recognized context, but at the deeper levels of theology, of history and religious sociology. Some important fields, notably that of Christian-Islamic relations, I have had almost wholly to ignore; while others are dealt with only very partially. Criticism and disagreement of some sort there cannot help being, but it is not as such that the whole is offered. It is intended as the collaboration of a pen-pusher in a work to which many, missionaries and Africans, have dedicated themselves with a faith, a heroism and a single-minded perseverance that the present author knows only too well he has never begun to emulate. With personal permission given just before he died, the name of the first African bishop in modern times, and the writer's own most affectionate father, is placed upon the dedication page. May this book contribute to the building up of the Church of God in Africa with the fullness of the divine gift and the fullness of the human response that across our fumblings in time, so fickle and so uncomprehending, we may yet attain the better to the unimaginable blessedness of the eternal kingdom.

I

Missionary Principles

"O RIGHTEOUS FATHER, the world has not known thee, but I have known thee; and these know that thou hast sent me. I made known to them thy name, and I will make it known, that the love with which thou hast loved me may be in them, and I in them" (John 17. 25–6).

The Word of God came upon the Father's mission to mankind to bring us truth and love—a sharing in God's own incomprehensible life of knowing and loving. Christ was sent to us, and as we are beings of time and space and vision, he came to us within these dimensions: he was made flesh and dwelt among us and we saw. The mission is from the divine Father but it follows the ways of men. This mission Jesus passed on to the fellowship of his disciples led by the twelve—a fellowship transformed by the covenant of cross and Eucharist into God's new people. The mission to the world is not a praiseworthy activity of God's people in the Church, it is the whole root and purpose of their fellowship. The mission is to draw men into the divine life of truth and love, but that life is already incarnate in the Church's communion which is both a living together of a human kind and "fellowship with the Father and with his Son". The Church's temporal mission is meaningless without this temporal communion: each is for the other and together they are the sacrament upon earth of God's fellowship and God's mission. Coming from God, they lead back to him. The mission is to enlighten the world that it be reborn in God; the communion is the fellowship of his love already established upon earth of those reborn, the initiation into eternal society.

The word "missionary" has customarily received a far narrower connotation than this. It refers to the work of establishing this

Church of God in lands and among human societies where she has as yet no home. This is but part—a privileged part—of the Church's total mission: the particular effort to actuate her universality more completely, to fulfil the Lord's command to teach all nations, to raise the sacramental sign of salvation amid those peoples where it has not as yet been known, to manifest the overflow of God's Spirit in the Christian community which forces it to spread itself ever more widely. Missionary activity is in a special way the sacrament of the universality of God's love.

If its specific purpose is the establishment of the Church in areas where she does not yet exist, the way to its fulfilment might seem obvious and simple, yet in practice this has hardly proved to be so. There are two central aspects of missionary work which need examining. The first is that the aim is to establish *the Church*; now this requires an adequate understanding of what the Church is, how she exists in a place and time, what is required that it can truly be said: "The Church is now present here in this land, among this people". The Church has essential unchanging characteristics that have to be fully realized in her local unit if she is really to be said to be established. At the same time she is a human society, changing vastly in her character according to age and land, and this gives us our second aspect. Her unchanging essence has to be deeply incarnated in a particular milieu; this applies to the expression of doctrine and liturgy and personal devotions, to Church organization, art and music. In a Church which is long established in a country, these things may be expected to adapt themselves little by little according to the temperament and needs of the people, though this does not always follow: Church forms tend to fixation in the pattern of a certain age and hence to become increasingly unadapted to the needs of the same society in a later age. But the problem of adaptation is obviously greater where the Church is approaching a society from the outside, where her active workers are foreigners, brought up within a different milieu and inevitably, to a large extent, identifying their own familiar patterns of Christian life and devotion with Christian life and devotion as such. Hence the second great need: adaptation to a new human and cultural tradition and milieu.

Failure to appreciate the first aspect has resulted in the identification of missionary work with conversion work, with preaching and baptizing rather than with the establishment of a self-supporting, self-ministering, self-propagating unit of the *Catholica*, an active eucharistic community or group of communities, a living member of the universal communion. Missionary work has often failed to advance appreciably beyond the establishment of a passive Christian community, whereas essentially a true Church is an active thing: a society whose life is characterized by the reception not only of baptism but also of confirmation, matrimony and the ministry.

Failure to surmount the second problem has resulted in the practical identification of christianization with Europeanization— a common phenomenon throughout the post-Reformation period. And while this may not always seem to impede missionary work at the start, it will almost inevitably, later, produce a nationalist reaction which identifies the Church with a foreign power and the negation of national loyalty, and anyway such an approach will stifle a full and characteristic contribution of the new people to Christianity.

To start with the first and basic aspect. Failure here can produce, and has produced, permanently maimed Churches. If the ecclesiology of the missionary is one-sided, so will be his missionary practice. And this is what has happened. A defective ecclesiology dominant in the West for centuries has revealed itself in the shape of the new Churches which have emerged in this period.

The Church is God's People, a consecrated nation, a royal priesthood (1 Peter 2. 9). It is a worshipping community, the liturgy being "the summit towards which the activity of the Church is directed ... the fount from which all her power flows":[1] and the essential heart of this worship is the Mass. It provides the Church's characteristic *qua* Church of God. Other communities can pray, others can hold meetings and run schools, but only the Church can offer and receive the sacrament of Christ's redemptive sacrifice. It is this that makes her the Church according to every side of her being. It is the cause of her unity, it is the covenant that makes of those who participate in it the new people of God, it is the body of Christ that transforms those who receive it into itself and so makes of them the body of Christ. It is the one visible activity that Christians have to participate in and come together for, so that

---

[1] Constitution on the Sacred Liturgy, art. 10.

the particular type of society or association which is proper to her is determined eucharistically—it is a communion. The visible unity of the Church is that of men who, presided over by one with apostolic authority, break bread together, offering their gifts and then communicating at a single table, thus sharing in the sacrament, the visible sign, of unity. The invisible unity of the Church in grace-full charity is the proper and direct effect of receiving or desiring this visible sacrament. The life of Christ, the invisible reality, which it is the purpose of the sacramental Church to bring to men, is directly imparted to him who eats Christ's flesh (John 6. 55–8).

The universal Church of God, the world-wide sacrament of his presence, his body on earth, receives its character then from the Eucharist acting in and upon the local community. The Church consists of Churches; she is not just administratively divided into local units, she grows out of them at the same time as they represent her, and bear in themselves of their very nature the structural characteristics of the whole. Each local Church, each "altar-community" (to use a phrase of Rahner's), each eucharistic assembly and the continuing human community which meets when appropriate for this assembly, is a microcosm of the whole Catholic body. The Church is not in her essence a great administrative organization directed from Rome and performing a multitude of activities of roughly equal importance, such as running schools and newspapers and hospitals, and then also celebrating Mass. She is a eucharistic fellowship, both in her universal and in her local character. The liturgy of the bread of life, and its co-relative, the liturgy of the word of life, are central, both for the individual Christian and for the community as a whole. Everything else—and the complexity of human life necessitates that there must be much else if Christ is effectively to sanctify the human condition—has to be ordered to this central experience.

There are, first of all, the essential things: baptism, foremost of all; this is the sacrament of entry into the divine community established on earth by the passion and resurrection. Then the five other sacraments, the purpose of all of which is further to build up this community, each in its own special way. But the end of them all, the *"finis omnium sacramentorum"*, as St Thomas tells us, is the Eucharist (*S. Theol.*, III, 73, 3). All the other sacraments are directed towards this, at making men in one way or another ready for the full union with Christ which is both given and signified by the one perennial sacrament: the communion Mass.

Two sacraments in particular invite our attention. The first is matrimony. The people of God are a people, bound together not only by bonds of supernature but also by those of nature, and at the heart of these latter is marriage. All our basic human relationships grow out of this, and the effective existence of the Church implies precisely the presence of God's people as people, sanctified in matrimony as they are sanctified in communion. The two inevitably go together among men of flesh and blood, and in practice the state of matrimony is the best indication of the real establishment of the working *Laos* of God, and not of a mere horde of baptized individuals.

The second is orders. The Church as shaped by Christ has always required presidency, a teaching authority, that is to say the ministry, whose function it is to break bread, to see that the other sacraments are duly administered, the word of God taught, the community of the faithful guided in its needs. The ministry must be both universal and local. Apostolic authority is single—the one college of bishops, centred upon and led by the pope—but this authority has to be present at the local level, the actual worshipping community: the individual bishop surrounded and helped by his own presbyterium.

Around this essential structure of the Church's life centred upon the word of God and the sacraments, many other things have grown up, according to the particular needs of age and place: other prayers and devotions, schools, institutions and associations of every kind. They enable men to enter better into the essentials and then transform their social environment. They build up the Church's communion and they express her mission—the essential service which the Church must give the world.

Ecclesiology is never irrelevant to missiology. The formation of new Churches must be based on a right conception of what the Church is and of the hierarchy of things within the Church, otherwise they are bound to wither up or grow into strange shapes. This indeed is what has happened in the past, and the prime cause of it was that the conception of the Church and of Christian life in the home Churches themselves had got out of focus. In the Middle

Ages the Church had come almost to be identified with the hierarchy or the clergy, the regular communion of the laity had ceased, and the Mass was looked upon as something done by a priest rather than as a genuine community action. Inevitably the great missions of the post-Reformation period carried this sort of Christian life abroad, and consequently tried to create new Churches on principles which were partially defective: men could even be regularly baptized but not admitted to communion.[2] South America presents the most striking example of this. If communion was often withheld, far more so were orders.[3] There was no true vision of what the Church really must be, everywhere and always, if she is to be true to herself. Instead of the formation of new local altar-communities, the Church obtained a vast fringe consisting of a sort of second-standard citizenry, baptized and obliged to conform to the moral law, but almost deprived of the Eucharist, except in danger of death or other special circumstances, and dependent upon a ministry recruited from far away. Again, translation of the Scriptures hardly entered into mission work at all; it might indeed be regarded as reprehensible. What went wrong in the missions was really a sort of caricature of what was already wrong in Europe. The results were disastrous: the Church could not grow healthily in such a way and either petered out entirely or declined into torpor.

It is clear that we are past such glaring mistakes today, yet it seems to me that a juridical type of ecclesiology rather than a eucharistic or sacramental one is still there behind very much missionary work in the modern period. Old misconceptions about the Eucharist as being a valuable extra rather than as the one and only possible centre for a Christian community, large or small, have survived, backed up in practice by the difficulty of obtaining enough priests to implement any other vision of the Church. The blame here, obviously, in no way rests with the individual missionary, but rather with the Church's norms for the formation of clergy. Those norms were only defensible with a juridical type of ecclesiology, which considered the Church as a great organization and did not really worry too much about the impossible difficulties which

---

[2] See S. Neill, *A History of Christian Mission*, p. 173; John McAndrew, *The Open-Air Churches of Sixteenth-Century Mexico* (Harvard University Press, 1965), pp. 84–5.
[3] Cf. Neill, *op. cit.*, pp. 173–5, 203; J. McAndrew, *op. cit.*, pp. 40–2.

were being set in the way of creating new altar-communities in mission lands. But if the Church really is both universally and locally a eucharistic fellowship, then our methods, ways of recruiting and forming clergy, and so on, must be geared to the basic theological facts. At present Africa is full of communities of Christians, living far away from a priest, regularly attending only a catechist's services, and able to share in Mass only very occasionally when a priest visits them on safari. We realize this is not the ideal and devoutly hope that sooner or later more priests will come; but we do not seem to realize just how wrong it is, how opposed to a true ecclesiology, and how it demonstrates that our very methods and deep pattern of mission thinking remain defective—the hangover of the even more glaring defects of past ages.

No ministry, no Church. The strategy of extending the Church and of founding new Churches is integrally bound up with that of extending the ministry quickly and effectively to members of the new community. One cannot build up the Church by granting baptism but withholding orders. Yet this is in practice what we have largely done in the past and are even still doing today. It is not, of course, the intention. Missionary doctrine is quite clear about the importance of forming a local clergy; it has been stressed in every one of the great missionary encyclicals, beginning with *Maximum Illud* of Pope Benedict XV in 1919. Everyone realizes the importance of this work. It was widely realized in the past too, and constantly emphasized in the directives of the Roman congregation of *Propaganda Fide*, ever since the congregation's foundation in the seventeenth century to supervise mission work. The founders of individual missionary societies were equally clear on the subject. Thus the aims of the *Société des Missions Etrangères* of Paris were stated officially in a document of 1700: the primary intention was "... to hasten the conversion of the heathen, not only by proclaiming the Gospel to them, but above all by preparing ... and raising to ecclesiastical orders those of the new Christians or of their children who are considered best suited to that holy state; in order to create in each country a clerical order and a hierarchy such as Jesus Christ and the apostles have appointed in the Church. They realized that is the only way in which true religion can be established on a permanent footing; and that, moreover, it will be difficult for Europe to go on for ever supplying priests, who take a long time to learn the language, and in time of persecution are easily recognized, arrested, driven out, or put to death. . . . "[4] Again, Monsignor de Marion Brésillac, the founder of the S.M.A., wrote in 1842 during the retreat before beginning his missionary career: "Above all, I implore the blessing of God on my desire to use every possible means to direct all my own work and thought towards training a native clergy . . . which has hardly been thought about yet at all. It is a pure dream, more brilliant than solid, to think of converting any people without a native clergy."[5] And many more have said the same in almost every age, and also made real efforts to achieve something in this line. As the Paris missionary society said, the example was given by Jesus Christ and the apostles: Jesus chose his apostles immediately from the ranks of his disciples, weak and uncomprehending as they were. They were not to be the crown or the culmination of his work of founding a community of believers, but its foundation stone. Church and ministry went together. It was the same for the apostles: how quickly Paul and Barnabas returned to Lystra, Iconium and Antioch, which had only just been evangelized, in order to appoint presbyters (Acts 14. 22). As is said in the first epistle of St Clement of the apostles: "Preaching in different regions and different towns, they established their first fruits as bishops and deacons of the future believers, after having tested them by the Spirit" (1 Clement, 42, 1–4). They established their *first fruits*: the giving of the ministry has got to be done at once. A Christian community must have its Eucharist from the word go; a community that can bear the gift of the Spirit in baptism is *ipso facto* worthy to communicate, and among those who are worthy to communicate must be found those who can celebrate and communicate others. The mistake has often been, while firmly believing in the importance of forming a local clergy to consider it as the crown, the culmination of mission work, whereas it has in fact to come in right from the start. In fact we have not, and still do not, follow apostolic example in mission work. Cardinal Costantini was quite right when he urged the restoration of the "liberty and methods of apostolic times to mission activity".[6] It is

[4] Quoted in S. Neill, *A History of Christian Missions*, Penguin, p. 180.
[5] Quoted in J. Todd, *African Mission*, Burns & Oates, p. 19.
[6] *Va e annunzia il Regno de Dio*, Brescia 1943, II, p. 24.

sad, however, that as Secretary of *Propaganda*, he did not lead us more effectively to that restoration.

The reasons why delay, ever more delay, has in fact time after time prevented the good intentions of Rome and of missionaries from coming to anything very much in this field were doubtless many. But I see two as particularly important. One, a psychological one: the desire to play safe, the fear of being imprudent, lack of trust in new converts. People can always fail one, even after years of preparation, but the Church cannot grow except in an atmosphere of trust, trust in new converts, when they have been reasonably tested, and trust in the Holy Spirit. Sometimes we seem to trust only in some sort of fool-proof system, and not in the Spirit of God. The second reason is that the training for priests imposed by the Council of Trent was far too hard for new Churches. It just was not possible to establish Tridentine standards of seminary formation and a long course of Latin in many mission lands. A few priests might be trained in this way, especially in a westernized place like Goa, but by and large it was not possible. Mechanisms suitable for adult Churches, and indeed for adult Churches of a particular character and culture, were being imposed in quite different conditions. The human character of the ministry and ways of training for it must vary and do vary according to the society and the condition of the Church in which it has to function, and norms which could apply fruitfully to the old Christian countries of Europe simply stifled growth when applied in mission lands.

Lack of trust in new Christians, especially non-European Christians, and a bad system explain why the good intentions of many missionaries came to so little. At the beginning of the twentieth century there was still no Latin-rite Catholic bishop of Asian or African stock. The same thing can be true today and for the same reason: the theoretical desire for vocations is not enough to obtain them: the system of recruitment and training and the subsequent life they are to live must be related to a given society. Failure to do this has produced a situation in mission lands which we have taken basically as normal, even though everyone believes that ideally it must be rectified: the existence of thousands of baptized Christians living without regular priestly ministration. The unit of the Church has ceased to be an "altar-community" and if the Church is visibly represented at all in the local African community, it is generally by

a catechist. The local community is, maybe, one that prays together but it is not one that regularly celebrates the Eucharist
together.[7] The majority of the faithful are quite unable to join in the
Mass even once a week. Priests strain themselves to the utmost to
get round the villages as often as possible, but they and their people
are basically victims of a mistaken ecclesiology and a mistaken
attempt to regard one pattern of the ministry as necessarily always
and everywhere valid. The mistaken, or defective, ecclesiology is
one which does not have the Eucharist as the very heart of both
the universal and local Church. The mistaken pattern of ministry is
a too European, post-Tridentine, Latin one. It practically comes to
this that for the sake of keeping the Mass in Latin, said by a well-
educated celibate, we have deprived countless people of having any
regular Mass at all: the educational standards we have demanded
for all the clergy without exception have made it impossible to have
a clergy at all adequate in number to perform its most essential
(and simple) tasks. Instead of the ministry being ordered to the
Church and her needs, we have subordinated the Church to a particular pattern of ministry.

To turn now to the second aspect of missionary work, the aspect
of adaptation, an opening can be provided by some striking pages
of *Requiem for a Parish*[8] where Father John Foster has described
the Church's modern missionary technique as he believes it to be:

> Much of what we know today about the mystery of adaptation
> in the life and mission of the Church has been revealed to us in
> recent years through what has been taking place in her "labora-
> tory" of the foreign mission fields. . . . In pagan countries of
> Africa and Asia she could break free of fetters which, in Europe,
> had tended to impede her natural developments and to conserve
> her structure at the expense of her inner growth.
>   . . . In the mission fields, the Church was able to reveal again
> something of her rich personality. By examining with clinical

---

[7] The position in other communions is often not much different. Dr Brown,
former Anglican Archbishop of Uganda and Rwanda-Burundi, writes: "When
I arrived in my own diocese I found one priest, with no ordained assistant,
responsible for ninety congregations, but I suppose the average with us
may be about fifteen" (*Relevant Liturgy*, S.P.C.K., p. 53).
[8] The Newman Press, Maryland, 1962, pp. 97–100.

precision every human condition, she could uncover the deep affinity of correspondence existing between the authentic expression of "human-ness" and the fullness of her own truth and life. . . .

True to the first principle of her missionary action—"to understand and to be understood"—the Church, on entering pagan countries, had first to find points of contact at which she could insert her truth of faith into their truths of actuality. Her work was not primarily to build mission stations, erect churches, schools, and hospitals. Wherever she came, she had first to be the pupil, to sit at the feet of the native people, to understand their ways, their wants, their aspirations and hopes, their culture and civilization.

Again it was not merely a matter of knowing their language, of being able to communicate her doctrine in their tongue. She had gradually to take on their mentality, to be incarnated in their culture, to propose Christian truth in their thought forms, to give Christian supernatural life as something which was a complete answer to all their human needs. . . .

When Christian missionaries came to Africa, for example, they found an authentic human art which had that universal quality making it a valid interpretation of their way of life. . . . Lacking our modern techniques, African native art could still be distinguished by a natural spontaneity absent in modern Western decorative art, with designs which were alive and spiritually moving. . . . The missionary could not ignore this universal value in a pagan people's art. . . . He learned to respect and reverence it as the expression of the life and beliefs of a people, and made it the under-pinning of the new Christian order offered to them.

It is a delightful picture of mission work that Fr Foster presents, but it seems to me, alas, to be largely make-believe. As a whole, and with exceptions, the mission work of the last 100 years has been almost exactly the opposite of what Fr Foster describes. Many missionaries have become masters of linguistics and some deeply knowledgeable in social customs but most have at least seemed uninterested in the art and handicrafts, the music and songs, the history and folk-lore, the herbal knowledge and traditional medicine of the peoples they are busy evangelizing. And all these things have wilted before them. The sort of approach Fr Foster speaks of was truly that of Ricci or de Nobili in seventeenth-century Asia, but of very few missionaries in modern Africa. It certainly has not been characteristic of them "to sit at the feet of the native people", to make African art "the under-pinning of the new Christian order", to break free of the structural fetters that the Church has worn in Europe. Her teaching has been almost universally expressed in Western scholastic formulas, her liturgy has not been adapted at all, her churches are full of cheap European art of the poorest type, her hymnology is a hotch-potch of popular melodies picked up from the missionaries' homelands, her development has been constantly fettered by the canon law and types of Church structure which were worked out for long-established Churches in western Europe. Today there is indeed in some restricted circles an intense concern for African art and music and thought patterns, the adaptation of every aspect of Church life. But such things could not possibly with honesty be said to be characteristic of the Church's mission work as it has in fact been carried out, and as it manifests itself today in the normal character of the new Churches which have arisen as a result of that work.

Most probably it would be naïve to imagine that, substantially, at least in sub-Saharan Africa, anything else could have happened. Throughout eastern and southern Africa there was little visual art beyond the simplest decoration of mats, pots and similar objects. Except along the West African coast and among certain tribes of the Congo basin "designs which were alive and spiritually moving" were simply not to be found, though in the matter of the vocal arts it was indeed a different story. But even the great artistic traditions that did exist—as at Benin and Ife—were almost incomprehensible to, and in fact largely ignored by, all missionaries before, say, the last thirty years. Again, African cosmologies are difficult enough to understand even for the trained anthropologist, and in the nineteenth century the science of anthropology was still in its infancy. In the East missionaries could, if they wanted, study the great classics of religious literature without too much difficulty, but there was nothing similar to be found in Africa. But above all, in an age when the Church in the West was more than ever wedded to a single way of expressing doctrine—the neoscholastic—and before the biblical and liturgical movements had begun to have any effect, it would have been next to impossible for missionaries really to have worked out the sort of approach which Fr Foster describes. In earlier ages readiness to accept variation and to make adaptations had come almost naturally to churchmen, but the development of canon law and the enforcement of Tridentine regulations steadily eroded the areas in which adaptation could be allowable, while the whole psychology of Europe in the second half of the nineteenth century—the Victorian age—with its enormous self-confidence, belief in progress as incarnated in its own achievement, and consequent sense of superiority, was most inimical to a supple missionary approach or to the commencement of what today we describe as dialogue. Missionaries inevitably shared this general psychology just as they shared the ecclesiastical attitudes of their age and country.

Today, these attitudes both secular and ecclesiastical have largely passed, and it might be thought that from many points of view we have now an almost ideal situation for a really intelligent missionary policy with a deep adaptation of all that is changeable in the Church's teaching and life to the mentality and circumstances of missionary countries. We are now very willing to recognize the values in other cultures—we no longer believe in the inherent superiority of the West; secondly, we have in the modern sciences of anthropology, comparative religion and religious sociology, instruments to help us both in the understanding of other religions and milieus and in the subsequent tasks of adaptation; thirdly, within the Catholic Church herself we have today an enormously increased willingness to modify inessentials and to admit diversity.

Yet, in fact, the difficulties in the way today in Africa of effectively actuating a policy of missionary adaptation seem to me almost as overwhelming as those of the past. Without a searching examination and appreciation of these difficulties talk of missionary adaptation remains superficial and unconvincing and its actuation somewhat naïve.

There is, firstly, the whole basic problem of adaptation in itself which—to be of value—is a process far more subtle than might be imagined. It is true that Church authority has repeatedly urged that all that is not openly opposed to faith or morals in a pagan culture be encouraged to pass across into Christian society. Religion is not culture and the adoption of Christianity certainly should not involve the adoption of a Western culture. But in fact though Christianity can certainly adhere in a great variety of cultures, that is not quite the same thing as saying that she can necessarily adhere in cultures already formed without her. This is very clear in the case of most African peoples which have been of a monolithic ideological type. Social life, religion, culture are all inextricably mixed, and indeed justify one another. The religious cosmology is expressed in ancestor cults, clan ceremonies, age-group initiations. Every aspect of the life of a tribe is bound together, and to make within it a division of culture from religion is meaningless. It can truly be said that to be a Kikuyu is itself a religion.[9] The acceptance of Christianity is bound to produce a fearful social and psychological dislocation; indeed if it did not, if Christianity was not seen as so supremely relevant to society and culture that it is bound to over-turn an order of things which has developed apart from Christ, one might ask of what significance it can really be for human life. The "adaptation" required in missionary work can never then be seen as the relation of static entities: Christianity and a native culture. It is rather a dynamic struggle of religious, cultural and psycho-logical dimensions in which Christianity, as a human phenomenon, must change its appearance and a new society and culture must come slowly to birth. Thus, though it is surely wrong to impose some outside existing culture (French, Portuguese, English, etc.) on new Christians as part of the conversion process, as has so often been done in the past, the reverse of this cannot mean that Chris-tianity can simply be grafted on to some existing, more or less static native culture—the very idea being a denial both of what Chris-tianity is and what a culture is.[10] Religious revolution must, in short, involve social and cultural revolution if it is itself to be worthy of the name. For culture—the intelligent use of material things and the significance given to them within the pattern of a particular society—inevitably grows out of the accepted world view or

[9] Cf. F. Welbourn, *AFER*, January 1965, pp. 58–60.
[10] Cf. the trenchant judgment of a professional anthropologist speaking of a Congolese tribe: "There can be no question of grafting the spirit of Chris-tianity on to an old society, and expecting that, apart from the excision of a few incompatible institutions, the old culture will survive the operation. Lele culture, christianized, would be quite unrecognizable, changed from top to bottom and in its most intimate recesses", Mary Douglas on "The Lele of the Congo", in *The Church and the Nations*, ed. A. Hastings (Sheed & Ward, 1959), p. 89.

standard of values of that society. A revolution in the standard of values and ideals has to be expressed culturally. Missionary adaptation basically means allowing a new pattern to evolve both ecclesiastically and culturally. One will sin against it as much by identifying it with the surface adoption of certain native cultural motifs and pinning them on, so to say, to a really unchanged Christianity—as some missionary circles now seem to advocate—as by the old-fashioned impressing of foreign cultural motifs on a new Christian group with the "*assimilado*" method.

Secondly, a great difficulty arises from the rapidity of change under the impact of external pressures, that is characteristic of Africa today. This impact has even been presented under missionary auspices; for the importation of a completely new system of education, which, more than anything else, has become the characteristic element in missionary work, has certainly had at least as much cultural as religious effect. It was missionaries who originally took the lead in teaching Africans mathematics, biology, history and the rest, and the effect of the injection of such teaching on a large scale into a pre-scientific society is obviously to break up very much of its traditional way of life and culture. The children with their arithmetic books and their home-work have no longer the time or inclination to learn the old songs and the old ways of singing or the laborious old technical skills—they hope to buy what they want in the village shop instead. If, *per impossibile*, the missionary had tried from the beginning to insert the religious teaching within the rhythm of life and a pattern of other instruction that really belonged to the society he was approaching, things might have been different. But then, anyway, he has not been alone; government and trade pressed on the old society as relentlessly as he, while young Africans have themselves sought the new vistas with all the energy at their command. One may not blame the missionary Church for all that she has done and yet it still remains naïve to suggest that she is trying to "preserve intact" "anything in these people's way of life which is not indissolubly bound up with superstition and error",[11] when in fact she is concentrating her personnel and money so largely on the development of educational and medical work of a Western type. Very possibly the Church

[11] Constitution on the Sacred Liturgy, art. 37.

cannot and should not do otherwise—she is assisting in a cultural evolution which Africa wants and needs—but she cannot at the same time glibly dissociate her work from the "cultural" field, for it has constantly been breaking up one cultural pattern and inserting another.

Today in Africa, the Churches are no longer the chief force making for this process of general change. Quite apart from any missionary influence, there is no tribal culture in Africa, except for that of some more isolated groups, that can long retain its integral character in the social revolution that is sweeping the continent. We are, in a way, in a more difficult situation than that of Ricci who had a clear social and cultural pattern to deal with in adopting the message and life of the Gospel. We have not. The old cultures of Africa were closely bound to the size of the society they informed and the mental horizons of the people. Today men are being drawn out of their tribal societies into new inter-tribal, national ones and the frontiers of knowledge are infinitely greater. The old ways cannot retain their collective hold even though parts of them do retain in one way or another enormous influence on individuals and groups of individuals who at one and the same time share in the new society and the old. Ancestor cults, for instance, may temporarily assume a greater importance than ever for the urbanized African, as a help in a situation which gives him great psychological insecurity but does not provide him with a substitute world view.[12] An anthropological training remains vital to help missionaries to be of use in the confused psychological and social evolution Africans are now undergoing individually and collectively. But in the circumstances of today, the aim of missionary adaptation cannot be simply the relating of the Church to the old society and culture, for though the anthropologist may still be able to describe the latter as a living whole, it is in fact quickly ceasing to be recognizable as such, except among the more remote peoples. Adaptation has rather to be essentially *ad hoc* and be aimed at relating Church life, consistently with its own inherent principles, to a new society, whose general pattern, ethos, culture, cannot be clearly expressed because they simply do not as yet exist.

[12] Cf. J. C. Mitchell, "The Meaning in Misfortune for Urban Africans", pp. 192–203, in *African Systems of Thought*, ed. Fortes and Dieterlen, O.U.P., 1965.

The coming pattern of African life and thinking will certainly not be simply Western; the element of African tradition will remain a determining force, though what it will consist of is not easy to say precisely: so much of what one calls typically African is really typical of a pre-scientific, pre-industrial society; so many characteristic "African" attitudes are also characteristic of medieval Europe.

Certainly Africans today are being drawn more and more into the new great cosmopolitan culture of the modern world: a culture that, in its chief lines, is non-national, infinitely complex and yet ultimately unified. African schools and universities are shaped upon European ones; within them the future leaders of the continent receive some sixteen years of concentrated mental formation of a Western type; while what is most dynamic throughout the continent is moving rapidly in the directions characteristic of the rest of the modern world, still largely inspired and directed by the Americo-European West, it would be dangerous and pointless for the Church to move effectively in another and contrary direction.

Thirdly, if it can be said that there is coming into existence today a vastly complex and diversified, but still basically one, world culture, it is also true that the same sort of thing is happening within the Church herself. Missionary adaptation in the past generally presupposed an already existing pluralism of religious tradition within the Church: the piety, religious practices, theological attitudes of Antioch were different from those of Alexandria; those of Ireland differed from those of Italy, those of Spain from those of Germany, and so on. But today again we are tending towards a complex homogeneity of theological outlook and devotional practice. Current theology, modern liturgical devotion is in no way national. One chief effect of the modern movements both in theology and in liturgy has been to rub away long-standing national divergences. And what is happening within the old Churches must happen too within the new ones. In an age of rapid translation, the mass diffusion of new books, the overwhelming weight attached to the popular name, it would be as bizarre to expect the growth of a characteristic African liturgy or theology as to expect the growth of English ones. The same would seem to be true in the fields of religious and liturgical art. In the modern globally-minded atmosphere both of Catholicism and of culture generally, the very presuppositions of missionary adaptation have to be re-thought.

Fourthly, in our work of Church building in Africa today, we cannot, almost anywhere, start with a clean slate. The Church of Africa already exists, and we must thank God that it does. But it exists, inevitably, as the missionaries of the last seventy years have formed it, and the work was strongly done. The Church of Africa, as it now exists, is undoubtedly an unnecessarily Europeanized one, formed on the exact canonical model of the Church in Europe, its priests formed over long, long years to adhere faithfully to the theological manuals, the devotional practices, the aesthetic standards that the mass of the clergy of Europe took for granted until, say, twenty years ago. And the winds of ecclesiastical change have hardly been felt as yet in large sections of the so-called mission field. To be realistic, mission policy has to proceed, not according to ideal principles, but from the existent situation and in some ways one has to admit that the discussion of missionary adaptation as it is often carried on today can become an unreal one. There are, of course, many areas where pioneer work is being done among less developed tribes and basic issues of adaptation can still be tackled vigorously and imaginatively within the initial stages of a new Christian community. But by and large the adaptation which is needed urgently in Africa today shares as much the pastoral character of the contemporary *aggiornamento* of an existing Church as one of ecclesial initiation into a new society. It is not, of course, any the less urgent for that. What is special to the African situation is the scale of the Church's growth, the foreignness of so much that has already been deeply built in and is still being so, the lack of committed personnel and at all adequate resources, and a certain passivity of the local Church.

The basic obligation to be relevant—to these people, to this society here and now—does not alter. Nor does the obligation to present the Church in all her completeness. We have to give the Church *fully*, and we have to give the Church *relevantly*. These are the essentials of a sound missiology. It will be the aim of subsequent chapters to examine their bearing in detail upon the history and present state of the Church in Africa.

II

Placing the Mission in the Context of Today[1]

THE MODERN WORLD, and indeed the modern Church, have their own exigencies in the field of mission. Our work has surely to undergo a thorough renewal, it cannot continue to be carried on with either all the presuppositions or the attitudes and methods that have prevailed with relatively slight changes over the last century. Without doubt the need for this renovation is well recognized, but its why and how have still to be thought through, even the conciliar contribution in this field appearing not wholly adequate. The fact that an earlier draft had to be rejected outright, despite its having been presented with the full approval of the Congregation of Propaganda, suggests how far even the official leaders of mission have been lagging behind in constructive missionary thinking. The rewritten decree is surely a great improvement, but the most valuable decrees of the Council are those which have followed upon a great deal of careful thinking and writing by theologians. Brief conciliar discussion cannot remedy the lack of this, and in our case the preceding thought was still not sufficient. There remains, then, a wide gap between the mission thinking and Church structures we need today and the actual pattern that still exists.

The character of mission work is being altered not only by all the very great social and political change that is going on in the receiving lands of the missionary apostolate—Asia, Africa, South

[1] Some ideas in this chapter I owe to a fine paper by Dr Visser 't Hooft, "Missions as the Test of Faith," in *Witness in Six Continents*, ed. R. Orchard, Edinburgh House Press, 1964, pp. 20–28.

3

America—but also by a world-wide mental revolution. There is a change of mentality in Western countries, or rather in the whole climate of world opinion, and this new *Zeitgeist* is on the whole decidedly anti-missionary; again, there is the whole theological renewal within the Church and its new insights into the nature of mission, together with the ecumenical movement. It is these mental and theological changes that we will consider here.

It may be noted that there has nearly always been a very considerable and regrettable gap in the Church between the work of theologizing and the work of evangelizing. The theologian sits upon his chair of theology at the centre of the Church, in some well-established Christian citadel; seldom has he personal experience of the missionary context, while the missionary, far away on the frontier of the Church, has had little time or inclination to express himself. There has been almost no dialogue between the two, hence a certain lack of missionary perspective within almost all the tradition of Christian theology. Only St Paul himself really combined the life of the missionary with that of the theologian. Since apostolic times, with the exception of St Athanasius, it would be difficult to name a Christian theologian of the first rank who has really had a personal commitment to the Church's contemporary mission to the non-Christian world.

The gap between Christian thinking and the mission to the world beyond was certainly greatest among the Protestant reformers of the sixteenth century; with most of whom there is no glimmering of a consciousness of the Church's world missionary dimension. They could blandly deny that universality was a characteristic of the Church: "Go into the world" was a command given only to the first apostles, it does not bind the subsequent Church; while instead Matthew 23. 15—"Woe upon you, scribes and pharisees, you hypocrites that encompass sea and land to gain a single proselyte," was applied to the Catholic missionary effort of the time. Certainly in the sixteenth century the divorce between the new theology and mission was almost absolute, as modern Protestants will sadly admit. And it lasted a long time. As late as 1796 the Assembly of the Church of Scotland could pass a motion that "to spread abroad the knowledge of the Gospel among barbarians and heathen nations seems highly preposterous, in so far as it anticipates, it even reverses, the order of nature".[1] Catholic theology could never go to these lengths, though the sense of world mission had largely disappeared from the ecclesiology of the later Middle Ages and that helps to explain its continued and accentuated disregard by Protestant theologians. But in the sixteenth century the Counter-Reformation was not only a theological revival but also a missionary one. The Jesuits took the lead in both and there was a genuine cross-fertilization. There is a real sense of theology behind the work of seventeenth-century figures like Matteo Ricci, and Francesco Ingoli, the first secretary of *Propaganda Fide*, but even then little sense of mission seemed to penetrate back the other way into contemporary Catholic ecclesiology.

Today, again, we live in an age of "new theology" and the word "mission" is certainly a key one in it. But its contemporary use has often seemed to missionaries, accustomed to its unique application to the evangelization of the non-Christian world, as somehow a belittling of their own task. The "France, *pays de mission*" school seems to them in a way to have undermined the sense of the primary mission to peoples among whom the Gospel has not yet been preached.[2] Hence a modern work such as *A Mission Theology* by Père Henry, O.P., is not concerned only with the missionary in the old sense, but rather with pastoral work in places where the Church has been long established. In essence this broadening is right and inevitable. The "mission" of the Church is indeed a universal work; it cannot be limited theologically to those priests and Christians working outside their own countries or in lands where there are very few Christians. Mission and Communion are the two fundamental aspects of Church life, and both involve everyone. An idea of mission which restricts it to the "foreign

---

[1] A. Vidler, *The Church in an Age of Revolution*, Pelican, p. 248.

[2] Cf. the complaints of Fr E. Hillman, "On Missionary Activity", *The Clergy Review*, October 1964, pp. 625–30, and Bishop De Souza in a Council speech. Fr Hillman has developed his argument in *The Church as Mission*, Herder, 1965. See also his article "The Main Task of the Missions", in *Concilium*, March 1966, pp. 3–7. Much that he says is most valuable and enlightening, but to maintain that "mission" should only be used to refer to work among peoples where the Church has never yet been established would be misguided. For another approach (but not the last word), see M.-J. Le Guillou, O.P., "Mission as an Ecclesiological Theme", in *Concilium*, March 1966, pp. 43–67.

mission" is theologically quite inadequate, but equally an idea of mission which does not manifest the specific importance in the Church's life, and for the manifestation of her nature, of the mission in the traditionally accepted sense—of action not only going out from one's own eucharistic community but also going out of and beyond the human community within which one's own local Church (or even any Church at all) has been enfleshed—fails to do justice to the full scope of the catholicity which is, and always has been, essential to the Church's mission properly understood. A notion of mission which does not do real justice to the special need to reach out to "the ends of the earth" is a defective one.

Practically speaking, a gap between theology and missionary work still remains. Our great theologians lecture in the Catholic universities of Germany, France, the U.S. and elsewhere; they have seldom the experience in depth of the missionary situation in a world where the environment does not share in that of traditional Christendom.

The new theology has very much to offer the missionary today, and even precisely in his missionary perspective—as is obvious when one thinks of names like de Lubac, Teilhard de Chardin, or when one reads the important two-volume work of Fr Le Guillou on *Mission et Unité*—but one still feels the need for the Catholic theologian not only to lecture about mission but also to share more directly in the missionary experience at its most acute, together with the growing of the young Church in the world of Afro-Asia. A serious theological work such as Fr Hillman's *The Church as Mission*, written by a practising missionary, is still something quite exceptional—and all the more to be welcomed on that account. But, frankly, at present, one often finds the comments of even distinguished theologians on these topics somewhat jejune. Perhaps this will not change until these lands bring forth their own theologians, as India is at last beginning to do. Raymond Panikkar is a striking example. But these too must beware of dwelling in new Catholic citadels rather than combining their theologizing with a living missionary confrontation. It is necessary for the health of Christian theology that the mission should not only receive from it, but also give to it; that the leaders of Christian thinking should share in its experience of Church-building and of the non-white world.

Missionary work certainly does not appeal much to the modern secular mind. There is a passion for giving help without "strings", while the missionary's work may be characterized as one of imparting strings—strings of the mind. He does not only intend to give help of an educational or material kind, but also to win belief, loyalty, a new commitment. The world today seems divided between the internationalist and the nationalist, and neither has much time for the missionary. The nationalist sees him as trespassing on the cultural and ideological autonomy of his own nation, denying the legitimacy of the totalitarian State he may be in the course of building. The internationalist sees the missionary as a little absurd, a survival from the past: international harmony is not going to be promoted, he argues, by people in one group trying to convert those of another. The missionary may be of some value in helping to establish an educated and orderly society among primitive conditions, but his primary aim is simply ruled out of court. If these religious beliefs have any validity at all, the modern approach is to recognize them as all of more or less equal value, and so we are back at a syncretism which seems to appeal far more to the tolerant, uncommitted modern mind than the ultimate exclusiveness of the Christian missionary.

There are many Catholics who surely feel a good deal of sympathy for this attitude. One senses a certain *malaise* even among believers where missionary work is concerned. There are a number of reasons for this besides the general one of infection by the climate of opinion surrounding them. There is with some a feeling of irritation at the naïve approach of much missionary propaganda, at times carried on by priests who have never been on the mission at all, while a fair number of their hearers may have worked in Africa or Asia and know a good deal about actual conditions there. At a deeper level there is a change in beliefs and attitudes. In fact it must be admitted that much of the missionary incentive in the past came from the belief that it was either impossible or next to impossible to be saved without baptism, faith and explicit membership of the Church. The reason for evangelization was then extremely obvious: countless souls were constantly falling into hell throughout Africa and Asia because there was simply no missionary there to instruct and baptize. Altered attitudes towards salvation outside the visible Church and towards the whole positive content of non-Christian religions has changed this and may seem for many to knock the very stuffing out of missionary work. Again, the European outsider often notices how much more religious and spiritual those seem to be who have been brought up in, and adhered to, their traditional beliefs, say Muslim or Buddhist, than many new Christians who have received baptism and some meagre instruction in mission schools, but whose traditional religious sense seems rather to have been impaired than strengthened as a result of it. As a matter of practice the arrival of the Christian mission—a big organizational unit, often providing inevitably a mere minimum of personal contact between the Christian missionary and his new converts—can upset not only traditional religion but also natural moral attitudes. Instead of growing up in *pietas* the young men are cut off from and despise their pagan parents. Disrespect for the elders, in no way taught by the missionaries, may yet arise almost inevitably from their influence on the young and introduction of so many new ways. Baptism comes to be seen as a step towards schooling and the new (in fact, despite the missionary, largely secularized) society of the twentieth century rather than as entry to eucharistic fellowship with Christ and the members of his body. All this makes some doubt the religious point of the missionary effort in Afro-Asia. If Christian conversion is not required for salvation after death, and in this life appears as a disturbing rather than consolidating force in non-European society, what is the justification of the "foreign mission"? The approach of the *consecratio mundi* may be extolled, but that of evangelization, of direct conversion is felt to be alien to the modern mentality. It is given the dirty name of "proselytism". It will be agreed that if an individual wants to change his religion, he must of course be free to do so, but should we make a vast and deliberate effort to multiply such cases? Many modern Christians would prefer to give their money to OXFAM, to the non-denominational assistance of men's bodies, rather than to a missionary society whose primary object is to convert their souls.

It can be answered at once that much of this is due to sheer misunderstanding. Catholic tradition as a whole never did rule out the salvation of the non-baptized; the intrinsic justification of the mission depended on quite other reasons. Christians have a mission to the world and whatever exact pattern it may take it must, if it is to be genuinely Christian, concern *truth,* witnessing to men's minds as well as having a concern for their bodies. As regards practical effects of missionary work today, the fact is that it is generally just those Afro-Asians who have become Christians who have also encountered the full force of Western secularist influences. These forces would have broken down the old pattern of religion and morality whether or not the Church had been there. That she has not been strong enough to counter them adequately and that many who have only come marginally and nominally under her influence have been more deeply affected by the impact of the new mental world which has struck Africa at just the same moment, is not her fault. The deeply religious and moral lives of many true Christians in the new Churches is the true effect and proof of missionary work.

However, the new ecumenical form of approach to other Christians seems now to offer a solution for the mission field as well, and some would propose to pattern future work more closely upon it. This approach is thought almost incompatible with deliberate attempts at conversion, though an individual's change of allegiance is recognized as possible. But instead of proselytism the requisite attitude would be one of dialogue, and the two are seen as opposites. Is the ecumenical attitude to separated Christians to be applied analogously to other groups of equally convinced people: to Islam, to the Buddhist and Hindu worlds, to agnostic liberalism? Is dialogue to replace direct evangelism everywhere? There is a feeling that it should; that the only satisfactory approach to people of other great religions may be a sort of diaconate of mental and material service with the aim of drawing truth slowly out of their own traditions rather than the producing of any immediate or manifest confrontation with Christ.

Let it be noted that this has not been the traditional attitude of the ecumenical movement itself. Its thought, on the contrary, has been that Christian unity is needed precisely for evangelism. There has been a very clear differentiation between one's attitude towards other Christians who believe that Christ is the Lord, the Son of God, and therefore have "the root of the matter" in them, and all others who do not. The tragedy of Christian differences in the eyes of the ecumenical movement is that they are minor, and preoccupation with them is blocking the really important thing: the evangelization of the non-Christian world. Ecumenism in the Protestant context really began with the World Missionary Conference of 1910 and has always been for the sake of mission: only a unified Church can bear adequate witness to the One Lord. It cannot be said that Catholic ecumenism has, hitherto, shown much of this mission preoccupation. Certainly, while nearly all the great Protestant ecumenical figures have a personal missionary background and are acutely conscious of the overriding demands of unity for mission and in mission, Catholic ecumenical figures are mostly personally untouched by missionary experiences, and they are far more Western-minded than their non-Catholic counterparts. This has appeared true also of the thinking of the Ecumenical Council itself in comparison with the World Council of Churches. Despite the large number of bishops from Africa and Asia present at the former, the concern for the Church's evangelical mission to the world seems to have been a far more subsidiary thing in Rome than in the W.C.C. As has been said, the withdrawal of the original schema on the Missions and then the rejection of the only Propositions to which this subject had been rather oddly reduced may suggest that the bishops themselves felt that there had been a lack here—not only of words but of preoccupation—and that some deeper rectification was needed. Fine as the missionary decree is, it came almost as an after-thought in the mental process of the Council. The ecumenical movement itself, however, has never lacked this preoccupation and its coupling of ecumenism with the evangelical and missionary witness is something we should not ignore, but imitate, as Archbishop Zoa of the Cameroons declared in the Council. The need for a genuine dialogue that goes far beyond Christian divisions to include all men must be reconciled with the continuing duty to bear full witness to Jesus Christ.

The existence of a separate conciliar decree on the Missions would be harmful if it was seen as somehow perpetuating the old geographical dichotomy between Christian lands (Europe, etc.) and mission lands (Africa, Asia, etc.). In the past one imagined that certain countries were somehow of their nature Christian, the rest pagan. The actual situation of the Middle Ages became a mental fixation. Europeans became missionaries and went to convert the pagans of Asia century after century, and yet Europe always remained Christendom, Asia always a land of mission, the whole ecclesiastical régime of the Church in these two parts being somehow different.

A good deal about this division was always mistaken; it grew out of a quasi-identification of the Church with the West and also out of defective missionary methods and a rigidity of approach to the problems of young Churches which imposed upon them norms only suitable for mature Churches and by so doing effectively prevented them from growing into maturity. Today the division is coming to an end. The Churches of the former mission lands are recognized as equal brothers, both as a matter of ecclesiastical organization and of the public opinion of the Church. The condition of the two areas is in fact becoming much more similar. For the most part both in and out of the West the believing Christian community is a minority and can no longer be practically identified with any society as such. What Karl Rahner calls the "diaspora situation" is common to the Church almost everywhere. In the past it was a fact that in some relatively small areas of the world everyone or almost everyone was visibly a member of the Church, whereas in most of the rest of the world there were no Christians at all. There was an obvious geographical and social foundation for the ecclesiastical division into Christian and mission lands, though the failure of long-continued missions outside Christendom to form whole, healthy new Churches shows that the geographical and social fact not only expressed but also had somehow come to control the theological fact. But all that has changed today. The practising Church community is now a minority in Paris, London, Bombay, Tokyo. Its fundamental condition in one of these places does not seem so different from that in another. There are few countries or areas now where the Gospel is not preached at all or some sort of Christian community does not exist, and there are few too whose integrally Catholic character could seriously be maintained.

If all this is so it might seem that the missionary himself, even in Christian thinking, has indeed become an anachronism. If any specifically missionary perspective seems to enter little into the work of some modern theologians, the answer might be given that it can exist no more, in the traditional sense, now that the Church is existing in a universal diaspora.

To some extent this is true and it does certainly impose the necessity of a psychological revolution upon those engaged as missionaries. Nevertheless we must not exaggerate. The Church exists in history and history does not deal in the *idée claire*. It is easy to overstate the character of a consecrational Christendom as it did in fact exist in Europe some hundreds of years ago, and it is easy by contrast to overstress the uniformity of the modern diaspora situation. Historically we may all be moving in this direction, but the actual condition of the Church in different parts of the world today still varies so much that the differences must enter into the very planning of the Church's mission and pastoral work and in the way her image is expressed in different localities. There are enormous areas where the Church cannot be said to be established as yet in any meaningful way, and these areas are not only ones of Muslim domination. The fact that the Church does exist in one part of a large country does not mean that she is genuinely established in it as a whole. And where the Church can truly be said to be established, in a rather bare way, the difference between this and the complex life of a great Christian community in some other part of the world may remain very striking. Even a strong Church like Bombay, with its many faithful and its numerous local clergy, still remains a tiny island in an enormous non-Christian sea around it. There is simply no equivalence between the numbers of priests working among the millions of Africa, Asia and South America, and the numbers working in Europe and North America. There are more priests and sisters in France alone with its fifty million people than in the whole of Asia and Africa with their two thousand million. The Gospel cannot be brought anywhere within reach of the vast majority of the people of Asia, as it is brought near to those of Europe. Hence a very real difference between the two remains.

It remains, furthermore, at the level of the cultural milieu. In Europe, North America, Australia, even in South America the cultural and social background is shared by Church and society. They have grown up together. The Church can use a language and concepts which she herself has helped to form. A non-Christian of the West in turning back to his own tradition and roots from the storm and strain of living today, as people must from time to time, finds the Church in front of him. He can refuse her but he can hardly ignore her. She is still there, a living part of the world he has inherited even if that world is changing drastically today. In Morocco, in India, in Japan this is not so. The Church is there not only a tiny minority, she is also an outsider, trying to grapple with a society and an approach of mind she herself has had small part in creating. Her dialogue with the world she wishes to inform must proceed far more tentatively, and she has at the same time to be able to transform herself liturgically, aesthetically, in the pattern of life of her clergy, and in many other ways if her dialogue with such societies is to be a convincing one. But of course, again, this cultural division of the world has no longer anything of the absoluteness of the past. We do indeed live today in a planetary society heading towards a fantastically complex uniformity. The young Japanese is not solely a product of the cultural tradition of Japan. Shakespeare, Sartre, Graham Greene, may have formed part of his reading. Nuclear physics does not vary from country to country. Marxism, a Western philosophy, is now a universal phenomenon. The culture and social structure of the modern West are imposing themselves upon every part of the world at the same time as they suck up into themselves whatever seems of value in other more localized traditions. In Africa this is particularly obvious, and the missionary to the educated can make use of the culture of Europe, specifically of England or of France, just because that, and practically only that, has been imbibed there in school and university.

The difference remains again in the human condition of the people of "the third world". For the great majority of them it is one of poverty, hunger, the prevalence of disease from birth to death. All human needs concern the Church: the more needy man is, the more the Church should seek him out. Yet in fact the parts of the earth where Christians are numerous are also those which are affluent. The really needy are generally far away, but unless the Christian community truly turns her face to them, enormously strengthening her missionary consciousness of service to those beyond, both in soul and body, she can only be identified with the wealthy—the haves. In the past the gap between the haves and have-nots was a class one within a territorial community; today it is far more a geographical one and provides a new point for "foreign" mission: the essentially Christian mission of human service: "I was hungry and you gave me food; naked and you clothed me; sick and you cared for me". We have to express the great Christian principle of "From each, according to his capacity; to each, according to his need" in inter-ecclesial and inter-continental structures fitting to the human needs and economic pressures of the twentieth century.

Though the condition of the Church in what used to be called mission countries is far, then, from being wholly different from that in the old Christian lands—and the two may, in the future, become more and more alike—there still remain, at least for the present time (and the Church's mission concerns the present time), vast practical differences both on the spiritual and on the material level. These differences require powerful recognition within the Church's structure, for the places where she is most needed, to perform her essential mission of witness to Christ and of help for the poor and the suffering, are just those where the local Church does not effectively exist or is quite unable to carry out the task unaided. Inter-Church aid is an essential in the nature of the Catholic communion but the present age requires that this essential be far more strikingly expressed in her contemporary structures, as Chapters V and VI of the Council's missionary decree make very clear. The need of the young Churches must be generously responded to, as in the Gospel story "they beckoned to their partners in the other boat to come and help them" (Luke 5. 7).

The duty of mission, of proclaiming and giving effect to the Gospel outside the existing fellowship and throughout the world, is something which belongs to every Church and to every one of her members. The quality of catholicity is not to be obtained as an aggregate of individuals who are themselves not catholic. The disciple, and the local Church he belongs to, have to share in the universality of the Lord's mission, if they are not to fall into the satisfied state of particularism—a temptation for the modern European diocese just as it was for the Church of Jerusalem. One cannot limit one's concern to local needs. The disciple of the Saviour of all men has to share in the quality of all-ness. Being missionary today means being globally minded, and our perennial duty of catholicity binds more than ever, for the very universality which is becoming a characteristic of secular society would otherwise put the universal Church to open shame. But, as we have seen, owing to the new conditions of things in which local Churches do now exist on a world-wide pattern, this duty can often best be fulfilled *across* another Church: the older Churches have as great a duty of evangelization and service beyond themselves as ever but they must fulfil this largely through the younger Churches. In the words of the constitution *De Ecclesia*: "Bishops must be willing, in a universal fellowship of charity, to offer the assistance of a brother to other churches, their needier neighbours in particular, after the admirable example of antiquity" (para. 23). If the character of the missionary work of the greater Churches is now to be more an inter-Church one, this certainly requires of it an added delicacy, for young Churches are sensitive and on the lookout for some sort of ecclesiastical colonialism. In the modern development of mission work from the mid-nineteenth century on, there was inevitably a domination of the home based mission and of *Propoganda Fide* over the missionaries in the field and over the first shoots of the young Church. Today the pattern has to be a quite different one, of respect for the new Church and its authority, and yet at the same time of help in making up its deficiencies. Such a task is no easy one. And it needs to be performed not only by specifically missionary societies but also more and more by the whole Church herself in her properly ecclesial and Christian character. There has been a certain split and even antagonism in the past between the Church in her normal diocesan form and the mission societies, even if the existence in many countries of a national missionary society originating from the secular clergy has helped to control this. But today the work cannot be left to specialized societies of any kind, necessary as they remain; the local Church as diocese is called upon to manifest its Catholic concern, its interest in mission beyond its own frontiers, and a small number of dioceses are already doing this. Bruges provides a particularly fine example. For the greater part, however, the missionary concern of most European dioceses remains entirely marginal: one or two parish collections a year, the odd sermon, perhaps a priest volunteering to help overseas for a few years. All this is entirely inadequate and even frustrating. What is far more effective is the pairing up of an affluent diocese with a needy one and then of particular parishes and schools within each. Edinburgh archdiocese in accepting a continuing responsibility for the Bauchi district in the Kaduna diocese of Nigeria has offered an excellent example. Several things have to be avoided in this sort of arrangement: first, haphazard help; but secondly, the domination of one diocese over the other; thirdly, the tendency of diocesan priests doing missionary service abroad to "hive off" and form a new missionary society must be absolutely resisted. What is important is to maintain a living relationship of service and sharing between two local Churches, both comprising laity and clergy. One wonders whether every young secular priest in the dioceses of Western Europe and North America might not be sent for three years on overseas mission. Similarly, the lay church member, simply because he is such, has to try to integrate a living missionary concern with his personal Christian life: he may do this in a great variety of ways—by prayer, by voluntary service overseas, by participation in the work of OXFAM and so on. But he needs to do it as the deliberate expression of the mission character of his own eucharistic life.

But the spearhead of the Church's mission must be today the young Churches themselves. It is they—little Christian communities amid the vast non-Christian masses of Asia and Africa—who have to be the prime evangelizers and servers of the people of their own continents. And one of the most serious things in the Church today is that just where this fire should most be, it may be lacking. Often the young Churches seem to be rather inward-looking, concerned with the preservation of their own institutions and sectional interests, rather than on fire to carry the Gospel they have received themselves to other tribes and localities. Missionary concern is not absent in the young Churches, but it is not nearly as strong as it should be to make of them what they ought providentially to be— the very centres of today's missionary effort. At times this is a consequence of the futile rivalries of the missionary societies themselves which have greatly impeded the growth of a truly Catholic spirit. Today the local Church needs to remember most firmly that to it, and not only to the Church in Europe and America, applies the Lord's own maxim: "It is more blessed to give than to receive" (Acts 20. 35).

This danger is made worse by being to some extent encouraged by foreign missionaries. There is growing up a sort of division of work whereby in many parts the pastoral care of the new Churches is left, in so far as is possible, to their own clergy, while specifically missionary work remains the concern of the foreign society. There are often practical and sound reasons for such a division, but the consequence and continuance of it could nevertheless be disastrous: failure to develop a missionary perspective among the new Christian communities. One obvious, immediate way of countering this is for the missionary societies to recruit for their own ranks from Africans and Asians. Some do so: the Jesuits in many places, the Society of the Holy Ghost in Nigeria, the Oblates of Mary Immaculate in Lesotho, and others elsewhere. But there are other missionary societies which have still made little effort in this direction. Doubtless one very commendable reason is their anxiety to build up a sufficient diocesan clergy. But the two need not be irreconcilable, and it would be disastrous to help create an idea that missionary work, that is to say the apostolate outside one's own community, is somehow specially the job of the white man. Perhaps in the circumstances of today the best thing would be the establishment of a specifically African missionary society: African based and African recruited.

The Missionary decree of the Council has stressed that the traditional missionary institutes are still required. They are indeed, but they do need an enormous internal re-adjustment. For one thing one may ask how far their continued separate existence is justified, with separate recruiting systems, training centres, missionary magazines. For another, there is the question of the basic training provided. They are societies specialized in their purpose for this single work, yet they have provided for their members a training which is almost wholly unspecialized. The White Fathers, in regard only to their North African work, afford the great exception, and the recent breaking up of the training centre at Manouba, in Tunisia, is a real tragedy for the Church's work in relation to Islam.[3] The missionary societies can no longer monopolize the missionary apostolate; but transformed they must still represent its core—a body of men dedicated for life to this particular aspect of the universal Church's work; and they must manifest that dedication by a specialized training and proficiency consonant with that expected of any such group in the contemporary world. Only very marginal efforts have

[3] The closing of the White Fathers' other great institution in Tunisia, Carthage Cathedral, is no disaster at all: Manouba represented the best in Cardinal Lavigerie's missionary approach, Carthage Cathedral the worst— the pseudo-re-establishment of the Church in North Africa as an adjunct of France's political presence.

been made hitherto to relate the studies in most missionary
seminaries to the specific work they are meant to be preparing for,
while the selection of men for post-ordination university courses
appears for most societies to be incredibly haphazard (both as
regards the men, and as regards the courses chosen). The serious
study of ethnology is almost entirely ignored. It still seems to be
felt that a society is doing well if it sends a few of its brighter
members to obtain honours degrees, whereas perhaps 50 per cent
of its members need a first degree and the abler ones need not just
a B.A. but a Ph.D. What is urgently necessary is to have men who
can (*a*) bring the most developed modern sciences, particularly
ethnology and sociology, to the service of the Church and the
shaping of her work; (*b*) secure appointments in the new universities
of Africa, and so exercise their apostolate in that milieu, because
their own academic training is up to the level required; (*c*) train
African priests in our seminaries in a similar way to share confi-
dently in the leadership of the new graduate society. At present,
with one or two shining exceptions, such men hardly exist—not
because there is not sufficient ability within these societies, but
because neither missionary superiors nor bishops have yet come
to realize the academic level a fair number of priests now need to
attain. Evidently committed lay Christians, of super-graduate standing, can and do help to fill a gap in the university field. They too,
however, are far from numerous, and while their presence may be
quite as valuable in an African university as that of the priest, it is
not a substitute for the latter.

The missionary apostolate to which the Church worker, both
indigenous and expatriate, is called today in Afro-Asia as in
Europe and America is one whose outward shape is clearly changing. More and more it is coming to involve a deep and constant
dialogue with the world about us, with the beliefs and ideologies
that are moving men. Dialogue does not change or replace the
central intention of bringing men to a new conviction, to faith in
Christ, but it does place the work of conversion in its proper
human setting. In many places in the past Christian missionaries
have worked in a sort of ideological vacuum. This vacuum could
be of two kinds: the first type seemed to surround the missionary
himself in the sense that until very recently he largely failed to
relate his teaching effectively to existing beliefs or to be aware that

those beliefs really mattered. In Asia, as a consequence, people remained entrenched within them, and few became Christians. In Africa such entrenchment has often not been possible. Local cosmologies have not stood up so effectively to the presentation of the Christian world view, especially when this was coupled with the acquisition of so much else in the material and social order. The only credible (or respectable) alternative to Catholicism might be the teaching of some other group of Christian missionaries. Here we find the second type of vacuum: the absence of other active ideological propaganda, though of course the forward movement of Islam continued in many places. But today the world is everywhere different, and men are faced not only with the possibility of many diverse Christian allegiances, but also with other alternatives that have much weight behind them. In Asia and Muslim lands this was always basically true, though the great Eastern religions seemed for long to be in a very quiescent state. Now they are wide awake, as are the new ideologies of Marxism, Moral Rearmament and agnostic humanism, and the adult mind in Afro-Asia will certainly not turn with any particular inevitability to Christian conviction. Indeed the Western associations of Christianity and the European pattern of life that has generally seemed to go with it render it at least initially suspect in the eyes of many non-Europeans, especially Asians. Conversion is in process of becoming a less easy thing than it was thirty years ago, but also consequently a more personally meaningful action. The mass conversion which has been characteristic of much mission work in the still recent past will have less and less place in the future.

The weakness in the traditional missionary approach has derived not only from the Western-ness of the Church as presented for acceptance, but also from the practical ignoring of the possibility of entering into contact with another mental world. Now at last, with our privileges gone, prestige reduced, doors slammed in our faces, we are ourselves beginning to understand how we should carry on a genuine dialogue, and its immediate aim cannot always be one of conversion. It has at times to be rather that of the White Fathers with Muslims in North Africa: one of pre-evangelization, of preparation of the ground, a contacting of minds where hitherto deep antipathies have made a conversion to Christ almost unthinkable. Mental and social situations vary so enormously from

4

Morocco to Japan that it is quite impossible that there should be any one norm of apostolate except that everywhere we must convince the world in the language of the world, and to do that we must know it. The work of evangelization must grow out of one of interpretation, of dialogue, of the contact of minds. In some places there is plenty of room for direct evangelization, but in others little or none.

At the end of it all, however, our goal remains the same. We do preach Christ and we must. "It would go hard with me if I did not preach the gospel" (1 Cor. 9. 16). The Church, in the Council's words, is "under the compulsion of the Holy Spirit to co-operate in giving effect to the design of God, who set up Christ as the principle of salvation for the whole world".[4] We are like St Peter, "We cannot but speak the things which we have heard and seen" (Acts 4. 20). The essential character of missionary work cannot change. It is to bring Christ to the world and the world to Christ. We respect the truth in other religions, we recognize that in them men have found something of the fatherhood of God, and that God has worked and works through all these things for the sanctification of mankind, but we have to hold that there is a qualitative difference between Christ and all the rest. We believe that Christ is the saviour of every man: so simple is the justification of our missionary work. It is a position of faith; it is indeed the core of being a Christian. That God can save men apart from the ministrations of the visible Church we do not doubt for a moment, but that he has also confided to us his prime and universal plan for mankind we are equally certain. All our dialogue, all the works of mercy, the Church's diaconate of the world must still lead back to this: to know Christ Jesus. The conditions of the world in which our task of evangelism is to be carried out, the methods to be used, the structures the Church erects for its implementation are all changing today, but the task itself is of the essence of ecclesial life. For the Church in her deepest nature is a communion on mission. She is a sacramental fellowship of faith and love, visibly and invisibly united by the breaking and eating of the bread which is the body of the Lord, but this fellowship is a sharing in Christ's mission to the world. Gathered together in the upper room, the apostles were

[4] Constitution on the Church, 17.

driven forth to witness in many languages. "Do this in commemoration of me", but "go and teach all nations". Communion and mission, these are the two fundamentals in the being of the Church, and if the organization of her missionary work can and must change, its necessity remains as ever. Together we have broken the bread of life but not for ourselves alone in an inward-looking community, for the life of the bread is the life of the world, and the Lord who died for us and gave us his flesh to eat has given it not for us only but for many.

III

The African Church: from Past to Present

1

IT IS widely held among Christians that the Church is always making progress, that her missionary effort is continually bringing the world more within her doors, that the command to convert the nations is necessarily carried out successfully. Alas, the opposite seems at times nearer the truth: time and again the Church's mission to the nations has, by the measure of human judgment, proved a failure. The tragic history of Christianity in China seems one striking example. That of the Church in Africa could be another. Has it been a story of steady "advance through storm" or does it not rather, if examined very coolly, appear as one of many missed opportunities? It is important to examine history coolly because what has happened in the past can do so again if comparable mistakes are made. God does not guarantee his Church fruitfulness or even continued existence in any given area; he works by grace through the movements of history and the free will and intelligence of the Church's members. It is on such things, things involving human and Christian responsibility, that the survival and growth of Christ's body among the nations depend.

The Church entered Africa in the apostolic age. The city of Alexandria, with its great Jewish population, must have been one of the first to be evangelized, and quickly Christian communities grew up throughout the African provinces of the Roman Empire, from Egypt in the east to Mauretania in the west. By the fourth century there were two great Christian communities in Africa: one, that of Egypt, centred upon Alexandria, now ruled by Athanasius, the second, that of "Africa Proconsularis" and Numidia—the Churches grouped around Carthage, strong in the tradition of Cyprian. This fourth-century African Christianity was numerous, rooted, dynamic. The hundreds of dioceses both in Egypt and to the west are proof of numbers; its vitality is demonstrated not only by its quarrels—Arianism in Egypt, Donatism in Numidia— but by its creation of new forms of Christian life in monasticism, and in its episcopal and intellectual leadership: Athanasius, Optatus, Augustine, and later, Cyril. Carthage offered a non-Roman contribution to the Western Church before Gaul was in a position to do so, while Egypt provided, in the East, a counterweight to Constantinople. The mystery is, what went wrong with these two vigorous and brilliant Churches? Why did Donatism sap the vitality of the Church of Cyprian and Monophysitism do the same for that of Athanasius? In a story that remains obscure much seems to hang on the growing identification of Church and Empire, Latin in the West, Greek in the East. Donatism was, in part at least, a nationalist protest of native Africans, of the peasantry of Numidia against a Church which was too Roman, identified with the unpopular imperial government; still more clearly, Egyptian nationalism in its protest against the domination of Greece and Constantinople took religious shape in Monophysitism. The imperial pattern for the Church, accepted by its more central communities, proved stultifying to those further away, but their reaction of schism—the national prolongation of doctrinal disputes for reasons quite other than those for which they originated —was no solution; it merely accentuated decay.

In the seventh century the Arabs poured across North Africa, bringing with them their new and simple creed of Islam. Their numbers were small in comparison with those they conquered, and it should not have been beyond the heirs of Augustine and Athanasius to convert their conquerors. But exactly the opposite happened. Islam proved more vital than Christianity; the uneducated converted the more sophisticated, the few converted the many. To accept this as almost inevitable, just because of a military conquest by a group of Muslim marauders, is surely a very strange thing. Something more than the imposition of taxes upon Christians is required to explain it. If Christianity failed so tragically it must have been because something was already very seriously wrong with those Christian communities. Rent by schisms, both the sense of united fellowship and that of mission seem to have faded from them. They had indeed considerable powers of resistance: the Church did not finally disappear in North Africa for some five centuries; in Egypt the important Coptic minority has remained to this day. But the force, the dynamism, the expansive power of the Church had disappeared before Islam even arrived, and without mission a communion must always be anaemic.

Doubtless there were many reasons for the decay, but of the fact of it there can be no doubt. Earlier, in the fourth century, Christianity had spread into the mountains of Ethiopia and in the sixth century up the Nile into Nubia:[1] in the fourth century missionary expansion had gone together with theological activity and the creation of new Church structures, but even then it seems to have had too personal and haphazard a character. The Church of North Africa never really got to grips with the conversion of the inland tribes, let alone with mission work well to the south. Internal quarrelling rather than evangelism is the impression given by the Christianity of that time and it was to pay dearly for it. The following centuries were a time of continual retreat. The Ethiopian Church survived but in a very restricted sphere, while that of Nubia, like that of North Africa, was finally submerged by Islam in the fourteenth century. Apportion the blame as you will or deny that there is any blame, the facts remain the same: Christianity had a six-century start on Islam and complete mastery of the whole northern coast of the continent. She failed to use this as a springboard for missionary penetration across the Sahara and finally lost almost everything to the new religion from Arabia so that the old Christian provinces of the north have become instead the great Muslim lands and the Church has had to start again in Africa, very painfully working in from the coast.

Unlike Christianity, the Islam of the north did not become static. Little by little the Sahara was penetrated, and the Middle Ages saw the development of great Islamic empires—Ghana, Mali and Songhai—south of the desert. At the same time influence slowly spread down the whole of the east coast though it failed to go far inland. It is not the aim here to laud every aspect of Islamic expan-

[1] See C. P. Groves, *The Planting of Christianity in Africa*, Lutterworth, I, pp. 46–54.

sion or to suggest that Christianity could do just as Islam. The point is that though Christianity should have done much better and in other places did do much better, in Africa it missed a supreme opportunity, apparently because it had become identified with the unpopular imperial government and had come to lack unity, adaptive capacity and missionary dynamism.

The opportunity returned, on a smaller scale, at the end of the Middle Ages as a sequel to Portuguese maritime expansion launched by Henry the Navigator. The end of the fifteenth century marked the beginning of the second great meeting between the Church and the African continent, a period which closed in the late eighteenth century. In this period there was missionary work all down the West African coast from Guinea to Angola and up the east coast from Mozambique to Mombasa. At first nearly all the missionaries were Portuguese, but in the seventeenth century and after, Italians and French joined in as well on the west coast. Everywhere the number of missionaries was far too small and their arrival far too irregular, nevertheless the numbers engaged in all must have been fairly considerable and in many places, such as the Congo and Benin, there was considerable initial success—less in the East, where Islam was already strong on the coast and the number of priests involved in the work tiny.

By far the most successful mission was that of the Congo where the Portuguese discovered a large and well-organized kingdom. The story of its evangelization is one of the most tragic in Church history. Its great king, Alfonso Mvemba Nzinga, who reigned from 1506 to 1541, should be recognized as one of the really great figures of African Christianity. From his baptism in 1491 as prince of Nsundi he laboured for fifty years for the conversion of his people with an extraordinarily clear understanding of what he was trying to do.[2] His son, Bishop Henry, was consecrated in Europe, probably in 1521, and returned to the Congo soon after, but it is his father the king of whom we know most through his long letters to Portugal full of information and requests for help. Here, if anywhere, in a large well-organized kingdom, with a converted monarchy and intelligent people, was the chance to establish the bridge-head for a real penetration of Africa. Seeing the state of the Congo and the

---

[2] For a full account of King Alfonso see Mgr J. Cuvelier's *L'ancien Royaume de Congo*, Desclée de Brouwer, Brussels.

progress that was made there, it is impossible to maintain that the tribal confusion or backwardness of Africa necessitated European conquest as a prerequisite for effective evangelization. On the contrary, it proved a great advantage in the Congo that the Portuguese did *not* attempt to conquer the kingdom. An integrally African Catholicism could here have developed, and it seemed for some years that it would do so. In fact the opposite happened. The kingdom decayed, the Church failed to take really effective root. It continued with a trickle of missionaries for three hundred years but there was no real establishment of the Church, no growth in Christian life, and in the end it all petered out. The chronicle of kings and missionaries and enthusiastic papal letters cannot hide with all its mass of fascinating detail the stark fact of total missionary failure.

Neither in the Congo nor anywhere else in Africa was the Church established in these three hundred years of mission work. While the Portuguese occupied a place the Church existed there but it fell with them. Only in the Congo had it really seemed to flourish beyond their political rule, though their influence was strong there, and even in the Congo it all died away little by little. The Church's second great encounter with Africa proved almost more lamentably disastrous than her first. There was nothing effected by it except, possibly, that on the coast there was a hardening of attitudes against her preaching and a certain residue of traditions and superstition.

This failure is paralleled by a certain general failure of Catholic mission work from the sixteenth to the eighteenth century.[3] But elsewhere, in Asia, it was not nearly so absolute as in Africa. Something of value survived the wreck of eighteenth-century decay, even though the Christian Churches then created in Goa, on the Fishery Coast, in Ceylon, Vietnam and elsewhere may seem inadequate in proportion to the effort put into them. But in Africa almost nothing survived. The climate and the general conditions of Africa are hardly sufficient to explain this fact. Doubtless the Asian mission had greater attractions, it drew the greatest missionaries and by far the larger number. Nevertheless the West Coast of Africa was nearer, easier to arrive at and offered less for-

---

[3] For this failure and the reasons for it see my *World Mission of the Church*, Darton, Longman and Todd, pp. 25–38.

midable religious and cultural obstacles than those to be encountered in the Far East.

The very close identification of the mission with the Portuguese empire—the very reason for initial progress—was certainly a chief cause of failure. The whole thing seems summed up in the name the Portuguese found suitable for their grim castle at Mombasa: Fort Jesus. Besides, Portugal was short of priests for the work but for long put extreme obstacles in the way of the entry of non-Portuguese. The privileges of the *Padroado* tied the development of the Church hand and foot to the policy of the Portuguese crown, and Christianity could not easily appear as other than an assimilation to the alien world of Portuguese rule and Portuguese ways. There is always an attraction at first in that sort of assimilation, but there is, equally, always a reaction later on. But in this case there was a special reason for revulsion—the slave trade. King Alfonso himself was loud in protest against it, but the Portuguese were too strong. At the best time of Congo's evangelization, in the 1530's and 1540's, five to seven thousand slaves were already being carried off to Portugal every year.[4] Later on the number had risen to some fifteen thousand. Some individual missionaries took part in the trade and it is said that further down the coast a bishop of Loanda had sat in the harbour blessing batches of slaves as they were shipped off to America.[5] It is perfectly true that the Church in her central Roman authority had condemned the slave trade; it is equally true that such a condemnation meant nothing when the trade was carried on under the very royal authority to which the whole care of the mission Church had been entrusted, and when a royal tax on the trade actually provided much of the money which the State used to support the missions. Whether she liked it or not the Church was identified with the slave trade and not unnaturally her work suffered the consequences. It is the result of tying oneself to a machine which is controlled by the State, in the hope of gaining some titbits thrown to God by a generous Caesar.

As a matter of fact how easily the slave trade was acquiesced in by the Church is shown by the severe way she condemned certain accidental aspects of it. Thus, those who failed to see that

[4] Cf. J. Cuvelier, *L'ancien Royaume de Congo*, pp. 327–8.
[5] R. Slade, *English-Speaking Missions in the Congo Independent State*, p. 20.

dying slaves received baptism came in for a heavy reprobation:[6] equally to sell slaves to heretical Dutchmen instead of to Catholic Portuguese was considered a really serious matter, and a native king allowing "the sale of slaves to heretics" was to be refused baptism.[7] It is only too evident that the basic evil of the slave trade, and the fundamental requirements of justice and charity, were little considered. The real preoccupation was with quite other things. But it was natural that Africans who witnessed and themselves suffered from the trade in human beings saw things in a different light, and that the spiritual dynamic of the gospel of charity could hardly operate in such circumstances. What the Church and her Portuguese protectors built with one hand they destroyed with the other.

Besides this, missionary methods were themselves defective both in the attitude taken towards the people to be Christianized and towards what was being brought to them. Jerome de Montesarchio, a seventeenth-century Capuchin in the Congo, reported how, "On my way I found numbers of idols which I threw into the fire. The owner of these idols, a Nganga Ngombo or sorcerer, seemed very annoyed. To calm him down by humiliating him, I let him know that if he persisted in his anger, I should see that he himself was burnt with his idols."[8] Such ignoring by missionaries of respect for private property and the personal dignity of Africans is not at all an isolated case. This high-handed approach is not such as to endear one. At the same time little was done to make Christianity really intelligible to the people; for instance, nothing seems to have been printed in Kikongo until the seventeenth century. Missionaries were few; they were scattered over many parts of the African coast as well as in the Congo; they seldom seemed to realize that their whole task should have been the building up of a self-sufficient local Church rather than a piece of personal evangelism. The task set many of them was, doubtless, almost impossible. Though they were often heroic, they made no lasting mark.

[6] J. Cuvelier, op. cit., p. 233.
[7] Cf. M. Bane, Catholic Pioneers in West Africa, Clonmore and Reynolds, p. 102.
[8] Quoted by R. Slade, King Leopold's Congo, Oxford University Press, p. 7.

By the early nineteenth century it was all over, apart from a few tiny, ill-instructed groups in places like Ouidah and Elmina, and rather more in Angola and Mozambique. The Jesus of Fort Jesus was not loved by Africans; they had had precious little opportunity really to know him. The Portuguese empire had declined. Fort Jesus itself became, in 1729, a Muslim Arab stronghold. Missionary fervour had faded away in the Europe of the eighteenth century and finally the whole home Church was shaken to pieces by the storm of the French Revolution. Her second great opportunity in Africa had come and gone and there was almost nothing to show for it: a land still unevangelized, a continent dark because, effectively, it had never been offered the light. In 1800 as in 1500 the African Church had its ruins, its memories, its canonized saints, but where were its living members?

2

The way of teaching any set of ideas must depend upon the context within which they will be understood. If this context is very different for teacher and taught, deep misunderstanding is almost bound to arise. Christian doctrine can hardly be got across to Africans who have not received any appreciable amount of Western education—and that is even now the great majority—if the missionary has not first understood something of their own thought world. In some ways the missionary of the late nineteenth and early twentieth century was actually more likely to arrive at such an understanding than his successors of forty years later. The early missionaries could not open and busy themselves with loads of schools and hospitals. They were almost completely isolated from Europe and were forced to share closely in African society, once they had abandoned the attempt to create independent Christian villages. Very probably there was quite a long period before any considerable number of converts was obtained. In this period they had the opportunity to acquire a fine knowledge of the local language, customs and thought forms, and many of them did so, both Catholic and Protestant. In areas and tribes where evangelization began much later—during the last forty years—this has often not happened. Missionaries have rushed straight into the provision of social services and an extensive catechumenate without any adequate prior initiation into the local tribal mind. The inevitable effect is that Christianity either does not penetrate deeply or becomes seriously twisted; it may be seen as primarily a permit for schooling rather than as a way of faith and life. The only way to avoid this is by a deep understanding of existing African preconceptions and beliefs and by the explanation of Christianity in terms related to them, while at the same time making clear the absolute newness of Christian faith and life. One danger is to teach the faith unintelligibly because unrelated to the convert's existing thought world; the opposite danger is to allow it to be almost wholly assimilated to that same thought world, so that there is no real discovery of Christ. Now the avoiding of both these dangers requires a deep prior understanding of African religion.

In fact neither in the nineteenth nor in earlier centuries did missionaries give much thought in advance as to what they would find in Africa. What struck them, undoubtedly, was the darkness of the continent: its lack of religion and sound morals, its ignorance, its general pitiful condition made worse by the barbarity of the slave trade. Evangelization was seen as liberation from a state of absolute awfulness and the picture of unredeemed Africa was often painted in colours as gruesome as possible the better to encourage missionary zeal at home. This tendency was not, happily, universal: Livingstone came to appreciate positive religious and moral qualities in Africa, and indeed the more that individual missionaries penetrated into African psychology the more of value they found, as is evident when the early White Fathers in Uganda —Livinhac and Lourdel—stressed these religious qualities in their letters to Cardinal Lavigerie.[9] And since then some of the greatest field anthropologists, and students of African customs—men like Fr Crazzolara in Northern Uganda—have been missionaries.

Nevertheless the negative approach has been very strong and, in practice, it remains strong. The tendency continues to treat everything pre-Christian in Africa as either harmful or at best valueless and to consider the African, once converted from paganism, as a sort of *tabula rasa* on which a wholly new religious psychology has somehow to be imprinted. That there was plenty

---

[9] But Lavigerie's comment on this was revealing: "These details are contrary to what all travellers say about other Africans and to what you yourselves have said in the past" (letter of 10 February 1881).

to horrify one in the pre-Christian state of Africa is only too clear. Quite apart from the extra enormities of the slave trade, superimposed on African society, it is clear that cruelty and fear were strikingly evident: cruelty especially in great kingdoms like those of Ashanti, Dahomey and Buganda with their frequent blood-baths; fear, everywhere—above all, fear of sorcery, or of being bewitched by others. So much of the positive practice of African customs goes back to this fear of sorcery, to which almost all deaths and other misfortunes were widely ascribed, and to an endless struggle to protect oneself against it.

But the tendency to condemn African things *in toto* came not only from actual observation, but even more from ignorance on the part of foreigners. African societies are so different from anything he was hitherto acquainted with that without some special training in interpretation, the missionary found himself clueless and revolted. A special training in anthropology, in the study of such societies, was what the missionary needed and still docs desperately need, but what he did not, and still, for the most part, does not receive. So far as I know almost no serious attempt is even now made to train the young missionary in advance to understand and appreciate social and mental patterns so extremely different from his own. Instead of this, and for lack of it, many missionaries have been too simply convinced of the enormous superiority of the European West, and they have come unconsciously, but naturally, as bearers not only of the Christian message but also of westernization.

Much of that was obviously inevitable and Africans have gained greatly in the secular as well as in the religious sphere from the work and therefore the presuppositions of the missionaries. Africans today would be the last to denounce all the processes of westernization that have gone on. Nevertheless the educated African may feel that behind much of this there was a certain implied insult to the more humble but genuine values that were, and are, to be found within the authentic traditions of African society. We need to appreciate those values; they have not been obliterated by the wave of westernization (though their influence on the more educated is surely weakening) just as they were not destroyed by the vices which existed in African, just as much as in every other society. It is to such values that the present-day appeal to "négritude" appeals, and, with so many more facilities and opportunities for study than his nineteenth-century predecessor, the modern missionary has a duty to appreciate and to make use of such values in his building up of the supernatural society. Grace builds upon nature, and nature exists in Africa as elsewhere. There is much of enormous positive value in African traditions and religious consciousness, and there is still time to make use of it for the creation of a genuinely African Christianity.

The purpose here is not to provide an adequate treatment of this theme and its practical realization, but simply to offer a few lines of approach to the basic missionary task which is neither in Africa nor anywhere else the imprinting of the Christian thing upon a *tabula rasa*, but rather the conversion of a natural consciousness of things good and evil into the new vision of a world reformed in Christ.

A first point to make if one wants to get African society into focus is that it has a past, its own past. We do not speak now of the possible African origin of mankind, nor of ancient Egypt and subsequent societies possessing literary records, but simply of the tribal societies of Central Africa. History does not begin with the arrival of the white man. That event enters into an existing story, and for many peoples an old story. Respect for a people involves a consciousness of their past and in this we sometimes fall down very much. A good example of a long past is to be found in Buganda's story. Mutesa II, the present Kabaka, began to reign in 1939. He is the thirty-fifth king of Buganda and generations in that country are much the same length as elsewhere. Mutesa's great-great-grandfather, Suna II, began to reign in 1826, eleven years before the accession of Queen Victoria—great-great-grandmother of Queen Elizabeth II. Going back thirty-five reigns from Elizabeth II takes us to Henry III and the thirteenth century, and it is likely that it was in the thirteenth or fourteenth century that the Ganda kingdom began to take shape in the area around modern Kampala.[10] It extended in subsequent centuries. Not only the king-

[10] Roland Oliver puts the origin of Buganda's present dynasty in the fifteenth or early sixteenth century, cf. Oliver and Matthew, *A History of East Africa*. I would think a rather earlier date preferable, just as the kingdom of the Congo, which was excellently organized when the Portuguese arrived there in the late fifteenth century, must go back at least another hundred years.

ship, but the whole social structure of Buganda—the clans, the counties, the chieftainships—have a well verified history going back for centuries, and the shape of the country and the mentality of its people cannot be understood apart from its history. Their religion, both their present and their past religion, has to fit into this framework—just as the Christian religion can only be understood elsewhere in its historical context: "And there went forth a decree from Caesar Augustus...".

Buganda has a longer recorded history than many African tribal societies; that is characteristic of a monarchy, which always becomes a focus for the preservation of a people's story. West African dynasties, such as those of Benin, Oyo and Ife, go back still further. Where monarchies are lacking, memories are shorter too. But history is recorded of necessity in all institutions and ways of behaviour and it is such a society with a tradition and a way of life of its own that the missionary has to approach and respect.

If the past of Africa must be seen and respected, so also must her variety: tribal variety and individual variety. It is desperately difficult not to generalize constantly about Africans, but it is extremely dangerous. I am sure, from personal experience, that Africans differ as much among themselves as Europeans do and it can be as meaningless, and basically as insulting, to declare that Africans feel like this or like that as to say the same of Europeans. Of course there are important and recognizable tribal characteristics —common social structure, religious beliefs and so on—but these are not common to all peoples, but to a tribe or group of related tribes, a socio-cultural group. Belief in a unique high god seems common to most African peoples, as also does a preoccupation with sorcery, but there are many other things which are of crucial importance for one tribe but of none at all for others.

Kingship is a good example. It is very easy from the striking examples of the West Coast and Lacustrian monarchies—Dahomey, Ashanti, Benin, Yoruba, Buganda, Bunyoro—and others like the Zulus in the south, to start generalizing about the African's deep sense of kingship and to go on to seeing this as a wonderful foundation for the doctrine of the kingship of Christ and so on. I have heard it done. Where there is this sense of kingship, all that may be well and good, but the striking truth is that very many Africans are moved not at all by the aura of kingship. They had no kings, nor any equivalent in their society. Thus it is said that in Kenya, Uganda and Tanzania in pre-European days, of 101 tribes counted, 45 had no chiefs at all, 47 had only district chiefs and but nine had central chiefs—kings in a recognizable sense.[11] Great peoples like the Kikuyu had no sort of tradition of monarchy whatsoever, while other peoples like the Baganda are absolutely impregnated with it.

This is a matter both of practice and of idea. The two are not separable. Initiation rites play a very great part in the life of some societies and little or none in that of others; marriage customs, codes of politeness, all such things differ vastly from people to people. Evangelization should start to work from what a people holds and how they are organized. An approach which might be successful with a tribe organized on a clan basis could be strikingly unsuccessful when employed with a people whose society is grounded in an age-set system. Equally it is obvious that methods geared to sedentary peoples will not be suited to semi-nomadic, pastoral tribes. This does not mean that the latter cannot be evangelized, but that they cannot be evangelized in the same way.

All this is simply an appeal for the recognition of Africa's rich variety, a variety which missionaries can ignore, and often have ignored to their cost. The striking differences between the outward success of missionary work among one people and its failure for years with another can have been due to the uniform character of the methods used, which have proved suitable in one set of circumstances but have been adhered to throughout.

Something which is common throughout Africa is a way of expressing truth: the sapiential way. Proverbs, enigmatic sayings, mythical stories—these are the means whereby the traditional beliefs of African folk have been expressed and passed on. It is a way of thinking like that to be found in the Bible, and it at once makes of the Bible a book attractive and understandable for Africans. That should have been the greatest source of strength for the missionary, but it has often failed to prove so just because we ourselves have grown so unbiblical in our approach to religion: a scholastic terminology and way of treating things has coloured even

<hr>

[11] Huntingford in Oliver and Matthew, *A History of East Africa*, p. 91.

African catechisms. Here again what is necessary is the recognition of the value of the Biblical-African approach for its own sake. It is not enough to take a proverb as a starter for a piece of scholastic teaching; it is necessary to express Christian doctrine in the sort of way that really brings the start of recognition from the hearer, not merely a stunned acquiescence. Jesus himself, after all, is the best of teachers and his approach was the African one through and through; proverb, metaphor, parable.

What do Africans express through these things? One thing which is absolutely certain is that when the missionaries first came to Africa, it was not to an irreligious land: on the contrary, it was to a world already loaded with religion that they brought their message. That religion varied greatly and it is not the intention to try and describe it here, but only to point out a few of its primordial stresses which evangelization should make use of, rather than denounce or ignore. What is striking is that the deepest beliefs of Africans seem to have been good and right, and, when purified, a real foundation for a supernatural edifice. Certainly the great goods of African tradition—the belief in one high god, the close family solidarity, the co-ordination of spirit and matter, the basic moral values, education seen as the acceptance of the accumulated wisdom of the elders, and finally, in many societies, the deeply democratic recognition of the rights of each individual within the tribal community, so long as he fulfils his duties—these goods seem to outweigh the bad things—an exaggerated faith in the powers (often malevolent) of the ancestors, belief in sorcery and witchcraft, the dictatorial monarchies, the lack of a developed moral attitude to those beyond the tribal group—and to offer a ground on which the tree of the Gospel could fittingly grow.

Let us consider briefly the chief elements of really positive value, from the Christian viewpoint, to be found universally, or widely, in African religions. The first thing, most certainly, is belief in one, first, high god, the source and father of life and of all things.[12] What struck Europeans on first coming to Africa was the multiplicity of African devotions, the consciousness of spirits present in everything. And there were gods of all kinds, mostly ancestors

---

[12] Cf. *African Ideas of God*, ed. E. Smith, Edinburgh House Press, 1950; also G. Parrinder, *African Traditional Religion*, 1954, and *West African Religion*, 1949, where fuller bibliographies can be found.

or ancient heroes, now in some sort of deified state, but also other nature gods, of storm, thunder and wind, of earth and sea and lake. The concern of Africans seemed to be chiefly with praying to and placating these individual spirits or divinities. It often took Europeans some time to realize that behind all these, in the belief of every, or almost every African people, is the great god, the first god, he who made the other gods as well as all else, the limitless, the wise one, the one you meet everywhere. The most striking religious phenomenon of Africa is its basic monotheism and this we need to make far more use of than we have done. It is true that missionaries seldom tried to introduce a new name for God; they found the name already known and rightly adopted it. In doing so they recognized a great truth—that they were not introducing a new god to Africa but they had come to reveal more fully to Africans the father they had already known and about whom they had many proverbs and wise sayings.

If most Africans knew the one god, it must be admitted that he had become somewhat remote to them. Many tribes even have stories of how the high god had departed far away. Some have no worship for him at all, others little in comparison with the attention paid to lesser spirits. The first father is pictured as somehow uninterested in the world he has brought forth, benevolent but practically ineffectual. It is here that the Christian teacher can come in. Our Father in heaven, the one who made everything in the first place, is not as you have pictured him. On the contrary: he does still care for us, and to prove it he has sent us his Son. The coming of Jesus is both the confirmation and the reversal of African monotheism. And it is the reversal too of African polytheism. The world of spirits, of semi-deified ancestors, whose details and imagined power vary so greatly from one people to another, has all been built up to fill the gap created by the remoteness of God. Here is a mentality akin to that which St Paul criticizes in Colossians. The closeness of Christ, God with us, must fill the gap and must show too that neither is the Father remote. In the presence of the Son do we find the proximity of the Father.

Very much, however, of the cult of ancestors is not really a type of polytheism but simply a recognition of continued communion and a ritual way of commending parental authority and filial dependence in the family group. Man is not alone in life. From birth to death he is a member of a wide family with complex clan relations merging into the wider tribal ones. Here again everything differs in detail from people to people, but not the sense of intense corporateness which nearly always goes with simple rural communities. In life and in death man is one with his family, with his ancestors. We are in them and they are in us. It is a people not cut asunder by the valley of death. All this is expressed for the living by the customs of clan and extended family and for the dead by the cult of ancestors. For Catholics at least all this should be easily accepted as an intuition of value and something to build on; even if we recognize in much of its practice a fear of the dead that we cannot share, we too believe in a close communion of living and dead. We have thought it too often our duty to destroy, whereas in these affirmations of natural religion we should find rather the finger pointing to the fullness of communion of all men in Christ. God is the god of our ancestors, of Abraham, of Isaac, of Jacob: the long lists of names we utter solemnly in the canon of the Mass are those of ancestors in the faith. An outward ritual of respect for ancestors, whether ecclesiastically canonized or not, is both a human thing and a Christian thing and it is one of the great offerings that African psychology can bring to the service of faith but which we, perhaps, have hardly seen how to make use of.

God is the first source of life. It is life, strength, vital force that one receives with one's clan and must respect in all things. This is the idea that has been seen by some as central to traditional African religion, to what they would call the African philosophy: a life that comes from on high but that all men and all things somehow participate in. Natural intuitions perceive central truths without the distinctions that subtle examination later provides. That is very true of much African religion but the point is that the intuitions are valuable ones and that people whose minds have been formed in them need to be carried into the fuller sphere of revelation across, and not in disregard of, their first perceptions. And they have so much to offer. Take again the sacrifices of natural religion or the meal as a sacramental action. Many African peoples have a real consciousness of the purpose of sacrifice, of the sin offering, the gift whereby to re-establish communion with god or with the ancestors. Again a ritual meal may be seen as the means of restoration of peace between men: "Let us eat out of the same spoon, drink out of the same cup, and be friends again", say two Thonga brothers who have quarrelled and wish to be reconciled.[13] It is through such things used rather than cast aside that the Eucharist can be made meaningful. If something of the real meaning of traditional African practices has not been first understood, all will be condemned outright by the missionary, fearful of pagan superstitions, and he will then have to build a new religious structure where he has roundly rejected all that could make meaning of it in the minds of his hearers.

African religion was one of ritual functioning through symbolism. It is striking how important symbols are in Catholic liturgy and traditional prayer forms, and yet how in the course of time we have, to a very large extent, destroyed their practical effectiveness, both by blindness to their power and by tying them up with little rubrical details. The great symbols of life—water, the meal, light and fire—are really central to the practice of our religion. But you can hardly see it now. Baptism no longer *appears* as a washing, the Mass as a meal. We have taken these things across in their dried-up state and offered them to Africans and been surprised that they have not understood or been satisfied. One of the striking things about the African separatist Churches, which have grown up throughout the continent, has been their replacement of emaciated symbols by expressive ones that answer to the need for symbolism of the whole man.

All this is a very brief statement of the sort of thing traditional Africa has to offer in the religious field. Inevitably in such a statement the danger lies in generalizing when the beliefs and customs of different peoples remain so very diverse. It is the criticism levelled by the professional anthropologist at such books as Canon John Taylor's *Primal Vision* and Fr Tempels' *Bantu Philosophy*, and it is difficult to deny a basic justice in the criticism—yet difficult also not to attempt some such general assessment! Surely such books are useful for the European coming to work in Africa in, say, a secondary school or some other modernized context, but they can be dangerous for the missionary wanting to make contact with a wholly African society. For the latter, the worthwhile course is the study of the religion of this particular people. The more one

[13] Parrinder, *African Traditional Religion*, p. 87.

enters on such a study the less help *Bantu Philosophy* is likely to be. Guiding books here are rather the precise description of a particular tribal religion such as Professor Evans-Pritchard's *Nuer Religion* or G. Lienhardt's *Divinity and Experience* (The Religion of the Dinka).

Whatever the particular religious beliefs of a people may be, it remains a first missionary principle to start with them and work on, as Paul did at Athens. Evangelization needs dialogue. Now though some Protestant missionaries might have difficulty in finding a way of approach across many of these African attitudes, Catholics should not do so. There are stepping-stones towards understanding here: communion with the dead, significant symbols, sacrifices for peace, meals of reconciliation.... Our difficulty has often been one of initial understanding and communication. Paul could know the mind of the Athenians so much more easily than the modern missionary could enter into the mind of Kikuyu, Ewe or Zulu. But the principle remains the same, and if today we sense a certain anaemia in much orthodox African Christianity we may guess that part of it is caused by failure to adhere to this principle, to insert our clearly defined doctrines within categories sufficiently meaningful to the convert's mind.

Of course the old beliefs had to be not only added to, but also purged. Respect for ancestors had, at least in places, turned into their deification. Ritual sacrifice had been twisted, among some peoples, into a reckless destruction of human life. Consciousness of the spirit world had become a haunting fear from which man was never free. There is much to be put right, but it needs to be understood before it can be put right or made use of as somehow contributing to the building up of the kingdom of light rather than to be dismissed as the unmitigated works of darkness.

In the context of all this, what are we to say of the meaning of "conversion" for an African? What is he converted from—what to? It would not, as we see, be correct to describe his conversion as one from polytheism to the one God. For some that might indeed be a fairly true statement, but for most they knew the one God before they heard the Church speaking of him. In the Church's preaching they learn more about him, they see him alone, no longer half hidden behind a host of lesser beings, they learn to love him more, but they are not exactly or necessarily converted to him just as a

Muslim is not converted to the one God. What the African pagan is converted to—just as the Muslim is converted to—is Christ, and, in him, to the fullness of the Trinity. In fact the Christian missionary has never been sent to preach monotheism as such. It is on Christ that the preaching has been centred from apostolic times; it is Christ that we preach today and it is to Christ that every non-Christian is converted. From this point of view his religious *status quo* is indeed immaterial; whether monotheist, polytheist or atheist, he is converted when he comes to believe in Christ and to share in the fellowship of the Triune God, and such conversion is always necessary.

It is salvation in Christ and the communion of his body which we call the Church that the missionaries came to preach in Africa and that we have equally to proclaim today. But this unique proclamation that constitutes the Christian message in all places and for all times has to be expressed in a form that can be understood. If there is no faith without preaching there is equally no conversion without a hearer and a hearer with a past, with his own old testament awaiting the good news of the new. The new is always the key, the old is always the lock. But key has no meaning without lock, and it is to the wealth of tradition, of natural intuition or original revelation or whatever it may be, embedded within the thought world and practice of each African people that the Christian message in Africa must provide the key. The wisdom of old Africa is as vital to the health of her new Church as was the old law of Israel to the beginning of Christ's kingdom. Man must enter the new community, not as a stripped nonentity, but as the bearer of gifts for the new Adam.

3

On 31 January 1842 Monsignor Barron landed at Cape Palmas in West Africa. This seems the most appropriate date for the opening of the Catholic Church's third great meeting with Africa.[14] It did not begin propitiously. Mgr Barron himself resigned, discouraged, only three years later and, though he was replaced and the work carried on by Holy Ghost Fathers, little in visible terms

---

[14] Though work of a limited kind had begun earlier at St Louis in Senegal.

was achieved by the first missionaries. The first forty years, 1840–1880, were largely ones of renewed failure. They were years in which the missionaries seldom moved far from the coast, trying to relight the flickering remains of Catholic Christianity that had survived from the Portuguese period. In every way the coastal conditions were bad for evangelization: the climate was particularly unhealthy, the presence of European traders seldom improved things, while the connection of the missionaries with a European political presence could seem for Africans to make the process of conversion involve a social and political separation from their own people. There can be no doubt that almost nothing of lasting value was achieved in those forty years. The effective beginning of Catholic missionary work was about 1880 or later when the interior was at last penetrated and wider attempts were made to evangelize African society as a whole, and not merely ex-slaves and the coastal fringe.

Up to this time Protestant missions had been far more extensive than Catholic. At the end of the eighteenth century, just when the old Catholic missionary effort of several centuries was collapsing, the Protestant Churches had at last begun to turn to missionary work and new societies were founded both in Britain and throughout Europe. The exploration of Africa was closely linked with Protestant missionary activity. Catholics only became really active again in the second half of the century when most of the pioneer exploration was over. The initial areas of work for Protestant missionaries were the Cape and Sierra Leone, but they soon spread further afield. Krapf and Rehmann, sent by the Church Missionary Society, arrived at Mombasa in 1844 to reopen the history of the evangelization of East Africa. David Livingstone, sent by the London Missionary Society, had landed at Cape Town in 1841 to join earlier missionaries like Robert Moffat in the south of the continent; he pioneered the work through enormous new areas of the interior. In the wake of such men a network of non-Catholic missions had grown up across the continent by the close of the nineteenth century. Different denominations sometimes overlapped, but often divided the field between them. The Anglican C.M.S. was working very extensively both on the west coast and then in Kenya, Uganda, Rwanda and the Southern Sudan. The London Missionary Society had sent men to the South where strong Methodist, Anglican and Congregationalist missions developed. Methodists carried out important work also in Nigeria and the Gold Coast, Presbyterians established themselves most notably in Nyasaland, and Baptists built up an extensive mission in the Congo. The Paris Evangelical Society penetrated into Basutoland and Barotseland, while German Lutherans and the Anglican University Mission to Central Africa spread inward from the coast of Tanganyika. Only in French West Africa did Protestant missionary work fail to develop on a large scale.

Though Catholic missionary work of the nineteenth century began first in West Africa, it had little result prior to the 1880s, by which time serious work was being undertaken also in the East. Almost nowhere has the African Catholic Church a continuous history of more than eighty years, and in most places far less. The ineffectiveness of earlier Catholic mission work on the west coast should be contrasted with the far more successful activity there of Protestant missionaries. This was based on Sierra Leone and the Fourah Bay College for training ministers at Freetown; the Yoruba Samuel Crowther, bishop on the Niger from 1864, was the first fruit of their policy.[15] At this stage Protestants were about fifty years ahead of Catholics not only in their actual achievement but also in their understanding of mission method. Their immediate appreciation of the importance and feasibility of a local ministry is in striking contrast with Catholic West African practice. This is the more remarkable in that Mgr de Brésillac, a pioneer of the West African mission and one of its most immediate victims, had the formation of a local ministry as the first of his ideals. After his death (in June 1859) continued lip-service was paid to the idea but it is only too clear that no sustained attempt was made to bring it to fruition in spite of the Protestant example. A dozen priests were ordained in Senegal in the course of the nineteenth century. Elsewhere, almost none. The West African Church has paid heavily for this failure.

After 1880 the political scramble for Africa was on. In the turmoil of new ideas and new possibilities the missionaries too rapidly penetrated into wide and remote areas. New societies were joining

---

[15] For the later backsliding of the Protestant mission on the all-important point of entrusting authority to Africans, see J. Webster, *The African Churches among the Yoruba*, pp. 8–20.

those first in the field and the whole Catholic missionary force was vastly increasing in number. The Holy Ghost Fathers had been the first on both the west and the east coast. On the west coast they continued to work from Eastern Nigeria as far as the north of the Congo, and on the east coast in both Tanganyika and Kenya. In the west they had early been joined by Mgr de Brésillac's Society of Missions of Africa (S.M.A.), who took over much of the coast from Lagos to the west, including Dahomey and the Gold Coast. Meanwhile the White Fathers, deliberately rejecting a coastal policy, had struck out inland both west and east. In the east they built up great vicariates around the lakes in western Uganda, Tanganyika and the eastern Congo, and pushed on into Nyasaland and Northern Rhodesia. In the west they began work on the lands around the upper Niger. The Verona Fathers had penetrated up the Nile into the southern Sudan and, later, northern Uganda, while the Mill Hill Fathers joined the White Fathers in southern Uganda. In the western Congo the Scheut Fathers and the Jesuits opened missions, while in Southern Africa it was the turn of the Oblates and the Congregation of Mariannhill. Further gaps were filled with the arrival of German Benedictines in southern Tanganyika, of the Consolata Fathers in central Kenya and of the Jesuits in Rhodesia.

Thus remembering the equally varied groups of Protestant missionaries arriving at the same time, the ecclesiastical "scramble" for Africa appears as complicated as the political, and soon on the Catholic side a whole network of vicariates and mission stations, all finally subject to the Roman Congregation of *Propaganda Fide*, was created. The building of a new Church on an unprecedented scale had been undertaken. Not only had the Church never previously thrown on to the missionary front a comparable number of men, but also in organization and methods this new period of mission work far outstripped all preceding ones. As to organization, the new religious societies, specially founded for this type of work and entrusted with some particular territory, guaranteed an enormous advance on the more haphazard methods which had often prevailed in the past: this is especially true as regards the African apostolate in which the White Fathers, the Holy Ghost Fathers, the S.M.A. and others could soon become specialists. Methods came to be more co-ordinated and certain standards made normative. The training of catechists, a systematic catechumenate, the formation of a native clergy, a respect for local custom—such things might not be universally applied but their importance came to be widely understood and regularly insisted upon by mission authorities at home and in the field.

Church history is not enacted in a vacuum but forms part of the complex rough and tumble of social and political history. It would be possible to write a history of the missions which only referred to the activities of the missionaries themselves and of their converts but it would of course be quite misleading. The missionary penetration of Africa in the twenty years 1880–1900 at times preceded but at other times depended upon the general European penetration of the conquest. The two only make historical sense when placed together. If one group of white men coming up from the coast with a long line of native porters were White Fathers, another group coming up in much the same way represented their Protestant counter-parts, a third the new European administration, and so on. It was not easy for the native mind to make all the necessary distinction—nor indeed for the European mind.

> "People who subscribe will find
> Profit and Piety combined,"

wrote Belloc in *The Modern Traveller*. The trading companies often started off with a religious motive. Stanley taught Mutesa "the Ten Commandments of Moses" but he shot opposition out of his way without compunction and founded the Congo Free State for Leopold. In his famous letter to the *Daily Telegraph*, printed on 15 November 1875, he had painted the picture of his ideal missionary and added: "Mutesa would give him anything he desired, houses, lands, cattle, ivory. He might call a province his own in a day. . . . He must belong to no nation in particular, but to the entire white race." It was this appeal which prompted the Uganda mission of both C.M.S. and White Fathers. Later on, Africans might feel that some missionaries had accepted Stanley's picture rather too literally.

Stanley was the contemporary of David Livingstone and Cardinal Lavigerie but also of Leopold II, Paul Kruger, Cecil Rhodes. The interests that all these men represented were converging upon Central Africa. The Catholic missionary was competing in the religious field with the Protestant as well as with the Moslem trader in attempting to convert the native African; and he was doing it inside a world which was beginning to be integrally transformed by the power not only of God's word but of the word of the White Man: the man who could fire the guns, lay the railway lines, create government of inter-tribal dimensions in the name of some distant queen or emperor or president. The missionary's attitude to all this was necessarily ambivalent. On the one side he had much to gain from the peaceful conditions and protection that colonial governments brought, and in fact most missionaries were clearly in favour of the colonial scramble and some worked actively to bring it about. *"Pour Dieu! Pour la France!"* was a quite recognizable Catholic approach, while English Anglican missionaries put constant pressure on Westminster to incorporate new territories into the empire. At the same time the missionary knew that the European trader was often a morally corrupting influence on Africans, while the settler and his needs might overturn their whole society.

The vast majority of missionaries were entirely uninterested in politics, settlement or commercial advantage. Their zeal and their purity of motive shine out in their activity. Nevertheless one can feel sorry about the extent to which, over the years and in some places, missionaries failed to perceive the essential gap which should be maintained between their work and that of government and the ease with which they came to be mixed up in a single white-supremacy image. This was not so everywhere and nowhere was it absolutely so, but it tended to happen where there were many settlers—in South Africa, Southern Rhodesia, the Congo and Kenya. In the Congo the very special privileges which the Church enjoyed from the State linked her all the more with the strong colour bar and the very special type of paternalism which existed in that territory. There and elsewhere missionaries might come to give an undue amount of their time to ministering to the small white community and educating their children. It is not possible to deny the colour bar which for long existed unnecessarily in great Catholic colleges in both English- and French-speaking parts of Africa. And one is not now speaking only of South Africa. In the Union the religious colour bar could take even more painful forms, extending at times beyond anything the law imposed.

There is no part of the continent in which at least some missionaries did not get infected by racialist attitudes adopted from nearby settlers. At times it was attempted to give such attitudes even a theological justification as when African seminaries have been made to pray "that we be delivered from the curse of Cain": such things, as a widespread tendency to identify Africans' racial "blackness" with some kind of racial and moral inferiority, are painful to recall.[16] Reference to these things has its purposes, especially as such attitudes are still far from extinct among those working in Africa. They are mentioned here as forming part of the very serious shadow, of which we are too seldom conscious, that European colonialism has in fact often thrown across our missionary work. Where European rule has been objectively unjust, and felt to be so by Africans, the friendly external behaviour of missionaries with settlers and government officials may have done far more than we realize to prevent Africans from fully accepting Church membership. This can explain the proliferation of Independent African Churches in countries like South Africa and Kenya. In the words of F. Welbourn, "Even for missionaries there is a sense in which the ties of race and culture are a stronger actual determinant of behaviour than their membership of a body in which there is neither Greek nor Jew.[17] Sharing in golf and the sun-downer could be held to prove a fundamental complicity in the works of the colonizers. And when those works, as in the old Kenya land and labour policies, were seen as deeply unjust, and when to that was added the visible sign of the first-class segregated Catholic college, a bar was created, which though still permitting individuals to embrace Christianity most sincerely, could prevent the society as a whole from doing so. In the words of Tom Mboya, a nationalist politician who is also a Christian and a friend of missionaries: The missionaries' "social life has often reflected the behaviour of the European settlers and colonial administrators, and disenchantment has come when nationalists see in the mis-

---

[16] An example of the sort of innocent futility which reveals so much in basic attitudes is the following: An experienced missionary explains how he described heaven to a dying woman: "There for thousands and thousands of years you will be just resting, Akunia, eternally resting. Even your skin will become white and no one will know it has once been black!" (*Claver Almanac*, 1954).
[17] *East Africa Rebels*, p. 180.

sionary world itself the same system and attitude which prevail among the settlers".[18] It is no good pointing out that the slave trade in the sixteenth and seventeenth centuries killed the old missions, and at the same time being entirely silent about similar, if far less crude, factors in the situation of this century. Thank God, such things are passing now—not so much, alas, owing to any initiative from within the Church but because of the general evolution of politics in lands outside the Republic of South Africa. But in recognizing all that the Church's missionary work has gained from its alliance with secular European forces, we have to admit too how much in the unsullied strength of its message it has also often lost.

We have spoken of the European, of what he brought with him, and of how he set about the transformation, religious or secular, of Africa. But what of the African? The history of conversion should be after all chiefly the story of the one changed. It is perhaps a weakness in much missionary literature that the missionary remains the centre of the picture from first to last. This is certainly a weakness in most presentations of modern African history in general: they remain accounts of Europeans in Africa encountering Africans. The approach, growing out of the sort of primary source easiest to obtain, is very natural; it is none the less misleading. It has suggested a passivity on the part of Africans at this crucial moment of their history which was not in fact the case. The story of Livingstone's servants carrying his body all the way back from Chitambo in modern Zambia to the coast is surely proof of the very positive way in which some Africans responded to the new situation. Among those who had been with Livingstone at his death in 1873 was a young man named Majwala, whose home was not in Zambia nor on the coast nor anywhere where Livingstone had ever been. It was on the northern shores of Lake Victoria in the kingdom of Buganda. His father, Namumjulirwa, had been a famous warrior and Pokino (county chief) of Buddu. Thirteen years later, on 3 June 1886, Majwala's brother, Bruno Sserunkuma, a soldier in the royal bodyguard, was burnt to death at Namugongo by order of King Mwanga on account of his profession of Chris-

[18] T. Mboya, *Freedom and After*, André Deutsch, 1963, p. 19.

tianity. He is today a canonized saint. Men like these were as positive in their approach to new things as to old.

Of course the African reaction to the missionary-cum-colonizing thing has varied enormously from place to place. With some, for instance the Masai and Karamojong, it has been a matter of indifference almost from first to last. With many others acceptance, often at first a wonderful, hopeful, trusting acceptance both of the white man and of what he brought. The great, loving, laughterful eyes of Africans, the eyes of the young that we have all seen time and again, had been opened to a new world, full of wisdom and adventure. They were opened too in undoubted bewilderment: the ways of the white man were so strange, his orders so brusquely given, the things he insisted upon so difficult to make sense of. A troublesome new pace had entered into life, but also a new sense of purpose or—as light dawned—of a whole range of possibly conflicting purposes, each represented by some sort of agent with one or another of which, if you were wise, you would seek to ally yourself. But acceptance, a humble willingness to learn, was the keynote of the new Africa: the humility of the disciple.

This acceptance did not mean servility, never that. Africans had a world of their own and a dignity in it, a past, a home and its values to be fought for if necessary in East, South and West. Zulu and Musutto and Muganda and Kikuyu and Yoruba: they could all stand up and fight if necessary, at first with their own weapons, soon with the white man's weapons; and they could stand up and argue, at first from their own premises but soon with the white man's arguments. They were, indeed, bewildered by the mass of idea and technique and new social pattern unloosed upon them, but they seldom entirely lost their heads and they remained in their own estimation free men, not servants.

In their own estimation. For it slowly became evident that it might only be their own estimation; that the white man whom they so easily accepted as teacher, as elder brother, as inspired leader, often looked upon himself as master and upon them as upon mere servants, second-class beings, almost (if one in misery may say so) as domesticated animals. It was difficult for Africans to believe this, to grasp that their so open-hearted acceptance of the new teacher into their home and land should have been so misunderstood. It took time for the eyes of hope to turn into those of disillusionment, and not everywhere nor with everyone did they need so to turn. The implicit recognition of human dignity and equality was the touchstone, proved by the warmth of personal relationship, by respect for custom, by manifest signs that the foreigner implicitly accepted that Africa was for the Africans; denied by keeping Africans at arm's length, by limiting their possibilities of advancement, by land grabbing. The choice made by most missionaries is not hard for us to see. Despite a possible roughness of manner, they had come *"propter Afros"* in search of no material gain, and were often to open their mouths in defence of the Africans' social and political rights. In countries like Uganda, where there were no settlers and the government was genuinely and consistently benevolent, Africans could see very well into the hearts of the strangers, and acceptance never turned far to bitterness. But in countries where the land was being lost and the law was against them, and all white men clearly supported the law and only seemed to accept other white men as equals, acceptance could indeed grow bitter as the years passed and it became an acceptance of tools and techniques, of the *savoir faire* that the white man could offer rather than of the happy fellowship that at one moment had seemed open, but was then denied. And they were right. A common humanity involves a deep equality between men, while even more Christianity—apparently the religion of all white men—is a fellowship, a community, not just a doctrine: and if full fellowship was not genuinely offered (and that meant a fellowship not only with white priests but with white laymen) then indeed there could be place only for the deepest of disillusionment.

Everywhere the African expected and expects equality. No other status could ever have occurred to him. At first an equality of personal dignity—the equality that can subsist between master and disciple—was sufficient; later, the equality to be master too, the equality to come to the top, political equality, was bound to be expected; and bound, too, to be given, where the earlier kind of equality had all along been admitted; bound, too, to be rejected, where basic, personal equality had all along been denied. The crisis of the years of the struggle for independence has not really been one of new attitudes, but of the hardening and clarifying of old ones. But the old simplicity has passed. For one thing the teacher lost his glamour, his faults were revealed; for another the techniques were being mastered, and they gave a new sense of confidence, of being on the inside. Often in European eyes they were only half-mastered and the conceit of the overconfident newcomer can seem insolent and overbearing. Everywhere relations have become difficult, difficult even among those on both sides whose fundamental attitudes are right, but much more so with those who make themselves unnecessarily the slaves of old resentments. The European, missionary or otherwise, has still much to offer, much that the African really wants to learn, but an atmosphere congenial to giving and taking is often absent and the psychological strains involved in the situations of today can easily be overwhelming.

4

If one considers the history of these last hundred years of mission work in Africa in a rough, global way, four periods can be unmistakably distinguished. Each period is characterized by the pattern that mission work took in it, by the methods typical of the time; and each corresponds also with a certain social and political situation.

The first period lasted the longest. It began whenever the mission began: 1840, 1860, 1880 and it continued roughly till 1890 or 1900. It was the period of the coast and it provides us with the normal nineteenth-century missionary approach: that of the Christian village, the *chrétienté*. The missionaries were relatively few and were mostly in areas greatly upset by slavery and the slave trade and almost everywhere their work and outlook was controlled by this last phenomenon: they came out rightly inflamed against it, inspired as they were by the anti-slavery campaigners in Europe from Wilberforce to Lavigerie. *Propaganda Fide* sent them money from Rome to redeem slaves. And redeem slaves they did. Slaves were bought; runaway slaves were befriended; any other outcast of local society was also gladly received and a Christian village was formed around the mission where the new Christians would be safe not only from slave-traders but also from all the corruptions of pagan society. The independent Christian community, the vast farm of well-tended acres spreading around the mission station, was the characteristic approach of the nineteenth-century missionary: the most striking exception being the mission in Buganda. But in a number of West African areas too, this method was less used as the century moved on, especially by Protestants, and in general new missions opening up about 1890 moved straight, or at least quickly, into the second period.

Though very impressive at first appearance, and doubtless almost dictated by the circumstances of the time, this first method proved in general a failure. The Church was almost hermetically sealed off by it from the normal society which the missionaries should have been chiefly evangelizing. Their time was soon taken up with a thousand secular concerns: the administration of a large community and its farm.[19] The human material—in general the dregs of African society—unlinked by any natural social bonds of tribe or common tradition, did not provide a good foundation for a vigorous Church life. Far from offering a bridge into African society, the "Christian village" presented a cul-de-sac.

In the last years of the nineteenth century the state of the whole of Africa changed very rapidly with the penetration throughout the continent of European rule; the slave trade disappeared. Missionaries moved into the interior and lived longer than those on the coast. They began to concern themselves far more seriously with African society as such. In Fr Jordan's book on Bishop Shanahan of Southern Nigeria we can read of the forcible reaction of one very powerful personality to the old methods and an inauguration of new ones. Throughout Africa the same thing was taking place. The missionary was turning his interest outward from the Christian village to a network of catechists' schools, established roughly but vigorously over wide areas. The first twenty years of this century provide the golden age of the catechist. In very many places the impact of Western rule made the people amenable to new things. They were anxious to be taught. At the same time the governments had small interest in education; they praised mission efforts but did little to supervise or subsidize them. These catechists' schools were Church schools not only in their formal control but in their whole pattern and purpose. And the catechist at that time was the man of prestige in the community, the man who more than others had mastered the new ways. He could teach them to his people. 1900–14 was one of the most fruitful periods

[19] For an account of these nineteenth-century mission villages, see R. Slade, *King Leopold's Congo*, O.U.P., pp. 148–55.

in the history of African mission work. The missionary was still in the lead, unshackled by government, but filled with an immense inspiration. Deep foundations, within the traditional societies, were now being laid.

The second period ends with the years after the First World War. There is a new government preoccupation with schools growing out of the report of the Phelps-Stokes Commission.[20] The development of African territories was now requiring a far larger local educated personnel, and education could no longer be left to develop in the haphazard way it had been doing. Government offered money to mission schools but insisted on supervision and soon the new age, the age of the schools, had begun. The effects that control of schools would have on what was now being seen as a newly emerging society were obvious, and the missions both Catholic and Protestant rushed into the new work. The catechist's school became a government recognized primary school; the catechists' training centre a teachers' training college: the priority of school work in the field was a deliberately accepted theorem. In the words of Mgr Hinsley, the Apostolic Visitor, to a gathering of bishops at Dar-es-Salaam in August 1928: "Where it is impossible for you to carry on both the immediate task of evangelization and your educational work, neglect your churches in order to perfect your schools."[21]

Above the primary schools came the secondaries and the arrival of orders of teaching brothers without whom the Church's effort in this field could never have developed as it did. By the time the Second World War broke out the university level was being envisaged. The effect of the war was to delay it a little, but once the war was over there was a steady push forward at this level by both government and Churches. But whereas government had been willing in most places to leave primaries and even secondaries in denominational hands,[22] it was not willing to do so, and quite

[20] This is true of Belgian as well as of British Africa, but a co-ordinated French educational policy in West Africa began considerably earlier. Details of the educational policy of Colonial Governments can best be studied in Lord Hailey's *African Survey*, Revised 1956, Oxford.

[21] Quoted in R. Oliver, *The Missionary Factor in East Africa*, p. 275.

[22] The exceptions being French West Africa, where the majority of schools were always non-mission, and such large Muslim areas in British Africa as Northern Nigeria and Zanzibar.

rightly, at the post-secondary level; so lay universities blossomed forth at Dakar, Ibadan, Makerere and Legon. The exception to this was in the Belgian Congo. Catholic missionaries, full of legitimate pride in the fine system of Catholic schools which had grown up in the various territories, could hardly bear to be thus excluded from control of the apex of the educational pyramid, and a number of Catholic university projects emerged in the same years: not only Lovanium University near Leopoldville but also Pius XII University College at Roma in Basutoland. Other projects failed to materialize at Kisubi in Uganda and Onitsha in Nigeria.

This period, one of intense concentration on building up a complete educational system with externally recognized standards from primary to university level, may be said to have come to an end in the late 'fifties. Not that such concerns did not and do not to a considerable extent continue, but that the structure of the work is changing as a whole and a new pattern of mission work is beginning again to impose itself: the fourth.

There are two striking facts in the new situation: one, the coming of independence and all that that involves; the other, the rapidly growing expense of educational institutions staffed and equipped for the needs of the times. To take this second factor first, we may note that Roma University College was handed over to the government of the High Commission Territories in 1964 because the Church was unable to continue to support it financially. That is symptomatic. The Church can also hardly maintain a host of colleges doing advanced "A" level work. The religious orders who had developed the Catholic schools throughout the continent are unable to provide adequate trained staff to teach in them and the post-war years have been ones of a rapidly growing lay participation; but that has meant the payment of salaries which only the government could afford. Inevitably government support and government control have loomed larger and larger; Church control of the schools has grown increasingly precarious, in spite of much sympathy and restraint on the government's part. Clearly this situation leaves the Church little ground to stand on when the new independent governments do decide to take over the schools, or at least in large measure to de-denominationalize them. That tendency is now everywhere apparent.

Furthermore, in many areas the concentration on schools carried with it a neglect both of the formation of catechists and of that of the local clergy. Pressed by government requirements and the people's desire to be initiated into English and other secular subjects, the missionary turned his attention from the existing class of catechists to the new class of teachers. Little by little training centres for catechists were closed down, whereas teachers' training colleges were everywhere opening up. The earlier prestige of the catechist was gradually lost and people of character and leadership no longer came forward to take on the job, which was extremely poorly paid—relative to the new scales—and went to people of only slight education. Poor pay forced the catechist to work more for himself and his catechist's activity suffered proportionately.

Concentration of the missionary's attention upon schools equally brought with it very often a neglect of clergy formation. This most crucial of works did not go ahead nearly as fast in the inter-war years as it should have done. The whole stress was different: on a schools system, necessarily at that time (and even largely today) in the hands of Europeans, rather than on the building up of an independent, local-controlled Church. It is pathetic how little had still been done in most places, despite a lip service of fine words, to form an adequately numerous local clergy by the end of the 1940s: pathetic especially when contrasted with the magnificent schools system which had been erected. In the 'fifties, with independence on the horizon, the stress at last shifted back again. Archbishop David Mathew, Apostolic Delegate to British Africa in the post-war years, was a prime mover in the new policies. A reasonably large number of African bishops were appointed, large sums of money spent on the building of seminaries, and some of the Church's best men put into them rather than into the schools. But the effects of this are only now getting under way.

At the same time positive defects in the Church's preoccupation with efficient schools have come more into the light. Already in 1923 a young African Christian could remark, "If religion were not connected with education and getting on in the world, how many people should we ever see in this church?"[23] Christian education has too easily been equated with the Church's ownership and management of schools. The need for education has brought

[23] Quoted in F. Welbourn, *East African Rebels*, p. 62.

thousands into the Church's schools from pagan or semi-pagan homes and they have experienced there an endless struggle to pass exams rather than a meeting with Christ. The spiritual atmosphere has too often been one of sheer indifference or, where that has been avoided, a hot-house discipline whose effects pass quickly away when the child is no longer within the confined walls of a Catholic institution. Furthermore, concentration on schools has meant the considerable neglect of all those children, generally more than 50 per cent of the total, who either failed to get into a Catholic school at all or only stayed there for two or three years of primary education. Educated Africans without any noticeable religious commitment will often praise the Catholic Church highly for having contributed more to education than any other agency, but one wonders whether the evangelistic and ecclesial value of the Catholic schools effort has always justified the amount put into it.

It is certainly not the intention to deny the value of that work, or to ignore the number of educated, committed Africans who have come out of Catholic schools, but we have to see it in proportion as a method of work certainly suited to the condition of society as it was evolving after the First World War but less so today when the new type of government is no longer willing to give the missions the educational freedom that the old colonial governments often did, when other needs call desperately for our very limited personnel, and when we are anyway discovering throughout the universal Church other perhaps more effective, and certainly more economical, ways of building up Christian life.

It may be noted here that though we have been considering chiefly the pattern of Catholic mission work in past and present, that of Protestants has not been strikingly different. Protestant missionaries have on the whole encountered similar situations with similar techniques. There are, however, certain variations. For one thing, especially in West Africa, they started effective work in the nineteenth century earlier than the Catholics; moreover, they were, with exceptions, less attracted by the "mission village" system. Their general influence on nineteenth-century West Africa was far greater than that of Catholics. Another point: both in the last and in this century they have in most places made more consistent effort to develop a local ministry than we have done. From this angle, as also from that of Bible translation, Catholics have remained almost everywhere behind Protestants at least until the post-Second World War period. But, in general, techniques have varied less than might have been expected from the variety of home organization and past tradition of the Churches, and today we are all facing very similar problems.

A Ghanaian, Mr Adu, gave the following advice to the Christian Churches Educational Association in Nairobi in June 1963:

> The time has come for the Churches to re-examine their role in the education field. . . . Today the Church is faced with the problem of preserving Christian education in the face of nationalistic tendencies in educational policy. I have seen in West Africa a tendency for the Churches to regard the running of schools and the establishment of more and more institutions as the measure of success achieved in Church enterprise . . . to the detriment of the primary object of all Churches. . . . I think there is a danger in relying too much on the facilities provided in the schools . . . it makes the Churches vulnerable to State intervention and may even bring them into conflict with the State governments.[24]

The governments have very good reasons for taking a greater measure of control over denominational schools in their efforts to build up new nations; by far the greater part of the financial burden of the schools is theirs and denominational divisions tend to add greatly to overall government expense, which is a very serious matter in poor countries. From our point of view, moreover, the mixing up of denominational schools should allow us to carry our apostolate further than before, into non-Catholic institutions where it was hitherto not possible to go.

All this does not mean that schools cannot still be useful to us; they can, very useful. But it does mean that the backbone of African Church life in the 1960s can no longer be a school system, both because it is an inadequate backbone and because in today's situation it is a dangerous one. We must again place our priorities in the churches themselves which in 1928 Mgr Hinsley told us if necessary to neglect.[25] And we have better means today in the new

---

[24] Quoted by D. Robinson, "The Churches, Schools and Religious Liberty", *AFER*, January 1965, pp. 9–10.

[25] It is certainly striking how little attention the Conciliar decree on Missionary Activity devotes to schools.

instruments which the liturgical and catechetical movements are forging for us. No longer is preoccupation with control of a complex schools system to be seen as the key of our African apostolate; instead we need to concentrate on active and understood participation of the people in liturgical worship and on the effective preaching of the word of God itself in church, in school—whether government or denominational—and anywhere else that we can do so.

So the new pattern of Church work in Africa which is now taking shape, or should be, will be one showing far less concern with the control of institutions. The Church rather than the school must again be the centre of our thinking, a Church enlivened by kerygmatic preaching and a popular liturgy. But the liturgy requires ministers and the greatest of all problems facing the African Church today is the utterly inadequate number of ordained priests or of men now coming forward into the major seminaries. Fine new buildings are not enough if the system itself is not adapted to the social circumstances of today. More and more it is obvious that Catholic life requires the celebration of the Eucharist in every sizeable group of Catholics every Sunday. Our present system of priest formation will never even begin to achieve that, and a Eucharist-less Church is a lifeless body. The coming era, if it is to be a fruitful one, must set off from a profound re-think based upon the implications of the conciliar decrees on the Church, the Liturgy, Ecumenism, Missionary Activity and the Church in the Modern World.

Evidently the work of the century before 1960 has been a vast one, great alike in quantity and in quality. Nobody surveying the complex field of the African Church today would doubt that. A new Church has been built, made up of hundreds of dioceses, many of them ruled over by African bishops and archbishops, and by two African cardinals, and it has been built not only in bricks and mortar but also very much in the hearts and loyalties of Africans in almost every part of the continent. But it is not a completed work, it is still growing at an unprecedented rate; at the same time as accommodating this enormous growth, the yet young and fragile Church requires readjustment on a vast scale not only because of real defects which have been inevitably present in its building but even more because of the changes that are going on in the universal Church and in the African continent today. "The Africa of today is not the Africa of twenty years ago", wrote the great Bishop Shanahan in 1913,[26] and that has been true several times since then. The Africa of independence is not the Africa of colonialism nor is the Church of Vatican II the same as that of Pius XII, let alone that of Vatican I. Today the whole mental and psychological atmosphere, the very standards of the useful and the suitable have changed. It is in the light of these changes that we have to survey our situation today, enormously thankful for the work God has permitted us to accomplish hitherto, but aware that fidelity to his inspiration may call us now to take different decisions and recognize priorities different from those presented to our predecessors.

5

The church of Villa Maria is very old, one of the oldest things in all its countryside; it has been there longer than the memory of any but the whitest-haired can remember, and that—in a country like this and a time like this—is very long indeed. It stands amid the green hills and the banana plantations and above the papyrus swamps of the county of Buddu in Uganda. It is a dark place— dark at least in comparison with the bright equatorial sun outside —but vast and well able to accommodate beneath its interlacing roof-beams some thousands of the Bannabuddu. It stands unchanging in its great cross form with twenty massive white pillars, its little round-headed windows and the smell of countless bats inhabiting the inaccessible rafters.

Besides its age and size, this church possesses a great holiness, for it goes back almost to the age of the martyrs and it was here that so many had to come from afar, before the modern parishes were erected, for baptism and catechism and confirmation. It is here that the priests have been made year after year since 1913, hallowed, respected men who mastered Latin when learning was still something rare and wonderful. They were trained for years in the seminary of Katigondo on the hill above, and then they knelt here in the great sanctuary by the bishop's throne, and here they were anointed and priested—in more recent years by the African bishop of Masaka, but formerly by Munsenyere Stensera

[26] J. P. Jordan, *Bishop Shanahan of Southern Nigeria*, p. 94.

himself,[27] the apostle of Buddu, their grandfather in the faith. It was he who founded the mission back in the last century, at the very time of the civil war, he who began the baptism register whose opening entry is dated 1891; it was he who built this present church in the last years of the old century after its predecessor had been burnt down in 1897 in Kabaka Mwanga's final revolt when Gabriel, the general of the army, earlier the Catholics' own champion and war leader, had re-embraced the ancient loyalties in the last organized struggle of the kingdom against the power and the god of the white men. Yes, it was Munsenyere Stensera who founded the mission and built the church and ordained the first priests.[28] It was he, with simple faith, iron determination and effective planning, who made of all this land a Catholic country-side and impressed on it his own ideals and enthusiasm, the strength and the narrowness of the Catholicism of his own home-land far away in Alsace. And his residence is there just above Villa Maria church, cool and thick-walled and attractive, a farm-house of Alsace, still housing faded photographs and the simple furniture of a missionary bishop. But most important of all: he himself is there, buried close below the main altar, awe-inspiring still in his presence, a shrine where the people come to pray.

There are many new things which have come into this country in recent years and which are changing its traditions and customs —more and more motor-cars and schools and cotton ginneries; they penetrate out from the town of Masaka which is a government and shopping centre, typical of its kind, and they make people impatient, especially the young people, with the old pattern of life of which the church is seen as part. For Villa Maria and its church and the faith which it represents were all there and firmly rooted before the arrival of these new things. At one time it was the centre of Buddu: the bishop lived there and the county chief, Alexis Sebbowa, lived near by, but times have changed. Masaka on crown land grew big while Villa Maria on mission land remained small, and the county chief moved away to Masaka, and the bishop moved away too, but the place remains with its age and its mighty pillars and its holiness, and now too with its many schools and its

---

[27] The Luganda form for Monsignor Streicher.
[28] By the time the church was built he was no longer superior of the local mission, but Vicar Apostolic.

hundreds upon hundreds of schoolchildren and its new life as the vigorous centre of a small but thickly populated parish. Like old churches in Europe, but unlike many things in modern Africa, Villa Maria has a history. Indeed Buddu, the great Catholic county of Buganda, their refuge after defeat in civil war; Buddu, with its pride and its wealth and its own traditions, could not begin to be understood without this church which has mothered and formed it in the faith.

On one hill above Villa stands Katigondo major seminary, on another Bwanda, the mother-house of the *Bannabikira*. It is an order of over five hundred nuns, founded too by the old bishop, trained by the White Sisters, and now ruled over by their own Mother General. Still often bare-footed, most of them speaking only Luganda, they work in every parish, teaching the girls, look-ing after the church vestments, growing bananas. Their companion order, the *Bannakaroli* teaching brothers, are less numerous but equally devoted and together they help to provide a core for the life of almost every parish. Besides the church and the schools are three houses—one for the fathers, another nearby for the Bannakaroli, a third near the girls' school for the Bannabikira. Without these simple but sturdy auxiliaries, the priests would not achieve the influence they do, nor could the Church maintain so effective a control over the primary schools.

Beyond each parish the hills roll up and down, and round each hill there is a village, and in the village a little catechist's chapel, and beside it the catechist's house. The catechists are not well instructed and they have not so much to do, but they represent the Church at its most local and its most conservative. Everywhere here the Church is a rooted, native thing, co-existing in the minds of the people with superstitions older and more native still. The pattern of thought, both Christian and pagan, is narrow, old-fashioned, difficult to change; it is the life of a peasant community, still largely turned in upon itself and only very mildly interested in the world beyond. It has some of the strength and the weaknesses of conservative Catholic peasantry the world over, and its clergy have naturally partaken of its character. It is the natural product of the conservatism of the people, the devotions and religious out-look of the turn of the century, the zeal and rigidity of the old mis-sionaries. They were hard as iron. They had come up from the coast in journeys which took months, not hours; they never expected to return home; those that survived the first illnesses became almost invulnerable to sickness; they knew the language as few non-natives ever know one; they wrote hymn-books and catechisms and dictionaries. In a few years they had established a vigorous new limb of the Church. They and their like in other parts of Africa have achieved something for the Church which has hardly been done since the conversion of the Poles and the Hungarians in the early Middle Ages—although in few other parts of Africa has the Church so grown into the country as it has here in the county of Buddu.

The people responded to their preaching. Hardly had Mapera[29] arrived than the martyrs were there to shed their blood; and it was an active martyrdom, a martyrdom of men who were natural leaders, conscious of what they did and of their position in the chiefly ranks of their society, deliberately refusing to obey the traditionally absolute power within the State for the sake of a newly-discovered greater good. Joseph Mukasa Balikuddembe, Charles Lwanga and their fellows were the best that their society could offer to God, not only supernaturally but naturally. And this best was very good indeed. They were not alone. The cream of the young men of the chiefly class was soon pouring into the Christian Church, and when revolt succeeded to persecution, the Christians had leaders in men like Honorat Nnyonintono and Stanislaus Mugwanya far more capable than their adversaries. Having won, they quickly took over the leadership of the nation: a remarkable instance of a social revolution carried on inside a governing class, and modern Buganda is built upon this social *cum* religious revolution of the late last century, which was engineered from within the group, not imposed from without. Within a very few years of the fires of Namugongo and the chanting of hymns by the burning martyrs, the whole structure of the State of Buganda had become formally Christian: in part a veneer, of course, but not a pure veneer, and certainly not a meaningless one. At its pinnacle it was to be a Protestant State; the firing of Captain Lugard's maxim gun in the battle of Mengo had ensured that. The Kabaka of Buganda, his chief minister, and a majority of the chiefs were to be Protes-

---

[29] The Luganda name for Fr Lourdel, derived from the French *"mon père"*.

tants, sharing in the Anglican quasi-establishment which the British Raj has carried about with it everywhere. But all missionaries were to be free to work so that soon the Catholics could be far more numerous, while the great county of Buddu in the west of the kingdom was to be politically their preserve. So it was decreed seventy years ago and so it has remained to this day.

In many parts of Africa Christianity has come only through the schools and therefore to the children, and its coming has meant a rupture between young and old, between the traditional tribal hierarchy and a new Christian society, and it has left both weak and unsure of themselves. In Buganda this never happened. It was adults, not children, who became Christian first, and far from being left out of their own tribal society, in one sharp struggle they captured it for themselves, and ever since then it has been rather the pagans and Muslims who have been left out of the nation's counsels and advancing life.

Though the Christian revolution was in the first instance the work of a small group of immensely wide-awake young chiefs and their immediate following, it did not remain merely on that level. This was the work of the missionaries' catechism classes at Rubaga and Villa Maria, the constant journeyings of the fathers, the founding of new stations, and soon the devoted teaching of a whole army of catechists. People in general embraced the faith almost as readily as did that first small group of young men in Mwanga's palace. Around the mission stations and catechists' chapels have grown up the circle of deeply sincere Christian homes. The homes of the Baganda are pleasant places. There is good land here; rolling land, never fiercely hot, seldom frighteningly dry; it is a land of regular rain, of green hills and valleys and plenty of fertile earth. The houses nestle on the hill slopes surrounded by the banana plantations and coffee bushes and patches of beans and ground-nuts and corn on the cob. The houses themselves are straight-walled earth constructions for the most part, with a wooden frame-work, small shuttered windows, and a roof of corrugated iron or red tiles. Around the main house are smaller outhouses for kitchen, animals and the like, and a rough courtyard where hens peck and the coffee berries dry in the sun. Such houses are neatly built and pleasant to look at, though the rooms inside may be small and there is little furniture. But they are homes, and many of them—houses

near the parish church, houses of catechists, and lots of others too
—Catholic homes where pictures of the Sacred Heart and the pope
greet you from the walls and a cluster of rosaries hang down beside
them.

The children who grow up in such houses with their rosaries and
their family prayers are many of them Christians of the third, and
even the fourth, generation, and may easily lack the fervour of their
parents and react against both the piety and the moral law that
they are taught, but these things are not alien to them, and the
religious vocation can seem natural too. How many of the young
seminarists have uncles and aunts or elder brothers and sisters who
are priests, brothers, nuns. How many are the children of ex-
seminarists, excellent men, still proud of their Latin and the
seminary which trained them, though they themselves never
reached its goal. And out of such seminarists has come a numerous
body of clergy, faithful to its pastoral duty and the norms the missionaries laid down, proud of the tradition of Masaka diocese which
has now been ruled by African bishops for almost thirty years. This
is a clergy, sure of itself, sure of its people, slow to move, hesitant
about new things both in Church and State.

This is a description of the best that missionary work has built
up; there are other areas more or less comparable like the Pera-
miho district of Tanzania, Dahomey, the Ibo country in Eastern
Nigeria, Lesotho, but in few places has so much been achieved.
It is well to see things at their best, but the best must itself be seen
within the context around it. Christian communities of this kind
provide a tiny minority in Africa today. Not only are Christians
themselves in all a small minority, but for the greater number of
them the new religion has not as yet entered in transformingly. It
has disrupted the old harmony between belief and society without
creating a new one. But even when the Church does seem, as in
Masaka, to have attained some sort of stability within society, it is
being plunged today into a new storm which is overtaking pagan
and Christian alike—a new unrest among the youth, new social
patterns and ways of government, a whole new world with vast
horizons which is seen to be determined as much by men in Wash-
ington and Moscow as by anyone locally. And it is to remote
places like New York and Moscow that the young boys who grew
up in these country ways and studied in the village primaries are

now departing for education. In the atmosphere of today both the traditional African elements of society and its traditional missionary elements are being called ruthlessly in question. The Church of Villa Maria, which was formed in an old world—the old world of Europe as well as the old world of Africa—is today open to all the winds of a new Africa and a new universe.

6

There are now in Africa not one but some three hundred dioceses, over twenty-eight million Catholics, many thousands of missionaries—priests, religious and lay—over two thousand five hundred African priests, thousands more of African nuns and brothers. It is a great achievement for eighty years. At the same time there are another twenty million Protestants, some eighty million Muslims, one hundred and seventy million pagans. These figures are not very exact; it is impossible that they should be; the religious loyalty of many people is anyway extremely tenuous. But some points are clear. One is that all Christians together in Africa form a small minority, though of course one with an influence out of proportion to its numbers because of its generally higher level of education. A second is that, quite apart from old traditionally Muslim parts (such as the Arab lands of the north, the Sahara, and the east coast strip). Islam has made much recent progress in a good many places, such as Yorubaland in Nigeria, though little or none in others. A third is that the evangelization of pagans alone remains a task in size far beyond the resources of the Catholic Church as they are at present marshalled. The majority of priests in Africa today have their hands more than full with pastoral and educational work for the twenty-eight million existing Catholics; they have precious little time left for the vast pagan majority. Unless and until we can drastically change our own internal organization and methods of evangelization, there is little point in moaning about the advance of Islam, for we often simply cannot present a feasible alternative. Islam can advance with little organization, we apparently cannot. There are indeed areas, particularly in West Africa, where one should ask why it is that Islam seems to spread so much more effectively than Christianity, even in places where the latter arrived before or about contemporaneously with the former. Sierra

Leone is one case, Western Nigeria another. But for the most part to weep over the strength of Islam in Africa is somewhat like weeping over that of Hinduism in India: it depends on circumstances now quite out of our control. It is part of the providence of God. The Christian conversion of Africa as a continent is not today within the realms of feasibility, and a Christian has as much reason as anyone else to be a realist. When we look at the modern Church of Africa, it must not be with the eyes of the imagination but with those of Christian common sense. The function of the Church always has been and remains today within the realms of the possible. Though that is not to say that we might not make strides forward of a very remarkable kind if we were prepared to revise our structure of ministry and pattern of work really radically. To fulfil the Church's function effectively within a given situation, it is required to understand both her essential nature and that situation and then relate the one to the other.

Just as the missionary of the end of the last century entered a complex situation in which there were many different and conflicting influences, affecting both the people he had come to evangelize and their very interpretation of his own work, so today has the Church to work within a situation which is being remoulded by forces largely outside her control, but which shape the very pattern her own work should take. Many of these forces are either entirely new to the last few years or at least have now an enormously much increased strength; and a Church, the shape of whose work was largely worked out for an earlier, quieter and very different age, is inevitably poorly prepared for the pressures of today.

The four chief influences of which we must take account in any study of contemporary problems are: first, nationalism and the africanization of control; secondly, social transformation; thirdly, the population explosion; and fourthly, the new pressure of conflicting ideologies. Without a real appreciation of these four factors, it is quite impossible to consider the present needs of the African Church.

The psychological mood of modern nationalism is composed of many strands, but its central position here lies in the simple affirmation of the value of being an African. Too much of the European attitude towards Africans has expressed, sometimes very arrogantly, sometimes simply implicitly, the inferiority of African-ness. In the conditions of human nature and the enormous difference of skills that existed between representatives of the two races, some of these attitudes were inevitable. But no people can bear the imputation of inferiority, and the further it has gone the sharper must be the reaction. To be African is in no way to be a second best. Nationalism is not just a matter of politics, it is the renovation of society and the lover of Africa can only rejoice in what is deeply positive about it. Evidently it is made sharper where a colour bar or laws deliberately negating the dignity of Africans have been in force; the danger can then become real that the spirit of indignation, of repudiation, can go so much to the head that men discriminate no more, and the Christian Church and the deepest, most human, most formative things brought by Europeans may be rejected with their sins and defects and rule.

In fact in the day of Africa's majority it is remarkable how moderate the nationalist generally is. The Pan-African movement, the search for the African personality, the statement of African Socialism—such things are seldom carried beyond the bounds of what even the outsider must consider reasonable. The Church has to live with them and help to form the new outlook from within. But a missionary who is basically out of sympathy with these attitudes, who still regrets that African States have received their independence, or thinks that Africans are less intelligent than other people, or that they are out of place in wanting to enter effectively into the world of international relations and the U.N.O., such a missionary should really not be in Africa today—and in South Africa no more than in Ghana—for you cannot work fruitfully with people if you are not in harmony with their most heartfelt aspirations.

Let us remember too that if at times African intellectuals show what seems to us a rather perverse resentment and reaction against European civilization, the civilization that has been presented to them was not always the European achievement in its most humane or endearing form; indeed it is often presented, at least in Rhodesia and the South, as precisely identical with white domination! Certainly there is a side of Western achievement other than that of aggressive activism, but the educated African has been taught to sum it all up in three words: inventions, discoveries, conquests. We have harped on these things overseas. The history that is put into African history textbooks seems so often the history of the most exterior, the most obtruding side of European achievement. Africa was traditionally concerned with just the opposite: the immutable rhythm of things and of man sharing in the cycle of the spiritual and physical worlds. We should be able to sympathize with the reaction of Aimé Cesaire:

> Hurray for those who never invented anything!
> Hurray for those who never explored anything!
> Hurray for those who never conquered anything!

It is a natural reaction to the brazenly superior, the mastering, contemptuous-of-others thing that has been paraded as the European achievement. In fact, of course, most educated young Africans have themselves no sympathy at all for such a reaction! What is sad is that there has not been a wider questioning, that the projected image of civilization has been so generally accepted as the ultimate norm, and that so often even the Church's educational institutions have seemed little more than a machine for passing examinations and providing Africans with the crude elements of European technology. We have cared too little to share with them the more humane, less go-getting aspect of learning: poetry, drama, art, music, though one does notice that in recent years some schools (not all of them Protestant) have come at last to take such things much more to heart. As a legacy they will outlast *Baaskap*.

If at the same time there is a revived sentiment of Africanness growing, a mood of criticism, a desire to be different, to offer a characteristic contribution to the world, it is certainly not for the Church or her institutions to present themselves as bastions of Europeanness, nor can we—like the government of South Africa—lay down some appropriate "tribal" conditions for such manifestations. In the modern dreary race towards uniformity every emergence or strengthening of a national culture is to be welcomed. "For too long in our history," said Dr Nkrumah, "Africa has spoken through the voice of others." That is not a healthy state of society, and it is part of the Church's work to help form a rounded, healthy society. Just as it was the duty of the first missionaries to understand tribal beliefs and customs, so it is that of the modern missionary also to be interested in the poetry of Senghor, the novels

7

of Tutuola or Ekwensi, the politics of Pan-Africanism, the history of Songhai and Monomotapa and the land of Zanj.

It is to be accepted as equally desirable that the fundamental responsibility and control of African affairs should rest in African hands. That is the central political insistence of the nationalist movement and it is again something which we must not only tolerate, but rejoice in. The colonial system implicitly denied Africans a political life, except in its closing stages, but man is a political animal and a society cannot be built up across the negation of one of its fundamental dimensions. Whatever the temporary justification for the colonial system, it was essentially anomalous. There is, of course, no reason why the coming of independence should be practically disadvantageous to the Church. On the contrary. The close co-operation of colonial governments with mission agencies helped to give the Church a foreign and colonialist character, while the co-operation of the Church now with national governments will, instead, strengthen her image as being at home in every people. Or at least it can strengthen that image so long as she does not try to insist on all the privileges which were hers in the colonial past; so long too as her leadership is africanized— which is in fact happening, especially at archiepiscopal level. It is as fitting that the bishops of a country should mostly be its own citizens as that its Cabinet ministers should be. The reason for the two may be somewhat different but the conclusions are the same. It would seem very strange if the Church consistently appointed French bishops in Germany, or English in Italy. We have still some way to go before we can satisfy the quite reasonable desiderata of the nationalist outlook in this matter.

The second overriding factor in today's Africa is that of social transformation. The anthropologist can still study traditional tribal patterns in any part of the continent, and the missionary can still evangelize those who live in a way no different from their grandfathers, and yet the effective structure of African society is changing rapidly. The town, the university, the great mining area, the chain of big secondary schools: these are new and decisive aspects of African society and they require a different type of evangelization. A missionary training which has been geared to rural, tribal work and which has aimed at producing a mental formation suited to that work needs very drastic revision if it is to be suited to today's needs. The personnel at the Church's disposal in Africa is very limited in comparison with possible fields of work, and the danger is to go on concentrating too much on what we are used to—the rural apostolate—and to give far less than a reasonable minimum to new approaches. One might compare the large number of missionaries working in Lesotho, a rural, mountainous area, with the relatively few at work in the African locations around Johannesburg. Those locations have as big a population as has the whole of Lesotho, they even include very many of the young people of Lesotho who have come down to get employment; and it is surely in the great urban areas that the future of South Africa and its leadership will be decided. Certainly the urban locations offer a much more difficult field to work in, especially in South Africa, but it remains the decisive one.

It is not true of course that African society is now, or in the near future will become, a largely urban society as so much of Europe and America now is. Village life continues to be the norm for the great majority. But even here the bonds of society are greatly changing, becoming freer, more individualistic. Everywhere the young men are questioning the old accepted attitudes and need a new, very sympathetic, kind of guidance.

With this qualitative change in African society goes a quantitative one: the population explosion. It is of course the vast increase in numbers which explains in large part the emergence of new social patterns. There is not enough room for so many young people in the villages, and they flock to the towns. European medicine has really caused an African revolution quite as deep as European education, by producing millions more mouths and hands and brains. It is not, perhaps, an accident that it is the Congo, which had, under the Belgians, the best medical services in Africa, which has seen the most sudden and extensive urbanization.

According to United Nations statistics the mid-1964 population of Africa was 304 million. The present growth rate in most places is 2 to 3 per cent a year. It is further estimated that by 1980 there will be 450 million and 768 million by the end of the century: that is only thirty-five years away. If there are twenty-eight million Catholics now, there can easily be eighty or a hundred million by the year 2000—the present Catholic growth rate seems to be about 6 to 7 per cent a year. Such figures are frankly terrifying, at least when no one is doing the Church planning that such an increase demands. The shape of Church work and one's judgment on it has to be related to these essential facts. Missionary statistics, even if themselves accurate, which often they are not, can indicate almost nothing unless they are co-related with the general population statistics in a very exact way. This very rapid growth rate should force Church policy to be truly anticipatory. At present it is not so at all. Thus sound thinking about the ministry has to work from the number of Catholics that we both actually have and within a limited period can expect to have: much of the woolly thinking and unrealistic cheerfulness on the subject of vocations and ordinations is due to a failure of awareness of population facts: of how much more quickly the Catholic population is growing than the number of priests at the Church's disposal.

A vastly growing population, two-thirds of which is under twenty years of age, new cities, new universities, new governments—all that is characteristic of the Africa of the 1960s and with them goes something more: the incipient clash of ideology. One cannot compare today and yesterday without seeing the striking contrast from this point of view. The colonial régime was one, as far as possible, of ideological tranquillity. European governments did not favour unsettling ideas. Communist propaganda was carefully excluded, even nationalism might sound like a dirty word. The missionary Churches were widely awarded a quasi-monopoly of education below university level, and they found the arrangement a comfortable and satisfactory one. Things today are less comfortable. New universities are being opened all over the continent and they are seldom centres of a specifically Christian point of view. Economic and cultural missions from communist countries are frequent arrivals and their permanent embassies are large and important. There are thousands of African students in Britain, France and the United States, but thousands also in Moscow, Prague and Peking. In the past the fairly simple education imparted in the schools left the ordinary missionary still intellectually master of the situation; today the swift spread of higher education—not only in the universities, but also in the sixth forms of schools and other higher colleges—can leave both the missionary and the African priests he has trained in a state of educational inferiority to those with whom they come into frequent contact. This is partly inevitable in a developed society and not necessarily a bad thing in all circumstances, but we can hardly afford it on a large scale at a time and place of ideological conflict. I have met a young missionary priest who thought the world was created six thousand years ago. Such a lack of modern awareness might not have brought the Church to disaster in the past, but it can so today if it erodes the intellectual confidence of the young in the Church's representatives. The missionary Church has now to face a genuinely ideological struggle, whereas up till now she has tended to get away very well with the purely *ex cathedra* attitude: "we happen to know". That is not good enough any more. A revitalized Islam, presented as the natural religion for Africa, Marxism, extreme nationalism, every type of secularism: these things are genuinely competing today for the minds of young undergraduates in the universities, young workers in the towns, young students in our own church schools. To help them we have to be as educated as our rivals, as convincing, as appreciative of the moods of youth. We have to be awake in a world of ideological struggle.

One can of course describe the work and prospects of the Church in Africa in terms which disregard these great forces. One can still produce figures of baptisms and communions, of dioceses, of the number of hospital beds, of ordinations; one can describe some typical missionary's day; one can speak of the millions of non-believers awaiting the word of God. And all will be very true and important. But unless these things are related both to the practical possibilities and needs of the Church and to the great factors which are transforming the world around her, our picture will remain an unreal one.

IV

Post-Independence Africa

To THE European outsider the achievement of political independence in the last few years by most of the countries of Africa could appear as the ending of a story: the story of European colonization and overseas rule, and the story of the nationalist struggle for freedom. As these were now over, it was presumed that conditions of stability must have been achieved, and that an era of uneventful development was about to ensue. When this does not happen, and there is instead a revolution or other disturbance, one easily concludes that the country in question was not after all ready for independence. For some, every apparent deviation from Western normality becomes one more item in a terrible catalogue of the sins of independent Africa: a ghastly warning which the white leadership of Rhodesia and the South are only too right to heed. This view works on the curious supposition that a people not possessing economic and political stability should, *ipso facto*, be ruled by someone else. It seems to me that approaches of this kind to what is going on in Africa today present us with a dangerously false focus, implying as they do that the acquiring of independence should have marked the culmination of the great process of building the new society rather than be the condition for its initiation. In fact it is that process which is going on now and I find it far more interesting than what happened before independence, but it is of its nature something which involves instability, tension and the immaturity which is inevitable when people are just beginning to face, collectively and individually, a wide range of new situations and problems. All these things are well worth putting up with for the exhilaration of being no longer in tutelage and having the world before one, and anyone who wants to approach the African situation from the inside needs to share in that exhilaration.

Stability in a State is not obtained by the acceptance of a balanced paper constitution, but by the working out of a balance of power between the various elements in its society, and this is bound to take time to emerge. It was to be expected that in one form or another the post-independence epoch of African history would prove to be more revolutionary than the age which went before it, and this is not a cause for reproaches. Nations, like individuals, have to go through things for themselves, and there is much, both good and bad, that cannot be experienced under foreign control. The declaration of independence is not then the sign that the time in which a nation is obtaining its fundamental experience in the social, political, cultural or religious fields is over, but rather that it can now begin, and the gaining of this experience may be a costly affair. If we chopped off the heads of kings and archbishops in our golden constitutional age of the seventeenth century, without presumably forfeiting the right to be independent, we should not be surprised if things happen in a new country which would not take place in the matured and weary atmosphere of Westminster. Pride's Purge does not show that constitutional freedom had no lovers and no future in seventeenth-century England, nor did Nkrumah's most dictatorial acts show that it has none in today's Ghana.

The coming of independence to the particular African territories which existed prior to independence has done no more than set the stage for a vast process of evolutionary and revolutionary change, whose political element is not the most important. The deeper revolutions are economic and mental. Without them political independence may bring, as it did in Liberia, only stagnation. But equally, without political independence, all the rest would turn sour and lack the necessary thrust from within. They must, in fact, go together. Politics get more into the news, but behind them are great forces, inexorably changing the face of Africa, forces whose effects can be moulded in a variety of ways, but which cannot be denied or held back. There is, first of all, the population increase; secondly, a staggering expansion of schools and universities; thirdly, wider than this, though obviously closely linked to it, the mental revolution in horizons, in criteria of assessment, in expectations; fourthly, and wider still, the economic revolution in production, consumption, living standards. The political revolution of the last seven years is the curtain raiser for a social revolution that is still only beginning, but which is bound to bring with it further political change and upheaval.

Nevertheless the political revolution that has replaced white control by black in most parts of the continent has had a particular character which is bound to influence future developments most considerably. For one thing it has been, with some exceptions, a very peaceful change-over. One might perhaps regret this. A nation may value its freedom and independence more across and because of the struggle it has had to gain these things. The struggle welds the nation; for the most part the new countries of Africa have had little of this. Countries like Tanzania and Uganda will have no epic freedom fight to look back upon: no Easter 1916, no storming of the Bastille, no martyrs for freedom. Will a future struggle with southern Africa supply this lack, and most terribly?

In most countries the anti-colonial campaign cannot be said to have seared the nation's soul or produced a saga whose common possession would help unify the country. What is remarkable is how much sense of unity countries like Tanzania have nevertheless developed. Nor does a gentle advance through conferences at Lancaster House and a series of agreed constitutions help to stimulate the muses. It is the tension and emotions of conflict and resistance to tyranny rather than a régime of careful reasonableness which excite artistic creation and it may well be that the Africans of South Africa will produce from their more bitter experience a far richer literature and a national saga that their descendants will never forget. Suffering can bring with it a compensation in maturity.

Yet it is obvious how good are the effects of the mildness with which independence has arrived in most parts of Africa. Among them is the friendliness which persists between the new nations and their former colonizers, and makes it possible for European expatriates to continue making a very real contribution to the growing life of these countries.

The political revolution and the emergence of some thirty new independent States from Senegal in the West to Somalia in the East seems now to have consecrated a series of often rather artificial frontiers, which are going to be extremely difficult to change.

Throughout the continent frontiers cut ancient peoples into two, yet it is striking that nowhere do the new States seem prepared to consider frontier changes, however reasonable claims for cession may be in the light of traditional African history or ethnology, and however much the frontiers to be defended today are due to the greed or ignorance of European politicians of the late last century. The politicians are not only true to character but probably wise in this, for once changes began there would be no end to them and the difficulty of relating political to ethnic and cultural frontiers can be overwhelming; but remembering how considerable was the discontent over the territorial division of tribes in the past, it seems strange how easily the colonial pattern has in fact been accepted by dominant African public opinion.

Similarly, the earlier urge for the wider federation of States, on a regional or even continental basis, has greatly diminished with the grasping of the fruits of local independence. It is clear, for instance, how much less eager the leaders of the three States of East Africa are for federation now than they appeared to be a few years ago. These two things go together and point to a very important phenomenon which is that almost everywhere a new leadership quickly emerged, and hardened, and in doing so identified itself with the *status quo*, a position which could best guarantee its own continuance in the exact form to which it was accustomed.

This new leadership represented a certain group of people, mostly fairly young, who were ready to occupy the leading positions in each State about the time of independence. They entered into the establishment somewhat as an age-group, replacing not their elders but expatriates. They had a short apprenticeship but could naturally look forward to a long tenure of their position of power and they are not, collectively or individually, very willing to move. Their corporate emergence is related too to economic and educational factors.

It is doubtful whether at present the economic development of most countries of Africa is comparable in pace with the others mentioned above—those of population increase, education, and mental attitudes—and this may well have a decisive effect on social stability. At present there is a rather thin layer of economic development spread wide (represented on the production side by a cash crop, on the consumption side by bread, wirelesses, etc), and there is a thick but very narrow wedge. That thick wedge is one of industrial development and of key salaried posts in commerce, government and the professions. Both these things follow a closely Western pattern. Industry is limited to a very few places, and if it raises the Gross National Product considerably, it inevitably does so chiefly to the advantage of a very small section of the community. Much of the economic advance in Africa hardly affects the "underdevelopment" of society as a whole, at least in the present phase. It rather tends to enhance a "dual economy": a very small sector of opulence somewhat unconnected with a surrounding field of indigence. The same thing can come about in the professional and political fields. The salary scales of graduate teachers, government servants and company executives are those first given to expatriates, and are therefore geared to the economy of a West European society. Their (doubtless inevitable) continuation after africanization further contributes to a state of imbalance between the tiny few who may now live on the economic level of the British middle class and the rest,[1] though it is true as well that clan and family solidarity often does much to redistribute the high salary of the successful individual over a wide range of relatives.

This pattern of a dual economy is in some way related to that of higher education as it existed in the years before independence. The academic ladder proceeded to the very top: to Makerere, Ibadan, Legon, and even to London and Oxford, but its upper rungs were trod by very few. Secondary schools had a very small intake: the difference between the numbers in primaries and the numbers in secondaries being very striking. An élite was certainly formed, and it was that élite which took over the country at independence and guaranteed stability and continuity. Inheriting the loaves and fishes, it could have no desire to upset the system which produced them. It is interesting to compare this with the situation in the Congo, where no such élite had been formed, and independence was followed by chaos. No one had been equipped for leadership at a more than local level, and no one really saw himself as having a vested interest in preserving order. In British Africa this was not so. There was a double basis of leadership and of vested

---

[1] The recent decrease in all the upper range of Tanzanian government salaries is at least a fine symbol of the desire to remedy this, starting with the president.

interest: old tribal and new Western, and both were present during the change-over, ensuring general stability. As regards the first: great tribal chieftainships remained powerful in many places— Ashanti, Northern Nigeria, Central and Western Uganda, Barotse- land, and elsewhere, whereas they had been eliminated in the Congo (though not, of course, in Rwanda and Burundi). After years of integration into the colonial system, these chieftainships—the most African elements in the African power heaven of today— have generally stood out rather strikingly for a continuation of the system of the late colonial period. They, like the new élite, certainly worked for continuity and stability in the period of power tran- sition.

After independence the first clash for leadership between Africans in the new societies often appeared as one between these two groups—those possessing traditional tribal authority and the "new men". Where the political units involved were not tribal, but inter-tribal ones, and therefore a naked appeal to tribal authority would bring about the disintegration of the new States, it has been the new men, who—across Western electoral practice—have in- herited the central reins of power from the European inter-tribal authority, and who have generally seemed to triumph in the first struggles for leadership. However, this sort of clash may be less meaningful than might appear. The reason is simple. The new leaders were often recruited from the ranks of the old, and could even be identical with them, as in Northern Nigeria. How many prime ministers of Burundi have been members of the royal family? It is perfectly understandable that it was the chiefly families who first sent their sons for higher education and subsequently occupied the better positions in the new governing class as they appeared. In very many places there is a close family continuity between those possessing the traditional tribal authority and those who have come to the top across a political party and the process of elections. And this is surely what anyone who knows something of the historical composition of the British House of Commons might well expect. To a considerable extent, then, the traditional hierarchy effectively retained its grasp while adapting itself to certain external Western patterns of government. In such cases more genuinely radical elements were simply squeezed out.

Where there has been sharp leadership conflict between the new and the old, it has been more often an inter-tribal one, than an inter-class one within a single tribe. That is to say, either one tribe has feared domination by others within an inter-tribal State and has countered with a separatism centred upon traditional tribal groups, or—as in Rwanda and Zanzibar—the traditional rulers were identified with a privileged minority lording it over a tribally differentiated majority, and the coming of modernization almost inevitably brought with it a revolution at once social and political. It was clearly the fault of the colonizing power in these cases to leave largely undisturbed a situation of outdated minority privilege which could so easily lead to violent revolution.

For the most part the leadership that took over at independence in African countries was then a composite of old and new, with both plenty of reason for desiring stability and the strength to maintain it. There was usually nothing very revolutionary about most of this leadership, except the racial change—it was a replacing of white by black. It was, of course, committed to pressing on with national development, but its general character—though naturally open to much new blood—tended towards that of an oligarchy, in which, behind a modern constitution, traditionally important families often continued to be highly influential. Such an establishment can become identified with the social and political *status quo*, while its desire for security provided much of the reality behind the formula of the one-party State. These post-independence régimes quickly came to appear as more concerned with power than with ideology.

We can see then that in Africa the political revolution of the last few years produced, in the lines of territory, institution and personnel, régimes of some stability, based upon a power group whose emergence was not only political but was related to the economic and educational pattern of the years around independence. With some observers it is the custom to condemn the post-independence African leadership as selfish, cut off from the common people, and so on. Doubtless there is much truth in such criticisms, as there often is of governing groups, but I am not trying to make a moral point here. I want simply to outline a certain, very important social phenomenon, and, one may add, an inevitable one. Revolutions are nearly always made by minorities, and countries moving away from a very simple rural economy are inevitably led by minorities, and ruling minorities invariably look largely to their own interests. It is enough that this group represented the obvious natural rulers of their countries at the moment of independence.

But if the emergence of this group, riding the first wave of independence, was one social fact, the development of a far wider revolution, whose manifestation is only coming little by little, but which, in re-shaping African society in a titanic fashion, is obviously not going to leave the cosy world of the original revolution and its leadership unscathed, is another. New leadership problems are sure to arise—indeed in many countries have already done so—and they are closely related to the elements of stability and instability in society and to the locality of its growth points. It is important to analyse these problems, seeing how far leadership conflicts and the appearance of elements of instability may be basically due, for instance, not to communist infiltration, the perversity and immaturity of Africans, or any cause other than an almost necessary evolution that society is bound to undergo in the coming years. An approach of this kind might help to prevent too hasty ideological judgments on what is going on or the facile identification of the Church, or Western civilization, or the Christian cause, with any particular régime or power group.

In all independent African countries today a very high proportion of total government expenditure is being devoted to education and there is an enormous increase in the number of those studying at all levels, but particularly at higher ones. Thus, in Uganda, whereas in 1960 only three or four schools were preparing some hundred students for "A" levels, there are now over twenty preparing some thousands of students. There is similar expansion everywhere and it continues at post-secondary level. Instead of the few cautiously developed university colleges colonial governments provided, there is now a whole spate of rapidly expanding ones. Nigeria alone has five universities. New ones spring up yearly across East and Central Africa to join the original trio of Makerere, Lovanium and Salisbury: Nairobi, Dar-es Salaam,[2] Elisabethville, Stanleyville, Busumbura, Kabgaye, Lusaka, Blantyre. . . . Moreover, there are literally thousands of Africans undertaking university studies in Great

---

[2] Strictly speaking, Makerere, Nairobi and Dar-es Salaam are not at present separate universities, but constituent university colleges of the University of East Africa.

Britain, and thousands of others in the U.S.A., Russia, etc. Below these are the tens of thousands who have fallen from the race, but have obtained eight, ten, or more years of formal education, who no longer feel satisfied with village life and drift elsewhere, providing what is perhaps the greatest single worry for African governments today. This is obviously much stimulated by the rapid increase of population: the traditional village often simply cannot absorb so many young people.

But neither can the towns. In general the economy is not developing comparably with education and there is a real danger that higher education—especially if it is incomplete—will come to put people out of a job, rather than into one. This is especially true as so little of the educational effort is directed towards a trade or craft. It is academic, geared to professional work or to the white-collar jobs of an advanced industrial society; but that society hardly as yet exists in Africa. It is a striking fact that in Britain, and in Europe generally, in the nineteenth century, industrialization came first, mass education second. In most of Africa it is rather the other way round. It is far easier to extend an advanced system of education than an advanced economy, and the result of the present enormous educational expansion could well become a source of frustration. Such a situation can make good potential for revolution.

One might distinguish, very roughly, four social groups in the new Africa. The first, still by far the biggest, including most adults and many of the young—those still almost unaffected by modernization; the village people, including those with possibly some four years of schooling; this is the basic element in all African States, which are all still predominantly rural; the majority of the population, it has as yet gained little economically, politically, or educationally, from the last few years. But at least most of its young members are affected to some extent by the revolution in expectations. The transistor is impinging on their existence. Tribal absolutes are crumbling.

Secondly, the horde of young people who have finished primary school and may have something more—five to ten years of education. They have failed to reach their school certificate, and many have not really qualified to do anything, though they have picked up more than a smattering of English, maybe the ability to drive and mend a car, and so on. Very many of these can no longer settle down in the old society, and there may be hardly room for them anyway. They drift into the towns, their numbers increasing by leaps and bounds. Many are out of work, many take to crime. They can be a worry both for the government and for the Churches.

Thirdly, there are the new educated, now beginning to pour out of universities and high schools of one kind and another. There are many jobs waiting for them, for even government departments still have many Europeans on their staffs, for want of Africans. Business—the big companies, the banks—are equally anxious to africanize. Then there are the schools, at secondary level still largely European-run. Nevertheless the best jobs, the jobs at the very top, have already been taken and are not likely to be vacated. The system is filling up.

Fourthly, there is the group which we have already considered: those in possession. The men who came to office and power at, or shortly after, independence, many of whom represent the traditional chiefly families. It was not a numerous group, which helps to explain why opposition parties, existent at independence, mostly shrivelled up. There were few, if any, ideological differences to justify more than one party, and not enough people to man the government side let alone an opposition. Many of these did not have nearly so thorough an education as the latest generation are now receiving, but they were on the spot at the right moment when someone needed to be appointed, and there they hope to stay.

The one group had looked for independence, received it, and could personally enjoy all that it has brought about. A few of them were born to the purple and in spite of their enthusiasm for development, they could quickly come to represent a basically conservative attitude of local entrenchment and maintenance of the *status quo*. However, if a few years ago Africa herself might truly have been called a very conservative continent, this is becoming less true every year. Chou En-lai had a good deal of reason when he said on a visit to Africa that he found a situation "ripe for revolution", and that meant revolution against the régimes which settled in since independence. We can now see why. Quite apart from the particular tribal or racial conflicts which caused revolution in Rwanda and Zanzibar and which— with a different tune—make South Africa fundamentally unstable, the effect of a population growth which may actually be larger than that of the economy, and of a spread of education poorly geared to the immediate needs of society; rapid urbanization and the emergence of an under-employed urban mob of youth—the sort that worries Kenyatta in Nairobi; the revolution in expectations that the preaching of nationalism, the coming of independence, and the steady voice of the radio have brought about; the growing gap between a small group that has enormously profited by changes and the masses that have gained little; and finally, the arrival, more noticeable every year, of a quickly growing set of young men more highly educated but more plebeian than their predecessors, less involved with the struggle for independence because they can take it for granted, still on the make, open to conviction that the good of their countries is to be found in solutions of every kind, and even that the immediate heirs of the nationalist revolution have betrayed its deeper aspirations: all this explains Mr Chou En-lai's revolutionary situation.

If the opposition parties of the years around independence have mostly disappeared, there is material here for new ones; or when an entrenched establishment unwisely no longer permits legal opposition, for revolution, and 1966 has in fact proved to be a year of revolutions. What one might describe as the hitherto rather monolithic attitude of educated Africans is in process of disappearing. Just as the average Irishman of the nineteenth century could concentrate on little but liberation, so the educated African of the 1950s was heading towards one thing: independence, freedom. That being attained, unity of approach quite naturally tends to fade away. Ghana, the first independent country, provides us at once with a classic example. Dr Danquah, Joseph Appiah, Gbedemah, Adamafio, one after another old allies in the freedom struggle broke with Dr Nkrumah. That need not surprise one. Compare Cromwell's career, the parting of the ways with Hyde, Lilburne, the Levellers, Sir Harry Vane. . . . Ghanaians grew deeply divided, and even Dr Nyerere found it necessary to keep a number of Tanzania's most distinguished citizens in detention without trial.[3] I had a great friend from Togo, a most charming person, who hated European rule and all the selfishness, inadequacies, ruthlessness of government, which he attributed to the European character.

---

[3] But at present there are no political detainees in Tanganyika.

He believed in Africa and was sure once Africans were allowed to rule themselves, all that would disappear. I thought of him sadly the day President Olympio of Togo was assassinated. I am told that all copies of *Animal Farm* were confiscated from Ghanaian schools: the new generation of students was applying the moral too close to home. In Africa, as has happened elsewhere so many times before and as is bound to happen, the simplicity, the unanimity, the spontaneous conviction of a first movement is passing. A new generation is emerging, open to disillusionment with the power and politics of the establishment. All this is really a sign of growing up and the consequent inevitable discovery that things are more complicated and less susceptible to solution, original sin more all-pervasive, than one had thought.

It is obvious that in this situation Marxism has an enormous attraction. Traditional Africa—very religious, very rural—could not so easily be touched by it, but exactly in the measure that education and urbanization break up the old shape of things, reveal the total backwardness of the whole continent in terms of Europe or America, and create a mood of dissatisfaction among the young, whether educated or half-educated, so will Marxism and the example of China appeal as a fine way out for members of the third world.

A way out, but not necessarily the only one. The whole point is that the new generation of African students, freed from the monopolizing claims of independence-seeking, can enter more easily than their predecessors into the whole complicated dialogue of the modern world, in which Marxism is one voice, but in which there are others too, and among them Catholicism. Entry into this general dialogue is still of course being partially, and with many wholly, impeded by world-wide colour tensions and the particular issues of South Africa, Rhodesia, and Portuguese Africa. Basically we can call these things irrelevant to the internal problems of the new Africa, but they are left-overs far too large to ignore, quite capable of masking the real issues and problems facing African societies today and of driving everyone back into racial attitudes as soul-destroying for the black man as for the white. Obviously such issues can raise enormous emotional power, and when raised will re-create, temporarily, the black world's unity of mind and purpose. Indeed, perhaps the greatest question mark facing Africa
8

today is whether she will be able to develop according to the real internal needs of her society and an open participation in world civilization, or whether she will be forced both by the South and by racial discrimination elsewhere into a crusade whose dimensions it would be hard to foretell, but which might blight the whole social and mental growth of the continent.

Already today, however, it is basically mistaken to look on the internal events of independent Africa through the glasses of colonialism and anti-colonialism, just as it is mistaken to look on every sign of unrest as evidence of a great communist plot, or to be for ever glimpsing white civilization grappling with barbarism . . . all such interpretations are fundamentally misleading, the troubles that are bound to occur in post-independence Africa being basically due, not to the subtle machinations of communists, nor to the inability of Africans to govern themselves, nor again to neo-colonialism, but to the forces of social and mental change operating at high pressure in a situation that is still very fluid. Some troubles are directly due to tribal rivalry, but I have tried to show how others may arise in a clash between generations, between a Whiggish establishment with strong traditional roots which grasped power and meant to retain it, and a younger generation more open to radical ideas. To put it like that is, inevitably, to simplify, but it does indicate roughly a pattern that is emerging. A wise government may be able to avoid it, both by keeping the doors of the Establishment well open for people to enter and for people to fall out, and by its ability to maintain a convincing ideological lead that will satisfy the younger generation (Nyerere tries hard on both these points) but where there is failure to do this and serious conflict develops between a dug-in, basically conservative group of "haves" and a new more revolutionary group of younger men deeply dissatisfied with what independence has in fact brought, it would indeed be disastrous if—as could so easily happen—the Church let herself side with the present power group, and the forces pressing for a more radical revolution became identified as Marxist. We have to prevent social cleavages, whose basic character is in no way ideological, being interpreted in ideological terms. As a matter of fact communists are adept at identifying themselves with movements destined to triumph, and Catholics seem to do the same with régimes doomed to pass away! We often do so because we fail to analyse a given situation and to recognize the inevitability of change.

To get back from these rather general considerations, a care for what is spiritual and a care for freedom, for the way of consent not that of external imposition, are two concerns which touch many Africans very deeply. Neither leads to Marxism. If some form of totalitarianism has its advocates in Africa today, so has parliamentary democracy; and so have many intermediate attitudes. Patrice Lumumba is one political martyr of these years, but Dr Danquah is another. Again, the school education of Africa has been in mission hands—Catholic and Protestant—and if some real appreciation of Western values, Christian and humanist, has not been communicated, we must indeed be quite extraordinarily bad educators. Independence came first; that achieved, there is much else to master, and the young African today is more and more aware of it. Beyond the political kingdom, are there not others? The kingdom of sport, of literature, of original scientific work, of God? I feel that African students today have the chance to be interested in a far wider range of subjects than their predecessors, and can come to hold a wider range of attitudes. They have entered into the complex, many-opinioned twentieth-century world after the simplicity of the quiet village, the simplicity too of the old nationalism; they have entered our world more completely than ever before, and the first way we can help them, and the best, is by simply sharing with them our interests, enthusiasms, troubles, faith. There is one society, and we are all of it. The great crime of South Africa and Rhodesia is to deny the human community, while it must be our chief duty to express it.

Within it we have the further supernatural community of the Catholic Church. A very high proportion of the young educated class of Africa is Catholic, by baptism, by school, by some continued loyalty, but few have as yet obtained much sense of having a sure and positive place in the Church. The Church was not shaped in Africa with such people in mind: still largely determined by what was judged suitable for the assault upon tribal society, her character has been authoritative and fideistic. The conditions of today require of her a new suppleness, the provision of machinery for dialogue, an approach which does not stifle or alienate the person trained to think in the categories of the modern world and the secular university. The situation of today, as we have analysed it, is one in which many such people will be increasingly ready to hear the Church's voice and give her a committed loyalty, entering really responsibly into her corporate life, if they are shown confidence and given the opportunity. It is certainly upon the educated élite of the post-independence generation that the fate of the Church and all that she signifies in Africa will largely depend.

V

Christian Life

1. CONVERSION

CONVERSION—both the fact and the idea—is bound to take a central place in a missionary Church. "Are there many conversions?" is the stock question asked of the missionary home on leave by someone interested. It is my belief that the greatest obstacles to sound missionary work arise later and that the widespread practical identification of that work with "conversion work" is a mistake; nevertheless it is obvious that conversion is the great initial factor out of which the new Church grows.

The very idea of conversion is not, however, an easy one to make precise. Traditionally Catholics have tended to understand it in a very ecclesiastical sense—the acceptance of a Church allegiance; to Protestants it is a sudden, decisive experience of grace. Missionary conversion requires both outward and inward aspects, but I suspect that the full Protestant concept is particularly difficult to export in an immediate missionary context, though it easily reappears in the life of the young Church, as with the "Revival movement"—the *Balokole* (the saved) of East Africa.

It is clear that in Africa as elsewhere there are a variety of motives and factors operating to bring people into the Church. Grace works through a total social context, but little by little motives have to be purified if a true Christian (and not, say, a rice Christian) is to emerge through the process. It was presumably with this in mind that the Decree on missionary activity declares that "according to a very old Church custom, the motives of a conversion are to be examined, and if necessary, purified" (n. 13).

The following is a personal account of an adult African's conversion where little purification was needed:

My father had always believed that our people had not the truth, and he sought it in his heart. He had often mentioned this to me, and before his death he told me that men would one day come to teach us the right way. These words made a profound impression on me and, whenever the arrival of some stranger was reported, I watched him and tried to get in touch with him, saying to myself that here perhaps was the man foretold by my father. Thus I associated with the Arabs who came first in the reign of Suna. Their creed seemed to me superior to our superstitions. I received instruction and, together with a number of Baganda, I embraced their religion. . . .

When the Protestants arrived Mutesa received them very well; he had their book read in public audience, and seemed to incline to their religion, which he declared to be much superior to that of the Arabs. I asked myself whether I had not made a mistake, and whether, perhaps, the newcomers were not the true messengers of God. I often went to visit them and attended their instructions. It seemed to me that their teaching was an improvement on that of my first masters. I therefore abandoned Islam, without, however, asking for baptism.

Several months had elapsed when Mapera arrived. My instructor, Mackay, took care to tell me that the white men who had just arrived did not know the truth. He called their religion the "worship of the woman"; they adored, he said, the Virgin Mary. He also advised me to avoid them with the greatest care. . . . . The first time when I saw you nearby, I was very much impressed. Nevertheless, I continued to watch you closely at your prayers and in your dealings with the people. Then seeing your goodness, I said to myself, "How can people who appear so good be the messengers of the devil?"

I talked with those who had placed themselves under instruction and questioned them on your doctrine. What they told me was just the contrary of what Mackay had assured me. Then I felt strongly urged to attend personally your catechetical instructions. God gave me the grace to understand that you taught the truth, and that you really were the man of God of whom my father had spoken. Since then, I have never had the slightest doubt about the truth of your religion, and I feel truly happy.[1]

---

[1] Quoted in J. F. Faupel, *African Holocaust*, Geoffrey Chapman, 1962, pp. 30–1.

That is the account of the conversion of St Matthias Kalemba, a man in his forties, which he gave to Père Lourdel. There are surely many, many Africans whose conversion is basically the same: a search for truth and the conviction that they have found it in Christianity, a conviction much helped by the striking goodness of missionaries they encountered.

Nevertheless all missionaries have not had the beauty of character of Père Lourdel, nor do many Africans appear to have shared that dissatisfaction with their existing beliefs that characterized Kalemba. Among many tribes adult conversions were for long almost unknown, and it was only among children across the process of schooling that converts were made. The immediate attraction of the missionaries was not in such circumstances so much religious: it was that of people who could provide a number of other things whose point had begun to appeal. Stanley, the master of guns, curiously taught King Mutesa the ten commandments, but it was the guns, not the commandments, which Mutesa was most interested in. We should not blind ourselves to the fact that that situation has often been repeated.

Doubtless many different factors have assisted conversion to Christianity in Africa during the last hundred years. The missionary has made use of everything that he could bring with him from the West to draw men into the Church, but the school and the hospital have been his two most widely effective instruments of conversion. Both medicine and books provided an almost incontestable authority to those who brought them, once Africans began to appreciate them. It was not difficult to have faith in the word of these people, who were so evidently equipped with a wholly wonderful knowledge and power; and in the early days they had a monopoly of it. The only rivalry was between the different Christian missions, and that rivalry must indeed have presented problems for the Africans who witnessed it. Anyway, Christianity and the new techniques went together, and the latter helped to give an overwhelming authority to the former.

Another factor making for conversion has been the authority and sense of superiority of the missionary as a white man and even the sheer use of force. Often he seemed to be in open league with the new colonial government, and at times acted as if he shared in some general authority for the running of African society. The strength and importance of this alliance—so convenient in the short, so dangerous in the long run—has greatly varied. In the British territories of Africa a separation between mission and administration was usually fairly clear, at least as regarded Catholic missions. Catholic missionaries often felt a grievance in British Africa that they were less favoured than Protestants, but they ought to have been profoundly grateful for anything which could contribute a little to making their true character apparent to Africans, and which would, moreover, restrain them from making use of governmental pressure to bring about conversion. In Belgian Africa the opposite was true, and the following remarks by an anthropologist illustrate what could happen:

> At first the mission attracted very few converts. Lele told me that they resorted to capturing village children by force, threatening their protesting parents with prison if they stopped them. The mission fathers told me that this may have been substantially true as they had no other way to start the ball rolling. . . . Once the initial stage of coercion was over, the ball began indeed to roll along of itself. The young Lele became keen, intelligent pupils, and sincere Christians of whom their pastors were justly proud.[2]

This particular mission began only in 1939. The initial show of force was maintained during the two years' catechumenate:

> They invariably described that two-year period as one of hardship and hunger. They worked both to grow their own food and to supply the mission station with its needs. . . . For the two years at the mission they worked for no reward, they might be abused, struck or whipped for some, to them, obscure misdemeanour. Why they endured it needs some explaining. . . . The head of the mission averred that they were deeply attracted by the very idea of force as exerted by the Europeans . . . he emphasized the necessity of using force in relations with the blacks. He did not usually employ physical violence himself, but deputed the whipping of culprits to their own comrades. On the grounds that the natives were at the stage of social evolution at which we

[2] M. Douglas, *The Lele of the Kasai*, Oxford University Press, 1963, p. 264.

in Europe had needed public chastisement, public penances were meted out for grave sins revealed in the confessional. Thus I saw a confessed adulterer dressed in striped pyjamas loaded with two buckets of stones staggering round the mission ground.[3]

Such blatant use of force has not been confined to one mission, nor to one country, though the possibilities for it would seem to have been in general more limited outside the Congo, and the utterly tragic events which have taken place there since independence would seem in part a reaction against systems practised there previously.[4]

A valuable study could be made of the different patterns that conversion has taken in various parts of Africa. Factors operative in one tribe have been almost absent in another; their study would help to explain why missionary work has had so little effect upon some peoples and so much upon others. Such factors are often not specifically religious but social and psychological for it is especially in answering social and psychological pressures that the need for religious conversion can arise. The trouble here is that in some circumstances the acceptance of Church membership may have very little real religious significance. It can be seen as a step in the educational ladder or even as a stratagem in tribal rivalry.

It is clear that some patterns of conversion are healthier and will produce a stronger Church than others. Numbers are far from being the one criterion. Conversions, of the type described above, strongly influenced by outside authority and affecting chiefly the children of the tribe, will be far less valuable than those where the feeling of enforcement is absent and where adults have taken the lead, as in Burundi or Buganda. The maintenance of some sort of tribal cohesion within the process of conversion can be of great importance in avoiding a total social disruption whose bad effects adherence to Christianity may not be able to nullify, and some missionaries have refused to baptize anyone until a whole group wanted to be received. But there are difficulties here too. For one thing African societies are the integrated expression of systems

[3] *Op. cit.*, p. 266.
[4] For a parallel non-Catholic instance of the use of force one might refer to the early methods of the Presbyterian mission in southern Nyasaland (cf. W. P. Livingstone, *Laws of Livingstonia*, London, 1921), but such methods have remained everywhere the exception.

of thought and genuine christianization is bound to disrupt much of their pattern of life as their ultimate beliefs and standards of conduct change. For another, where tribal cohesion has effected a mass conversion, generally led by the chiefs, though missionaries are jubilant at the time, the Christianity which has developed in subsequent years has often been rather disappointing,[5] a sort of "tribal Church" can result, in which in a time of crisis tribal loyalties greatly outweigh Christian commitment. We cannot in fact canonize any one pattern of conversion. Different factors are bound to operate in differing circumstances; they have their various advantages and disadvantages. What is important is for us to recognize this frankly so that we can guard against the character of the subsequent Christian community retaining too much of the mark of the original circumstances of conversion, and so being unbalanced. If this happens and is not properly rectified a conversion movement which has lain heavily on some fundamentally secular impulse may create an essentially uninspiring type of Christianity which can fall an easy victim in a subsequent crisis.

In general it would seem that tribes with a centralized and monarchical system have turned to Christianity more readily than acephalous groups;[6] equally, patrilineal peoples more easily than matrilineal ones, tribes with a clan system more than tribes with a strong age-set system, sedentary peoples more than pastoral ones. These are wide generalizations, which need to be confirmed, modified, or disproved by more extensive examination and comparison. What is clear is that the immediate success of evangelization is closely connected with pre-existing beliefs and social patterns, as also with the recognition of new needs. One tribe perceived the social advantages of schooling and welcomed missionaries, another saw no gain and cold-shouldered them. We cannot understand conversion without some awareness of these various pressures which lead up to it, and we have to remember that a socially

---

[5] Cf., for instance, I. Schapera, "Christianity and the Tswana", *Journal of the Royal Anthropological Institute*, July-December 1958. But the fault here may lie too in the particular type of Christianity (mainly Congregationalist) imparted.

[6] Cf. B. A. Pauw, "Patterns of Christianity among the Tswana and the Xhosa-speaking Peoples", pp. 240–57 of *African Systems of Thought*, ed. Fortes and Dieterlen, Oxford, 1965.

favourable situation may produce many conversions, but will tend also to produce superficial ones.

The most widely effective of these pressures have undoubtedly been the inherent attractions of school and medicine and of the new and apparently superior form of life which they seem to represent. Outsiders have sometimes doubted whether across the excitement of the new medicines, across the grasp of new techniques in the mission schools and the vistas opened up of office work in government and commerce, across the sheer mesmerism of these new attractions, anything of the truth of God's word, of the liberation of the Gospel, of the gentleness of Christ, of the God who loves us, really penetrated. Anyone who has seen African Christianity from the inside will not think like that. In every age and every place God must use fallible and human means, our vessels of clay, to communicate the treasure of his grace. The faith and charity of so many new African Christians, the sense of liberation that the Gospel has brought to them, are clear as day. Nevertheless we have still to consider the factors and motives in conversion very critically—not only as part of the historical past, but as a legacy for the present. The quality of conversion can vary, and on that quality will depend very largely the vigour of the Church's subsequent life. The Council enjoins a purification of motives, a process whose effectiveness depends upon the institution of the catechumenate; it is to this that we should now turn.

2. The Catechumenate

It is *via* the Catechumenate that conversion leads to baptism and membership of the Church. Almost everywhere in Africa there are large numbers of adult people anxious to be received into the Church and so the catechumenate remains of the very first importance; indeed its use for the whole of the Universal Church has been recently recalled by the Council.[7] Nevertheless, behind a single name, the organization of the catechumenate varies enormously from diocese to diocese, and for many people there is now a good deal of doubt as to what shape it can best take. The norms laid down for it in the past had a situation in view quite different

[7] Constitution on the Sacred Liturgy, art. 64.

from that of today. They envisaged an unbroken tribal society, almost no existing Christian church, and no other institutions such as schools. There is no reason to think that those norms should still be applied unchanged; however, some clear pattern is required. In the absence of such a pattern the catechumenate has degenerated in some places into a few shapeless months of memorization and manual labour. How varied in fact our practice is can easily be seen by a comparison of diocesan figures for adult baptisms in a year with those for catechumens. According to the 1965 *Catholic Directory of East Africa* there are many dioceses which would seem to continue with the old four-year catechumenate, for the number of catechumens given by them is rather more than four times that for adult baptisms. But there are other dioceses, such as Arua and Gulu in Northern Uganda, where the two figures are almost exactly the same, indicating presumably a catechumenate of one year or less. There is then a third group which goes to the other extreme, where the number of catechumens is simply vastly more than that of adult baptisms; thus Nairobi archdiocese claims 56,000 catechumens but less than 7,000 annual adult baptisms; Kigoma in Tanzania has over 36,000 catechumens and a mere 1,300 annual adult baptisms. Evidently there are many people who remain for years as catechumens because, for instance, a polygamous life prevents baptism. Varying missionary attitudes towards what should be advised to people living in polygamy may help to explain some of these differences. Nevertheless even such a brief glance as this at the figures does suggest that it is time we should all reconsider the theory and practice of the catechumenate and one would especially want to feel sure of the justification for such a situation as that existing in Kigoma.[8] Here I try to map out the general pattern that this very important type of work could take today in the light both of changing social conditions and of the new understanding of catechetics and liturgy.

Cardinal Lavigerie's plan for a regular four-year catechumenate[9]

[8] A father from Tanganyika has criticized this "keeping people too long in the catechumenate" which discourages others from wanting to become Christians, in *AFER*, April 1959, p. 122. We need, of course, to distinguish between the catechumenate as a real course preparatory to baptism and the catechumenate as the state of those who are interested in Christianity but have not been baptized.

[9] Cf. "The Catechumenate as seen by Cardinal Lavigerie", by J. Perrardin, W.F., *AFER*, Jan. 1960, pp. 48–53.

has been at the bottom of most African practice in the last hundred years. Before him the catechumenate had varied greatly in length from age to age and place to place. In the earliest Church it will have been very short, becoming much longer by the third century. The Council of Agde (506) prescribed a period of eight months; St Gregory the Great in 604 one of forty days. In most subsequent periods it tended to be fairly short, until Lavigerie returned to what he considered early practice, instituted a total catechumenate of four years and divided it into three periods: a first one for postulants lasting two years when only principles of the natural law would be inculcated; the second and third periods comprising another two years to form the catechumenate proper when specifically Christian truths would be given, leading up to the immediate preparation for baptism. This long catechumenate was extremely useful in the first stages of founding a new Christian community on a sound basis, making sure that the acceptance of Christianity was not skin-deep, and its effective application was a practical proposition at the beginning of the mission when the chief work of the priest could be with adult catechumens because there was either no existing Christian community or it was small and newly formed. Moreover, four years did not seem so long in the slow pace of life of nineteenth-century Africa. Months could be spent living in or near the mission, wholly given up to the catechumenate routine.

The situation is quite different today. In many places it seems impractical to get people to attend a continuous catechumenate for four years. Few missions have space for them, while the people themselves have other occupations which they have to attend to. The course has got to be intensive rather than extended. Moreover, the old system whereby the catechumens were made use of as a cheap labour force for mission work of all kinds should be frankly abandoned as unsuitable in modern conditions.[10] It is anyway very doubtful whether a four-year period of waiting and of moral formation without the giving of any sacramental help is more likely to produce a convinced practising Christian than a shorter initiation. Moreover, four years of catechumenate should mean four different

---

[10] In the past it was, of course, in many circumstances entirely reasonable. There was no alternative to the catechumens living in the mission compound and their support obviously required considerable organized manual work; in some places this may remain the case today.

classes, each supervised by a priest, because the whole sharpness of the teaching is lost, as also the shape of the course, if people of different years are put together. But priests in a modern parish with thousands of baptized Catholic adults and hordes of children to look after find it hard enough to give reasonable attention to one adult catechumenate class, let alone four. For all these reasons, the conclusion seems to be that the regular catechumenate should not last much more than a year.

The greatest problem of the mass catechumenate is how to make of it an instrument for conversion in the personal sense, the achievement of a commitment to Christ. It is this which is too often lacking in the present-day African catechumenate which can degenerate into a largely routine process. This may never arrive at all at producing a personal decision, at conversion in an interior and evangelical sense. As modern catechetics stress, arrival at this must be the chief purpose of the early part of the instruction. Some may reply that the commitment can be taken as already there before the catechumen is enrolled for formal instruction at all, otherwise he would not have come. But in fact this is not very realistic. Initial motives are so very varied for entering on a course of religious instruction. Some people come in order to obtain a Christian name, as being a pagan now appears a sign of inferior status; some because their children are in a Christian school and they do not want to be different; some wish to be Catholics because members of a rival village or tribe have become Protestants: there are many basically non-religious and quite accidental reasons for being enrolled in the catechumenate. Evidence of this is that it is quite a common occurrence for newly baptized Christians to fall away from regular religious practice almost immediately after completing their course of instruction. Clearly too often our catechumenate fails to achieve a real commitment to Christ, the beginning of a new personal life, a conversion in the spiritual and not merely in the bare ecclesiastical sense. There is a regular course of instruction, the requisite answers are memorized, baptism imparted, a new name given, and that is almost all.

Such a disastrous mis-shaping of the catechumenate has grown too common to be overlooked. It derives from the large numbers often involved and the lack of priests to cope with them adequately, from the consequent leaving of the catechumens very largely in the

hands of poorly trained catechists, from the expression of doctrine
in a dry scholastic way, and too much reliance on the memorization
of certain formulas. Catechisms in African languages, like the
European models on which they were based, are still many of them
miniature scholastic treatises rather than a living account of sacred
history. Our weakness here has simply been the common weakness
of the whole Church in the period prior to the new catechetical
movement, but made much worse in practice by the huge number
of catechumens and the tiny number of ministers.

It must be axiomatic that everywhere the catechumenate has to
be an instrument for conversion and Christian formation in a personal sense; our problem remains how to apply this in African
conditions. The individual or small group instruction, so profitable
a method for forming new Christians in the European context, is
just impractical in most African situations. Nevertheless the system
of collective instruction must still be geared to the individual as
far as it possibly can be and more than we have tended to do.

In modern catechetical thinking three stages are distinguished
in the instruction of the convert.[11] There is first of all that which we
can call pre-evangelization. This is the time when one brings the
future convert into touch with the Church, presenting the Church
to him, making him realize his dissatisfaction with his present non-
ecclesial state. It must advance from what is positive in his existing
beliefs, especially, where it is present, the deep consciousness of a
single God Creator and source of life, but it must work through
them showing the inadequacies of the non-Christian state and in
one way or another thus inducing the individual to make the effort
to attend some regular course of instruction to be evangelized. The
period of pre-evangelization clearly has no set form. It is the making of contact, the insertion of an idea that faith in Christ and
membership of the Church may alone provide an answer to the
troubles and question marks of life, the plan that God himself has
given to men, the way of escape from the haunting fears of death
and quarrels and sorcery. With such motives for beginning a course
of catechumenate may go many other more worldly ones, as we
have seen. Most catechumens are not at the beginning really com-

[11] Cf. O. Hirmer, "The First Approach to Adult Catechumens", *AFER*,
Oct. 1964, pp. 383–92; A. Pierce, "The Adult Catechumenate", *AFER*, Jan.
1965, pp. 43–54.

mitted internally to a spiritual revolution in their lives, to the acceptance of Jesus Christ as saviour and lord. It is to that commitment that the first part of a regular course of instruction must be geared.

This part should be centred, in a general, global way, on Christ. Its aim is not to cover the range of the catechism; it should certainly not be to start by teaching particular prayers and practices whose true significance can only come later on. It is meant to introduce someone to Jesus as his saviour. Now the question may be raised whether this introduction does not need to be done across the Old Testament, which should always be introduced before speaking of Jesus, according to the plan of St Augustine in the *De Catechizandis Rudibus* and as is done in the fine South African manual for adult catechumens, *Africa's Way to Life*.[12] But it seems to me that a method suggested by St Paul in his speech at Athens, of treating pagan beliefs as the Gentile's own old testament and going straight from them to Jesus, is preferable. The Jewish Old Testament will, of course, come in later, but to deal with it straightaway seems to introduce much matter which may appear at this stage almost irrelevant. Every man is his own old testament and can come straight out of it into the one New Testament which is Christ.

The ideal African catechesis, undertaken in a tribal milieu, could begin its stage of evangelization with questions to the catechumens about their own ideas of God; out of these traditional beliefs the teacher would, little by little, draw a picture of the Father, re-explaining it in Jesus' own words, using the parables of the Father. From this one goes naturally to the question: who was this teacher who taught so wonderfully about God? One is then led to describe Jesus, the supreme teacher, the man who really knew about God, who had the words of eternal life. And how did he know? Because he came from God, he was his Son. Out of this grows a global account of the life of Jesus, his death and resurrection, combined with the Church as the continuing community of his disciples: those who have accepted his teaching, those who have been adopted by the Father as his brothers, those who believe in him and keep

12 Written principally by Fr Hirmer, and published by the South African Catholic Bishops' Conference, 1963. Fr Hirmer defends this "Old Testament from the beginning" approach in *AFER*, Oct. 1964, pp. 389–90. Jesus is not mentioned until lesson 12, after Adam, Abraham, Moses, and the Commandments.

his word. The global teaching must lead up to a moment of real psychological "shock", when a quite deliberate decision to change will be made, and so to the act of commitment. Do you want to keep Christ's word, are you for him or against him? The affirmation of commitment should be solemnized in a definite liturgical ceremony when the salt of wisdom is blessed and given to the catechumens, and only after that should they enter the catechumenate proper: the detailed view of the history of salvation. This indeed will begin with Adam and Abraham, it will include John the Baptist, Mary and Joseph in their historical places, and then Jesus' life, bringing out the different events more distinctly. Then Pentecost and the Church; in the Church the sacraments and commandments—the moral life of preparation for death, the second coming and the new Jerusalem. The doctrine of the Blessed Trinity is essential for Christianity; it must not be relegated to one brief, concise, scholastic section. It has to be seen as essential, and so it has to grow out of the whole. The person of the Father is met in the Old Testament, the Son in the New, the Holy Spirit in Pentecost and the Church. The encounter with each is an addition to, not a replacement of, the preceding one. The Trinity must be appreciated, not as an abstract doctrine, but as the supreme fellowship into which we have been brought progressively through sacred history.

It is most important that prayers should only be taught and learnt at a moment when each appears genuinely relevant. The "Our Father" must be the first prayer to be learnt, and prayed, and that immediately after solemn commitment. The "Hail Mary" can be introduced after Mary has been fitted into the picture at the Annunciation; the "Glory be" as an expression of thanks when Trinitarian belief has become clear, and the Creed itself only towards the end when all the great articles have been gone through and accepted.

Memorization both of prayers and of some catechism answers may be necessary, but memorization must always follow understanding, not precede it. Moreover, the understanding of the catechumen must not be tested chiefly by his ability to repeat something memorized: his personal grip on crucial points must be tested in a less formal way.

Knowledge of the Creed is the immediate prerequisite in the

9

intellectual sphere to baptism: the creeds are, in fact, essentially baptismal and once the creed has been grasped there is no reason to delay baptism further, so long as personal commitment, which the catechumen came to some months before, has been maintained in the quality of his life. Baptism should be followed by a further final part of his initiation: deeper instruction in the Eucharist and all other aspects of ecclesial life, this being done best when the Christian is able to participate immediately in what he is learning about.

The next question is how to integrate this course of instruction into the Church's year. This is most important. The catechumenate is not just a course of instruction; it must be presented as essentially a preparation for baptism, as initiation into the life of an existing community whose representatives—the baptismal sponsors—should be actually present at all the important ceremonies of the cate-chumenate. The life of the Church is a liturgical one, and this has to be made clear to the convert from the very beginning. It is clear that the central point here is Easter. Baptism is pre-eminently participation in the death and new life of the Saviour, and it is in the solemn rites of the Easter vigil that our catechumens should normally be baptized: not just one or two as a sort of gesture but all who have been brought through the normal course of instruction.[13] The initial rites of baptism will, of course, have been performed already in stages throughout the catechumenate.[14] Coming up out of the baptismal water—and plenty of it—on Easter night, the new Christians will solemnly partake of the Eucharist on Easter morning, communicating under both kinds.[15]

If there are so many catechumens that it is really impossible to baptize them all in the Easter vigil, the rest could receive baptism in the course of Easter week. What is important is that the Easter-baptism link should be taken really seriously, which is seldom the case at present. The last stage of the post-baptismal or mystagogical catechesis, as it is sometimes called, would be carried on between

[13] The Vatican Council's Decree on Missionary Activity, n. 14, takes this for granted.
[14] According to the Decree of the Congregation of Sacred Rites, 16 April 1962. Cf. "The Restored Liturgical Catechumenate", *AFER*, Jan. 1963, pp. 78–83; this is confirmed by the Vatican II Constitution on the Liturgy, n. 66.
[15] Constitution on the Sacred Liturgy, art. 55.

Easter and Pentecost. With Pentecost, which is the feast of the fully alive Church, their initiation too would be over and a new batch of Christians would take their place in the normal life of the parish, next to their fellows.

Pentecost should end the catechetical year. When should it begin? Let us remember the three stages prior to baptism, and therefore prior to Easter: pre-evangelization, evangelization, and the catechesis proper. The stage of pre-evangelization may, of course, have been going on for a very long time: a period of growing contact with Christians, with a catechist, with a priest even. But the clergy could concentrate on this stage in the time after Pentecost. It is a natural time for the more intense visiting of the villages, of both Christians and pagans in their homes. It is the time when new groups of potential converts are being got together, are receiving, maybe, some initial instruction in a village from a catechist, and then about October all these catechumens could be gathered together in the parish or some larger out-station, where after a liturgical ceremony of entry into the catechumenate, they will receive that global announcement of the good news which we have already spoken of. By Christmas they should have made their commitment, learnt to pray the "Our Father" and joined in a first ceremony whereby, in a personal and individual manner, each announces his intention, perhaps at the church door, of following Christ and going forward to baptism. From Christmas to Easter would come the formal catechesis, the most intense period of instruction, becoming steadily more so as Lent advances[16] until about Passion Sunday they solemnly recite the Apostles' Creed and the Lord's Prayer in church and are anointed with the oil of catechumens. In Holy Week they should receive special instruction in the meaning of the Paschal ceremonies and of their own baptismal rites.

However, some may feel that this gives altogether too short a period of formal catechesis. In which case one might follow instead a sixteen-month course, beginning the teaching in Advent and completing it at the Easter of the following liturgical year. The ceremony signifying commitment might then be placed at the intervening Pentecost.

It may be pointed out here that confirmation, too, is an essential

[16] For the baptismal character of Lent, see the Constitution on the Liturgy, n. 109.

part of Christian initiation and it should not be postponed rather indefinitely until some future moment convenient for the bishop. The ideal order for receiving the great sacraments would seem to be baptism-confirmation-Eucharist, not baptism-Eucharist-confirmation, and a real effort should be made with both adults and children to revert to the traditional and more meaningful order. The Pan-African Catechetical Study Week at Katigondo earnestly recommended that "Confirmation be administered to the newly-baptized adults within the framework of baptismal initiation and where the bishop is not available, a priest be delegated by him to administer this sacrament." That is to say, within the cycle of Easter ceremonies. At the very latest, confirmation should not be delayed further than Pentecost when the mystagogical catechesis ends. It is difficult or impossible for a bishop to confirm in all his parishes at Easter or Pentecost, or even in between, and it is therefore eminently desirable that a senior priest be regularly delegated to do this in each of the parishes where the bishop is not himself present. There would seem to be little advantage and many inconveniences in maintaining the customary bishop-confirmation link.[17]

Let it be noted that our whole way of approaching the formal instruction of the catechumenate is based on the history of salvation: Jesus Christ is placed firmly in the middle of the picture and everything is built up around him. Moreover, the whole is linked with the Church's present life as experienced through the liturgical year. This shape of teaching involves the explicit rejection of a course of teaching, or a catechism, based on a fundamental "Creed-Sacraments-Commandments" scheme. Such a scheme is not existential but scholastic, and it is not clearly Christocentric; it can easily suggest a division between faith and life, and also imply that our moral life as such is hardly specifically Christian. Sacraments and commandments must be seen as ways of entering into the Christ life. Evidently the commandments will come back several times. They will appear first in the rudimentary discussion *cum* instruction of a pre-evangelization stage; if you want to learn about God, you must try to please him, you must listen to your conscience and your conscience tells you that this and this is evil. Again, the com-

[17] Cf. Karl Rahner's opinion in *Bishops: Their Status and Function*, Burns & Oates, p. 29.

mandments return in the period of evangelization: commitment to Christ at once involves moral conversion, both do and do not. A third more detailed treatment of the commands, dealt with as positively as possible and all shown as expressions of the charity which is the essence of Christian life, will follow in the regular catechesis.

It is clear that the catechumenate arranged in this way, or indeed in any way practical for Africa, is still bound to be done with a strong concern for the crowd rather than for the individual. Yet conversion to Christian faith and living is an essentially personal thing, and some need longer to arrive at a definite commitment than others. We have to have an organized catechumenate, but we have also to make a real effort to keep it flexible, to be on the look-out for the special case. The priest must try to ensure some personal contact with each catechumen beyond his work of general instruction. It is to be recognized that some will need to put off the expression of their personal commitment, as also, later, baptism. The institution of our catechumenate can so easily become a thing in itself, something to which the good of individual catechumens somehow gets subordinated, instead of remaining a tool of service.

One thing which has in some places caused great confusion to the catechumenate has been the incorporation with the genuine catechumens of Christian children, teen-agers, who have not been to school. The religious instruction of many Christian children is now, of course, done in school, but there is still a large group of children in most places who fail to get to school, perhaps for lack of money, but have in some way to be taught their religion. There has been a tendency to throw these in, at some time or other, with the catechumens, as a relatively easy way of ensuring that they obtain a complete course of religion at least once. This seems to me to be disastrous. Their psychological needs are utterly different and their presence confuses the whole point of the catechumenate. Far from being given one complete course, they obviously need to be called back and receive different courses over a period of years as they are growing up. Clearly this is an extremely difficult matter. The very fact that these children are not in school may indicate that they come from less intelligent, less determined, or at least less accessible homes. It is not at all easy to collect and instruct them. Nevertheless it does seem that the attention of many missionaries has been concentrated so much on our schools that there has been a neglect of the large group of Catholic children who never get into schools at all, or at best for a couple of years. To swell the normal catechumenate class with these children will help neither them nor the catechumens. The least we could do is to set aside one month of each year, when the catechumens are not present, and perhaps even better when the schoolchildren are on holiday as well (and so the school buildings can be made use of) and give them some serious instruction according to their different age groups. August would seem a month adapted to this. Courses of this kind need as much planning as any school teaching. They must be made interesting, with other subjects included as well as religion. It is for such work that fully trained catechists are especially needed.

To return to the catechumenate, it must be stressed that it is a community involving a way of life, not just a course of instruction. It is a community of prayer, developing as it goes, as new prayers are introduced and deeper mysteries appreciated. In so far as is possible the baptismal sponsors should actively participate in this community, at least being present for the important ceremonies: the opening, the making of commitment and the solemn entry into church. The reading of Scripture and the reciting of the psalms should be a regular feature in the life of the catechumens, joined together in a Bible service. Indeed the best course is probably not to allow the catechumens to come to Mass at all for the first months. On Sundays they could still have a separate service of the word on their own: a service adapted to their present knowledge and status. Admission to presence at Mass might follow the cere-mony of commitment.

One might urge, furthermore, that the reading of Scripture take the form of a regular "*lectio continuata*". The exact matter could be worked out on a daily basis and read by a catechist—about half a chapter a day. All the catechumens should have heard at least one complete Gospel read to them before baptism. The course of reading could begin with some Old Testament extracts followed by the Gospel of Matthew, Acts (chapter 1 to 15), and then, in the time immediately before baptism, I Peter. If it is possible to keep the newly baptized for a few weeks more, they might then hear

John (chapters 20 and 21), Ephesians, and finally the First Epistle of John.

Certainly there are different ways of running a catechumenate and a great variety of needs. Numbers, occupation, density of population and climate all enter into the problem (it may, for instance, be impossible to get catechumens together in the wet season). There can be no single absolute pattern. What is important is that the basic elements of a living training in Church life be preserved: the making of a definite commitment after an initial period, the Easter-baptism link, the performance of the liturgical ceremonies at different stages, the centring of instruction upon Christ and the history of salvation, the joining together of doctrine and prayer in a meaningful way, the insertion of a really serious scriptural element in the instruction, the linking up of the sponsors with the whole catechumenate period and not only with baptism itself. If all this is done in one way or another, the catechumenate will be indeed a balanced initiation into the life of Christ and of the people of God.

3. SACRAMENTS AND SCRIPTURE

Baptism is the entry into a eucharistic community. Christian life is centred upon the Mass. Yet the terrible truth is that in practice, with the shortage of priests, the Mass must remain for very many African Catholics an almost peripheral part of their religious life. While this is the case, it is difficult to see how we can build up healthy Churches. The implementation of the Conciliar decree on the Liturgy involves for us far more than adaptation in the way those who are present join in; it must mean a radically new approach to the task of making it possible for all our people regularly to offer Mass and receive communion at all. All the decrees about popular participation in the Mass remain unreal in a situation where so many people can only hope to be present at it once in several months.

Even so it remains true that a vast amount can still be done at present to increase the reality of popular involvement in the liturgy. First of all, we priests have ourselves to be re-educated. The attitude of the people to the Mass will depend largely on the attitude of the priest. If it is not felt as a community action by him, it will not be so felt by them. We priests have come to see the Mass far too much as a sort of private possession, the centre of our personal devotions, and this is inevitably strengthened by so often saying Mass all on our own. It is "my Mass", not "our Mass". This is reflected in the extremely devout but clearly "private" way that public Masses are often said. Recollection can even withdraw the priest from the community, from visibly and psychologically presiding over the gathered assembly. It is difficult to think that this will disappear while the "private" Mass remains the norm for so many priests. The *sacramentum unitatis* has got to be lived, and firstly at the very sacramental level, and that by its consecrated ministers. While priests—especially the priests who form and train other priests in seminaries—regularly prefer to divide just at the central moment of their religious lives, celebrating apart from private devotion, instead of sharing in a common altar, it is next to impossible that they should get across to others the full sense of the Eucharist.

Next, for a really corporate Mass, it is obvious that the canon too should be said audibly and intelligibly. To exclude just this focal point of the community's action from the principle that what is done in community should be understood by the community will be disastrous if persisted in. The canon concerns the people just as much as the rest of the Mass does, and is more important; they must be brought into equally manifest contact with it. The Church will have to brace herself for the universal acceptance of this final stage in the use of the vernacular.

Our primary pastoral need is to make effectively true within the human community the Church's essential centring on the Eucharist and the Word of God. To do this requires, as we have said, an adequate number of priests, suitably dispersed. It next requires understanding—hence effective instruction; the use of the vernacular, active popular participation in the liturgy, and finally, a renewal in the use of symbols.

Liturgical renewal and catechetical renewal—a programme for the Church's essential needs always comes back to these two central points. The battle for the vernacular in the universal Church has been won, with the exception of the canon—and that also will surely come. Liturgical translation is everywhere difficult but particularly for languages which at present have little or no

Christian literature, and the Church in Africa is desperately short of competent people with time to do the work. It is obvious that the introduction of the vernacular presents very special problems in Africa, above all in the dioceses where there is not one but a whole series of vernaculars. Certainly that is not everywhere the case, and there are areas like Tanzania where one language, Swahili, is used by a whole group of dioceses or an entire country. But the language map of Africa is still enormously complicated, and there are not only multi-lingual dioceses but even multi-lingual parishes. This last is particularly true in urban areas, such as the Copper Belt, the Rand, Leopoldville, where people from a whole variety of tribes have gathered together to work. This fact of the multiplicity of languages has at times been used to justify the simple retention of Latin, but with insufficient reason. In every community some *lingua franca* is bound to emerge, and it will certainly not be Latin. Already in every church some language has to be principally used for preaching. Let whatever language is used for preaching be used also for liturgy. No principle can be simpler than that. In town areas it may often be best to use English or French—the official languages of most African countries. It is certain that some people will not understand, but that is better than that no one should understand. There should also always be a place for the singing of Latin, at least for special and solemn occasions when people from quite different areas are gathered together. Latin has, in fact, symbolized our unity for many very simple people, and that is a symbol which in Africa—a world of great tribal, racial and linguistic divisions—is still greatly needed. In countries of racial division it has helped Catholics to worship inter-racially where Protestants, using a variety of vernaculars, have fallen more easily into a pattern of segregation. Sometimes powerful symbols may be more valuable than total understanding of the details of what is going on. English and French have no valuable religious significance, but Latin signifies the spiritual unity of Catholics, white and black and brown, and their unity with the pope. For sophisticated people in Western Europe such a symbol may be expendable; I doubt if it is in Africa. There we have to reconcile much greater use of the vernacular than we have had hitherto with some continuing effective use of this symbol of Catholic unity, the Latin language. It would be very sad to think that we must bind ourselves to worship in a single language in a single place. There is plenty of room for liturgical pluralism. But our general aim must always be the same—the maximum of genuine comprehension and communal participation within any particular group of circumstances.

The introduction of the vernacular is far from the most difficult of liturgical problems; far more complex issues are posed by the question of a more drastic adaptation of the liturgy to the needs of Africa in the fields of prayer-forms, the use of symbolism, and the employment of dancing and drums. Let it be said at once that there is no single answer to these questions in Africa, and any attempt to provide one could only be disastrous. What can be suitable and effective among one people may be quite meaningless elsewhere; it all depends on tribal traditions and the present degree of Westernization. If the liturgy is really to be a living thing, it must be everywhere in Africa a locally adapted thing. It is local bishops and commissions of liturgy that must make the decisions in accordance with the individual needs of the particular cultural-ethnic area or town, and to do this successfully the local authorities need real courage and a sense of ecclesial confidence: it is this that seems to be lacking so much at present—the courage really to go forward and do something. However, certain considerations may be very widely true.

The first is that Africans want to express themselves on a solemn occasion in a solemn but dynamic way, and they customarily do this across the media of dancing and drum-beating. These are the natural external stimuli to their inspiration in almost every field and they respond at once. What part dancing could play in the Church's liturgy I do not know, but then I have not tried to experiment. What is important is not to make up one's mind in advance about the impossibility of the unfamiliar. Far easier to integrate into the liturgy than dancing is drum-beating, and it does seem extraordinary that so little has been tried in this field; and not only drum-beating but African music of other kinds, some of which might seem more suitable for the liturgy.[18] There is fine sculpture in some areas of West Africa, but as a whole there was a terrible poverty as regards the visual arts in most parts of the continent,

---

[18] As that of harps and flutes. One should note that drums have not the same importance for all African peoples, and pastoral tribes seldom use them.

connected with the limitation of material and objects to work upon. It is the sheer paucity of local artistic tradition which sets the basic problem of adaptation in most places; but for music this is not true at all. It has been, we can say, the characteristic art form of Africa; it remains vigorous today. It is in fact an aspect of life which seems to survive the pressure of Westernization rather well, and it has, of course, a special value for liturgy. From the viewpoint of liturgical action visual arts matter far less than vocal ones. It is obvious that in this field we should be very bold, not trying to produce one famous "Mass" for the European market, but a vigorous and varied chorus of local musical responses to the divine mystery. But how much has already been written on this subject and how little done! Frankly one of the obstacles is often African priests themselves, who have been personally accustomed for years in the seminary to plainchant and Church polyphonic music, and have no wish to change. The trouble is that someone who has docilely entered into a pattern of things, has come to put up with them, and then to like them, may still be suffering from a sort of "psychological suffocation", even without realizing it. And indeed in the docility, but also seeming lack of vitality, which does somewhat characterize the Christian African's acceptance not only of Western music, but also of a certain tradition of Western pictures and architecture, and so much else, one does sense at times something of a deep unconscious suffocation. What is typical is indeed acceptance, not creativity. That is not their fault—docility, not creativity, is what the missionary Church has asked for, and it is what she has received. But today we must seek for something more, and there is no field better than the musical one in which to set about it.

It is sometimes suggested today that the African Church should adopt an oriental rite, perhaps the Ethiopian, in place of the Latin rite. This is not realistic. A Church of 28 million cannot suddenly up and change all its central prayer forms in such a drastic fashion. Moreover, a rite is an expression of an ecclesial community and tradition. The Ethiopian Church, though genuinely African, has developed in an entirely characteristic way, and much about it could not be relevant to the young African Churches. It has strikingly lacked the dynamism that these Churches need. An attempt to attach them closely to the liturgical tradition of this Church just because it is in Africa would be artificial and surely lead to disaster. Nevertheless, without any sort of wholesale changeover, much could be learnt in detail and adopted from both the Ethiopian and other oriental Churches in the liturgy, church life and ministerial patterns of the African Churches.

With a renewal of music must go a renewal of symbols. There can be no doubt that in the current condition of Africa symbolism has still a very special power, and the desire for it—for founts of flowing water, and pillars of fire and the sacrificial meal that really is a meal—is shown strikingly in the practice of many of the separatist "Zionist" and "Ethiopian" sects.[19] Instead of minimizing the symbolic quality of so many of our liturgical functions, as we have in fact done, we need to maximize it. I can remember nothing so pitiful as the Easter vigil ceremonies I once saw performed in an African parish with some pathetically poor little fire, quite unperceived by the crowd, wholly unable to signal forth effectively the light of the Resurrection. We must have an enormous great light at Easter, a splashing of living water in adult baptism—not a drop or two out of a Pepsi-Cola bottle—a Mass that is a meal, with the priest upon one side of the table and the people upon the other, and an offering that can be perceived as bread and wine and will afterwards be recognizably shared and eaten in the communion. At present one has not only to believe in the presence of Christ, one has almost to believe as well in the presence of bread—so diminutive and dried-up has it become. These three great signs of life—bread, and water and fire—which Christ has made use of in his Church to teach us in body and not only in mind about the bread of life, and water flowing up into eternity, and spiritual light of the world, have been depreciated into mere tokens, shorn of the natural power that they should have to move us.

The symbolism of water seems particularly meaningful in Africa, and baptism has tended to become "the central act" in the Zionist Churches of South Africa.[20] These dissident Christians often return to practices of total immersion, and baptism is something repeatable. They feel the returning need for spiritual cleansing. In other parts of Africa one sees the great importance attached by Catholics to blessed water, but on the whole we have made rather little of it.

---

[19] See B. Sundkler, *Bantu Prophets in South Africa*, O.U.P.
[20] B. Sundkler, *op. cit.*, p. 215.

Yet it provides the natural and Christ-given symbolism for divine purification from sin and runs through baptism, the Easter renewal of baptismal vows, the Sunday *Asperges*, the Maundy Thursday washing of the feet. We have ample material here for the effective liturgical expression of the water flowing out from heaven and bringing life—the life of the resurrection—to men. It is all here, if we choose to use it: if, for instance, we place the font in a position of real dignity in the church and make of baptism a clearly parochial action, consciously linked with the Easter celebration; if we make of the Sunday *Asperges* something that the people can really enter into, with a procession that passes right through the congregation, and plenty of water and a vernacular chant—not just another dose of hurried clerical ritual carried out around a distant altar. Far from all this being true at present, I know of many well-established African parish churches which have no font at all, and where of course, the paschal blessing of the font is simply left out. So far are we from having attempted to make a really effective use of the symbolism of baptism and cleansing.

Today, for some, all this presents a problem. Can symbols still be valuable in the modern world? The de-mythologizers have come among us. "The debate on Bishop Robinson's *Honest to God* has proved beyond doubt one fact, namely that the images, myths and languages of traditional religion have become, or are increasingly becoming, irrelevant to men who are growing up into the views and temper and lingua franca of the modern scientific age."[21] Yet, even in Western, urbanized society what would seem to be needed is not the abandonment of images, but their purification. In fact a disuse of images would mean the effective abandonment of both the Bible and traditional liturgy, which are both impregnated with them. This sort of "language of traditional religion" is absolutely integral both to Semitic Biblical Christianity and to historic Catholicism. The Church cannot give it up, and does not need to. The return to the Bible is quite opposed in its deepest sense to a de-mythologizing movement. What we need is not de-mythologizing, but re-mythologizing, a rebirth of images rather than their consistent elimination. It is doubtless perfectly true that religious imagery as presented often means next to nothing to modern man,

[21] M. M. Thomas in *Witness in Six Continents*, ed. R. Orchard, Edinburgh House Press, p. 12.

but that is just because it is presented so badly—too sugary, and not effectively arche-typal. The filling of a church with over-painted statues and pictures does not satisfy the deeper imaginative requirements of the human psyche one jot, the bold presentation of the light of the risen Christ in the Easter vigil service will do so. What the catechetical movement is calling for in fact is a far more effective use of symbolism and image language; perhaps one trouble with the modern mind is, not that it does not need this, but that it does need it and has not really been getting it.

Whatever may be the psychological state of Western man in this matter, however, it is certain at least that in Africa the effective use of symbols is of the first importance. The scientific age has as yet impinged hardly at all upon the spiritual needs of the masses, while symbols, poetry, the language of images can speak to them with an overriding force. That is why the Pan-African Catechetical Study Week, meeting at Katigondo in 1964, when speaking of "the necessity for future liturgical adaptation" stressed especially "the importance of symbols in the Liturgy".[22]

Probably equally important is adaptability in prayer forms. One of the most tragic things not only in Africa, but also among Catholics elsewhere, is the poverty of prayer formulas. The "Hail Mary", the "Our Father", the "Glory be"—these most excellent prayers have become—especially in the shape of the rosary—the stereotyped reaction for every occasion: the anointing of the sick, thanksgiving after Mass, the blessing of houses. This is, of course, extremely bad for these prayers themselves. Because they are so important, the Lord's prayer especially, they need to be respected. Sheer repetition dulls the edge of appreciation. Nor does the addition of the "Acts" of faith, hope and charity greatly improve our prayer situation. Certainly the rosary has proved a most valuable help for raising up the minds and hearts of many to God, offering a sort of framework and background music for meditation, but we do need greater variety in prayer, and a greater relationship of formula to circumstance. There is a place, for instance, for *ex tempore* prayer, in providing new formulas suited to the immediate occasion. If a priest can be trusted to put together the language of his sermon, surely he can be trusted too to formulate

[22] *AFER*, Oct. 1964, p. 417.

special prayers for his congregation. But first of all far greater use should be made of the psalms, especially in para-liturgical services —for instance, Sunday services in a village where no priest is present. Yet in very few languages of Africa have we hitherto even bothered to translate the psalms—and a bishop could actually refuse to allow the use of the psalms when taken from a Protestant translation! Again there are beautiful prayers which have been customarily used in many African tribes. Here is a very easy field in which to adapt what is already existing to the needs of the Christian community. A fine example of the sort of old African prayers which could be most fittingly taken over by the Church may be found in the following Kikuyu prayers, regularly offered up at public assemblies.[23] Line 1 was spoken by an elder, while line 2 gives the responses of the assembly:

1. Say ye, the elders may have wisdom and speak with one voice.
2. Praise ye Ngai. Peace be with us.
1. Say ye that the country may have tranquillity and the people may continue to increase.
2. Praise ye Ngai. Peace be with us.
1. Say ye that the people and the flocks and the herds may prosper and be free from illness.
2. Praise ye Ngai. Peace be with us.
1. Say ye the fields may bear much fruit and the land may continue to be fertile.
2. Praise ye Ngai. Peace be with us.

This type of responsorial singing is both traditionally Christian and very characteristically African. Almost every tribe will have similar invocations that could fruitfully be brought into the Church's local worship, that it may be made genuinely African. The shape and sound of the liturgy should be renewed to achieve in every community a maximum of comprehension and deeply intended participation.

The greatest natural need of most African peoples is for rain. On the great sweeping uplands drought is the great menace and drought brings famine. Prayer and sacrifice for rain was of enormous importance in tribal religion. Prayers for this have always

[23] Jomo Kenyatta, *Facing Mount Kenya*, Secker & Warburg, pp. 238–9. *Ngai* is the Kikuyu name for God.

been a recognized part of the Church's liturgy, but they have become a fixed, formalistic part, tied to certain days, practically pointless in non-European lands—a seminary and convent exercise. Let us put the rogation processions at times when a concern for the crops is really being keenly felt, when rain or sun is especially needed. Let the litanies be of course sung in the vernacular with prayers that can be understood to relate to the needs of the time.

The great need is to escape from the fixation of the liturgy, and from the exclusively clerical character that so much of our ritual has tended to acquire. Africans hunger for ritual: groups breaking off from Protestant missions in South, West and East Africa have all tended to move strongly in a "Catholic", ritualistic direction: "Protestant Missions brought the Zulus into contact with a form of Christianity which was centred round a Book. The independent church changed the stress and evolved a form of religion centred round a set of rites",[24] and one of the chief reasons why Catholic Africans have so seldom broken away to form separate churches is surely that they have indeed found a helpful ritual within the Catholic Church. What we have to do now is to render this ritual more vibrant, more adapted to local circumstances, more open to popular participation and understanding.

These things, even when made more manifestly comprehensible than they are at present, still absolutely require explanation. Worship and teaching go together; the Eucharist at the heart of the one, Scripture at the heart of the other. Too often our religious instruction, whether given in church or in school or to some special group, has tragically failed to reach the mark, to get across the sort of unified vision of God's redemptive economy that produces conviction and commitment. Here again, the basic fault—as is well recognized today by many—lies in the teachers and in the sort of intellectual formation that is provided in the seminaries. Courses of scholastic philosophy and theology learnt in Latin seldom provide a healthy foundation for the subsequent explanation of the faith to common people, which is the chief work of the great majority of priests. The chief qualities that this work of explanation does need are four: first, it must be unified; secondly, it must be scriptural;

---

[24] B. Sundkler, *Bantu Prophets in South Africa*, p. 181.

thirdly, it must be organically related to the liturgy and corporate life of the Church; fourthly, it must be adapted to the age and culture of those receiving it.

Catechisms and traditional methods of religious teaching have been far too atomistic. A catechism consisting simply of a vast series of questions and answers seems to put everything on to the same level of importance and fails to relate all other doctrines effectively to the great central truths that really constitute the message of life, the good news: Jesus Christ has died and risen to reconcile us to the Father. Passion and Resurrection must be given the same importance in the catechism and in our own religious teaching that they receive in the Gospels. Other things, especially the commandments and sacraments, must be seen to share in and make manifest our covenant with God in Christ, instead of somehow seeming to stand upon their own.

Our teaching must be scriptural. This has two aspects to it. One is a copious use of Scripture and a scriptural way of expression within the general teaching of the faith; the other is the reading of Scripture on its own and consistently. Both are important. There are African catechisms, just as there have been European catechisms, where the place of the Word of God has been no more than to provide the occasional proof-text as an argument behind scholastic statements of doctrine, and the texts may not even be quoted, but only referred to! The language of Scripture is far richer than that of technical theology, and makes much more impression on the common mind. The Sunday homily is really the centre and type of all religious teaching, and its whole *raison d'être* is to be an explanation of the Gospel.

There is, secondly, the study of Scripture in itself, book by book. This can be done in school, in special study groups, or of course as a regular parochial activity in church. It would be an excellent thing to have an exposition of Scripture in Church, once or twice a week at some suitable time, when a book would simply be read through and explained systematically. The same thing should be done in special groups. As yet they hardly seem to exist. There are indeed many valuable groups of the Y.C.W. type which include a "Scripture enquiry" as part of their routine, but this generally relates only to very short extracts from the Bible, chosen because of some immediate appropriateness for social work and all together

10

very few in number. The same texts keep coming back, largely those already well known from the Sunday gospels. Such groups have their own value, but they are not Bible Study groups, and these are most certainly needed as well. Every parish, where there are a fair number of literate people, should have one or more. The aim is not to find some special practical application for the weekly passage, but simply to enter into it that it may help to mould one's thought and life.

All this may seem very simple and obvious, but it is still very far from the practice of the Church in Africa today. The reasons for this are two, and they are inter-connected. The first is the old lack of real scriptural interest on the part of the clergy, the second the state of existing Scripture translations into African languages. Certainly there has been marked progress, both liturgical and catechetical, in many countries, particularly since 1964, the year of the Pan-African Catechetical Conference. The lead which is being provided by the Pastoral Centres of Butare, in Rwanda, Kinshasa and Elisabethville in the Congo, and Lumku in South Africa, is particularly valuable; and other regional pastoral centres are urgently needed. Again, the recent publication of the very first complete Catholic edition of the Bible in an African language —a Chinyanja translation for Malawi and Zambia—is an event of the very greatest importance. Nevertheless old attitudes remain strong and in Africa they can be still more difficult to change than elsewhere, for here they have resulted in a very special way in the formation of a non-scripturally conscious Church. Whereas in other countries Catholic vernacular Bibles do exist and are there for those who want them, in Africa they simply do not exist. This was made so much worse by the rigorous refusal to allow Catholics to read Protestant translations, though in many places that refusal is now breaking down; a result of this has been that in many parts of Africa conversion to Catholicism has meant for a Protestant, who knows only his own vernacular, the actual immediate loss of personal contact with the word of God. As a Protestant he had his own Bible, becoming a Catholic he had to give it up. In practice the Catholic Church in Africa often seems to be hardly aware that the Old Testament really exists at all—at least as a book.

The situation can be expressed by a simple statement of the Catholic and Protestant translations that do in fact exist in any part of Africa. The best Catholics have achieved, in a very few of the most important languages, is the translation of the whole New Testament. The difference in the Protestant position is overwhelming. Here are the facts for Uganda, as they stood in 1962.

Language	Catholic translations	Protestant translations
Acholi	—	New Testament
Bangala	—	Complete Bible
Bari	Sunday gospels	Old Testament
		Luke, John
Kumam	Extracts O.T. and N.T.	—
	Sunday gospels	
Luganda	Extracts of O.T.	Complete Bible
	New Testament	
Lur	—	Complete Bible
Nkore-Kiga	—	Bible: production projected
Nyoro	—	Complete Bible
Padhola	Extracts of O.T. and N.T.	
	Sunday gospels and epistles	—
	(typewritten)	
Teso	Extracts O.T. and N.T.	
	Sunday epistles and gospels	Complete Bible
	(Gospels projected)	

For East Africa as a whole there were three complete Catholic translations of the New Testament to stand against many complete Protestant Bibles and nearly fifty New Testaments.[25] Yet Catholic mission workers are more numerous than Protestants and work quite as universally, but they have had an entirely different order of priorities. The position in the rest of Africa is no different.[26] We do not have to think that the Protestant translations are perfect—they would be the first to admit the contrary—nor need we agree with the Protestant attitude to the Bible as a whole, but there remains no way of justifying the undoubted fact that those representing the Catholic Church have been far less interested in bringing the Scriptures to the people than have those representing other separated communions. The Bible belongs to the Church; with the

[25] See J. Bessem, W.F., "Scripture Translations in East Africa", *AFER*, July 1962, pp. 201–11.
[26] For the situation in Zambia see an article of Fr Vermeulen, W.F., "Scripture Translations in Northern Rhodesia", *AFER*, Jan. 1964, pp. 66–73.

Eucharist it is her most precious possession, but we have lamentably failed to communicate it to our African Christians. Even today our attitude, when deeds are considered and not words, seems hardly to be improving in many places. Yet unless it does change quite drastically, our religious instruction is bound to remain deprived of its very heart.

Again, it is quite unrealistic to think that we can catch up on our own. We cannot, within the foreseeable future, and there is anyway no point in trying. Everywhere in the world Catholics and Protestants are now beginning to co-operate in this work, but there is no continent where such co-operation is so necessary as in Africa, because there is nowhere else where we are so behind, and nowhere else with a comparable number of languages involved. A big step forward has already been taken in Tanzania, where the Catholic hierarchy has agreed both to adopt the Protestant Swahili translation and to sponsor a joint Catholic-Protestant Commission to revise the text in the future. In the discussions with the British and Foreign Bible Society, it was emphasized that "a common Bible for the use of both Roman and non-Roman Christians would make an impact on the whole Christian witness to the nation which can hardly be over-estimated."[27] What has been done in Tanzania should be done everywhere. Most Protestant authorities will be only too glad to co-operate with us in the improvement of their own texts. It is obvious that first translations into strange languages, done largely by foreigners, are bound to have serious defects. Today Bible translation has high standards. There are extremely few Catholic missionaries, and even fewer African priests who have the biblical training necessary. This does not mean that nonspecialists cannot join in this work. They can—especially African priests—if the work is done by a team, not by an individual, and includes biblical specialists as well. However, it is better to have imperfect translations than none at all. The important thing is the determination to go ahead and this should everywhere be done through the close collaboration with Protestants that the Pan-African Catechetical Study Week asked for in 1964.[28]

Of course the many educated people in Africa can read the Bible

[27] W. Bühlmann, "Co-operation with Protestants in the Translation of the Bible for the Missions", *Teaching All Nations*, April 1965, p. 204.
[28] For the full text of the resolution see p. 245.

in English or French and should obviously be greatly encouraged to do so, where their own languages have not complete and adequate versions.

If our teaching must be scriptural, it must also be liturgical, closely interwoven with the Church's year. This follows naturally if the liturgy is itself celebrated with zeal and enthusiasm, and if our general teaching is genuinely Christ-centred, for it is above all across the liturgical year that we can enter into the great mysteries of Christ and the redemption. All the best teaching of religion comes in and through praying. It is by sharing in the Mass, understanding its prayers and thrust that we can learn best about the very core of our Christian reality. The same is true, at a lower level, of other prayers. That is an additional reason why it is so important to get the balance of our prayers right. Again, we need to examine ourselves very stringently about this. A prayer can be entirely fitting and very beautiful, yet we may still be giving it a wrong or an exaggerated place in the full pattern of life, while other prayers, such as certain acts of contrition, may even be presenting a false emphasis, especially for the young. Is the repetition of fifty "Hail Marys" every day for a month really very helpful for the religious life of schoolchildren? Just as one may ask whether the saying of fifteen decades of the rosary every day is really a suitable core for the spiritual life of nuns.[29] Then again there is the repetition of the Litany of Our Lady every day of October and on Saturdays (twice a day, in these circumstances, in some religious establishments). Will this sort of pattern for our prayer life really form a balanced Catholic mind? It is difficult to think so.

Finally, our teaching must be very positive, including our moral teaching. The Christ life is a life of doing, far more than one of avoiding sins. The mortal sin complex has already grown terribly strong in the Church of Africa, though of course, like all our other weaknesses, it has come from elsewhere. The most serious example of the misuse of teaching about mortal sin is in the matter of church tax. Failure to pay church tax, even by the poor, has been taught and re-taught over most of Africa as constituting mortal sin, and, moreover, a particularly heinous type of mortal sin, on account of which the sacraments are to be publicly refused. This

[29] In some convent schools even the children have to say fifteen decades daily.

is not only wrong in itself,[30] but also puts the whole attitude to mortal sin and the grace of God and the nature of Church life wrong. Wrong too is the widespread indoctrination of a direct link-up of confession with communion, so that many will not go to communion unless they have just been to confession. This begins with not allowing children to make their first communion until they have made their first confession, when the best order for the young to receive the sacraments is Baptism-Confirmation-Communion-Confession. Bad again is the absolute enforcement in so many schools of the routine confession, and even the issuing of confessional cards with the person's name on it which have then to be marked by the confessor. When such things are written down in black and white, it may be difficult to believe that they actually do happen, but such is the sad fact. All this is calculated to turn people away from confession, instead of finding in it a difficult but still valuable help. When the question of church tax is brought in, on top of the dislike which has already been inculcated for confession by such methods, no wonder that many young people simply give up the practice of the sacraments altogether. The religious mentality that such practices form is a wrong one—one more to be connected with the Police State—and if we want to build up a healthy Catholicism in Africa, we must change it before it is too late. Our chief insistence must not be upon attitudes of compulsion, upon the danger of committing mortal sins, but upon the positive freedom with which, as members of the people of God, Christians grow up in the image of Christ under the influence of the Eucharist and the Scriptures.

4. INSTITUTIONS

The life of a young Church cannot but reflect the circumstances and methods which have brought it to birth. Inevitably these will have been related chiefly to some particular side of Christian belief and living. One of the most important things that the young Church has to do once it has realized its corporate existence is to react against the one-sided stresses which have derived from the conver-

---

[30] Cf. E. De Bekker, W.F., in *AFER*, April 1963, pp. 110–21. I believe that the last three years have witnessed a real, and welcome, change in this matter.

sion process. There must be a certain special search for fullness, for the most central things in Christian life, and a gradual liberation from too much dependence on some of the secondary things which seemed so important in the initial process of conversion.

For us, of course, the school is the chief case in point. For forty years or more it has been the chief instrument of missionary work, and the result is a Church life in which the school occupies a place of quite overwhelming importance. Two quotations from priests working in Nigeria, where this seems to be quite particularly the case, can illustrate the situation.

> The total population of Nigeria is thirty-two million. The school population is about two and a half million. Of these approximately nine hundred thousand attend Catholic schools. These schools are owned and controlled by the Bishops, and are under the management of Fathers and Sisters. They have more than thirty thousand Catholic teachers on their pay roll. About 70 per cent of the total salary bill is met by Government. The remaining 30 per cent comes from school fees and various forms of organized contribution.[31]

Is it really conceivably desirable to have thirty thousand Catholic teachers on the bishops' pay roll? Is that likely to produce the right sort of relationship between the clergy and the leading laity? Nigeria is particularly short of priests, and yet so many of those she has are taken up in school administration. Another priest has commented on the same situation:

> Much of our effort goes into schools—primary, secondary modern, secondary grammar. Priests and Sisters are disproportionately cooped up in schools. Parish priests spend so much of their time dealing with primary schools that they are referred to currently as "Managers". One must be careful not to condemn this school work. Much of our expansion still takes place through the schools . . . in our present missionary methods we are heavily dependent on schools, perhaps too dependent.[32]

---

[31] J. P. Jordan, C.S.Sp., "Catholic Education and Catholicism in Nigeria", *AFER*, Jan. 1960, p. 61. The population figure given for Nigeria is not accurate.
[32] J. O'Connell, "The Church and Modernization in Africa", *AFER*, Oct. 1963, p. 330.

What is true of Nigeria has been largely true of almost all Africa. The dangers of the situation are clear; and have been pointed out above (pp. 84–7). Missionaries have seemed to use as a lever, to bring about the conversion of ignorant people, things that have very little to do with the Church. Education and medicine are not in fact the Church's own possessions and Africa today is waking up to the fact. Independent governments are no longer anxious to have their government-financed schools used as a means for securing the Christian allegiance of the young, be their parents pagan or Christian. Again, a vast schools system because of which priests are hardly able to fulfil their genuine sacerdotal ministry and become instead "managers" is bound to produce a great mass of very nominal Christians. And this in fact is what has happened. We have to ask ourselves today whether the Church's function is really to get the nominal allegiance of the largest possible number of people or the real commitment of a possibly smaller group. Thirdly, the precariousness of the Church's position today is very clear indeed. We have created a colossus, but with feet of clay. Deprive the Church of her schools by nationalization and in the present state of things far too much of our work could collapse overnight.

It is true that actually, despite threats, most independent African governments are not anxious today to carry out a vigorous policy of nationalization although a few, such as Congo (Brazza), have already done so. The advantages of mission help remain obvious. The Church provides a vast army of competent, hard-working, often poorly-paid, staff, and it is almost impossible in present circumstances to replace it. Hence for the present the Church is permitted to remain in largely effective, if not nominal, control of the schools. New African graduates go for the most part into ministerial or business posts. It is still difficult to get many to remain at the higher levels of the teaching profession. The secondary schools, which are also rapidly expanding, remain as a consequence very largely a preserve of expatriates. But even this is going to change. African universities are expanding at an enormous rate, and thousands of other students are overseas. In a few years the good posts in other fields will have been filled and a rapidly increasing number of people will be pressing into the teaching profession. It is at that moment that the Church may really find her present control of the school system slipping away for good. And when that happens, what will we have to replace it?

To generalize, the vast work of evangelization which has been accomplished in Africa during the last eighty years has been achieved within a situation and with means which we shall very soon have lost for good. The situation was one of privilege, sometimes gross over-privilege, of a near monopoly of the social services, of an authority which in many places there could seem no means of questioning. All this has gone. The Church no longer has privileges and monopolies, though she has often to suffer the backwash of having had them in the past: and the more she had, the more violent the reaction can be. Africans are coming to see today that the connection between the Church and the schools was in some way fortuitous. One can read and write, appreciate Shakespeare, study nuclear physics and still ignore religion. This does not invalidate every argument for having Catholic schools, but it does greatly affect the probability of education being a motive for Christian living, and it does call for a reappraisal of our methods and order of apostolic priorities.

This is no call to the Church to abandon wholesale her schools and hospitals. The good they can do at their best is clear, and institutions are needed in any walk of life to radiate personal influence. It is clear how much a parish school, run by a parents' association of parishioners, can do to pull the whole parish together. Nevertheless we have to do our very best to make church life less dependent upon them, not only because they are government-sponsored institutions which we may well lose, but because of themselves they are not adequate for the construction of a living Christian community and preoccupation with the sheer quantity of them is making the Church extensive but anaemic. The human and religious quality of our institutions is more important than the total number which we administratively "manage", but where we are allowed to keep them there can be no doubt of their potential value, both as a witness to our desire to serve society as a whole and as ways of building up and strengthening the Church's own life.[33]

[33] For this question one may refer with profit to Mgr Mullin's *The Catholic Church in Modern Africa*, Chapman, pp. 17–23.

They must offer a witness of service. Gone must be any attitude which sees them as a sort of lever providing health or education in return for conversion. They need to possess a quality of disinterestedness which is a virtue to be manifested not only in our personal but also in our group capacity. Both school and hospital can then remain, what they have always tried to be, real sacraments of a full Christianity.

The hospital witnesses to the Church's mission to the whole man, the body as such as well as the soul. It expresses her basic anti-Manichaeism. And it shows her loving care for any and every man; its ministrations can in no way be limited to the baptized. It is the sacrament of Christian compassion for human suffering, and human suffering is of a mind—joined to a body. As suffering is not a mere physical process, so the Church's medical mission is not a concern with the physical alone. It reaches to the whole man, to enfleshed spirit. That mission will always remain, but the exact part the Church's hospitals play in contemporary society can greatly change. When missionaries first came to Africa, there were of course no hospitals at all, and missionaries could do much useful medical work, even if they were very amateur. Today this has passed, and in most places—outside emergencies—medical services from a non-trained missionary can seem almost insulting. People are learning to expect the best, just as they do elsewhere.

Nowadays there are many government hospitals; the State, not the Church, has the primary duty to see to the health of her citizens, and the Church has not to intrude herself in pushing forward a rival *system*; she must be ready to give up hospitals, when asked, to the State. True service implies a willingness to be replaced, and the Church has no right to force her attentions on society, any more than on the individual. Her true mission to society can be fulfilled quite as effectively through individual Catholics, lay or religious, ministering within a general hospital as through the possession of her own controlled institutions, but of course in African countries medical services are still very inadequate and there can be little fear that the Church's organized services will not still be required. Her medical work is surely not something to be abandoned, for there is no way in which she can serve the developing countries better, but individual works are to be scrutinized as to how far a particular institution really renders sacramentally concrete the Church's general mission. It has to be recognized that things can change in this regard. As a hospital expands, becoming a large government-supported institution, it may quite possibly be more fitting to hand it over entirely to the government, leaving the Church's own workers free to run other smaller hospitals and dispensaries in which, because of the greater human contact possible, there may be more opportunity for the individual worker to manifest his Christian belief and concern and to be a personal sacrament of the Church's charity. What we are always in danger of doing is to allow services and witness to degenerate into mere management.

The school for its part is the sacrament, the visible sign in time and space, of Christ's and the Church's love for the young, of the Christian concern for all the things of the mind, for truth as such. We should certainly be most unwise to abandon our schools, where this is not forced upon us. To do so could certainly greatly damage our reputation in the opinion of the young countries, even if it is very probable that an unreasonable proportion of our very limited number of priests have their time at present entirely taken up either teaching in a secondary school or "managing" a school's organization. It is often strange in Europe to find ten or more priests teaching in a single school when people are complaining of the lack of priests for pastoral work, but in Africa, where we really are desperately short of pastoral clergy, this sort of thing is even more hard to understand and justify.

There are Church schools in Africa which are hardly more than nominally Catholic; this applies especially to some primary schools, managed by the diocese, but most of whose teachers maybe are not communicating Catholics. Their very existence may be simply an expression of an over-concern with numbers. But the genuine Catholic school surely does provide a real opportunity to form the young in a Christian mind, and this is especially valuable as the parents of so many of these young people can offer them little Christian formation, having themselves received little. The best Catholic secondary schools offer the field today in which the work of forming convinced committed Christians is perhaps being most successfully accomplished.

Again, in present circumstances, it is obvious that if the Churches do not help very considerably with the schools, other, possibly dangerous, agencies may well be asked to take them over. In general Africans do appreciate what the missions have done for them in the educational field, and feel happy about their continued activity. They realize the supreme importance of educational work for the social development of their countries, and they recognize both the enormous and self-sacrificing labour missionaries have put into it, and the near impossibility of finding equally reliable help from any other source. In fact our active collaboration in this development and in the educational field may well be the passport allowing a continued missionary presence in the country. In the words of a recent writer, "The educated élite of modern Nigeria, whether Christian, Muslim, or Pagan, judge church organizations by the amount and quality of the education they have provided in the past. . . . Favours which the élite will be prepared to sanction in the future will be bestowed on churches in recognition of their educational effort."[34] In such circumstances it seems evident that a very considerable educational effort on the part of the Church must continue, at the same time as we do try to free the Church's work from too much dependence on the school. We have to see our school work as an offering to the nation, to be accepted in the way the nation likes best, rather than as a private possession we must fight our hardest to retain. In practice this means an immediate willingness to accept non-Catholics into Catholic schools without putting on subsequent pressure to convert them, willingness to collaborate in multi-denominational schools by providing a chaplain or, if possible, other staff members as desired, willingness to make of all our school work a genuine service of the wider community and not a segregated activity. African governments will at least insist on this much, and in complying with their insistence we should make it clear that we are fulfilling not only their principles but our own as well.

Educational work can certainly not cease to be of the utmost concern to the Church, but it may increasingly take on a new pattern in which what matters is not the control of school management by the organized Church, but the effective witness that the individual Catholic teacher, priest or religious or lay, African or expatriate, makes within the school in which he is teaching.

Church and school and hospital: the old trio of mission work.

[34] J. Webster, *The African Churches among the Yoruba*, Oxford, p. 190.

They are all three valuable but to the extent that preoccupation with them means preoccupation with the things of bricks and mortar, we need to see deeper. The establishment of the Church is often spoken of so much in terms of bricks and mortar. They are deceptive terms, and these things are dangerous things, which we can certainly easily lose, in some countries of Africa most certainly will lose; and which—in the circumstance of today—we must not too much regret. The real establishment of the Church is in the loyalties of people. Schools and hospitals can be nationalized, churches burnt down, but if people are committed to the faith, what is essential remains. The future of the Church in Africa depends upon the number of committed African Christians that exist. They, and they alone, cannot be taken away from us.

When our control of a schools system is in fact not increasing but diminishing the loyalty of our Christians—for instance, through the monopolizing of headships for the clergy—when we fail to show a proper professional respect for the educated men who have come out of our schools, or for the susceptibilities of the maturing students within them, when we concentrate our energies upon numbers, upon obtaining examination results, but think little about surmounting the problems of human relations, we are our own worst enemies. What is important is not how many people out of fear of mortal sin have been got to come to Mass, but how many communicate and behave as living and responsible Church members; it is not how many pupils are enrolled in our secondary schools and attend there a compulsory Mass every morning, but how many when they come out continue to practise their religion in a mature way as educated Christian men. The Christian family, the local priest, the individual believer, these provide the only really reliable units of church life, sharing together in the Eucharist, learning from her teaching of the word of God, participating in the full communion of the Catholic fellowship.

While freeing ourselves to some extent from preoccupation with government-sponsored institutions, we need at the same time to create some more characteristic institutions of our own. What we lack badly in most parts of Africa is the well-run conference and retreat centre where laity and priests can meet for a whole range of purposes—places such as Spode House in England. There is almost no institution which, well placed and imaginatively directed, could be of more value for the Church today. Such things could be linked up with monasteries, of which we have also great need— and great lack. It is strange how the old missionary sense in the monastic tradition has faded out of large sectors of its modern representatives.

Equally great can be the need for social centres in towns or a student centre at a university. Again, nothing is more absent in most parts of Africa, both town and country, than good recreational facilities for young people and indeed for their elders too. To provide a tennis court, a basketball pitch, or a small library at the parish may have far more effect on the real life of the Christian community than the management of an extra school. These things need not be alternatives, but we do need to spread our efforts and our money-spending over a wider field than hitherto.

In conclusion it is worth proposing a theorem concerning apostolic activity and institutions: the constant tendency to create them and religious societies of every sort is a right one; initially they express and fruitfully canalize its dynamism, but the more they develop in size and the more time passes, the more do those same institutions tend instead to become a barrier to real Christian work: no longer channels but ends in themselves, sucking up the full time and attention of ever more workers in the business of administration and self-perpetuation, but offering ever less in the way of apostolic and pastoral fruit. This is true of religious orders, of schools, of hospitals, of almost everything. We cannot dispense with institutions, but no more must we submit to their domination.

5. A WORKING LAITY

The laity are the people of God and the people of God are the Church. We have certainly still some way to go to get across this understanding of the fundamental equivalence of Church and laity of whom the clergy are a specialized group, as against an equivalence of Church and clergy with the laity as a sort of subjected attachment.

In practice it is clear that in Africa, as elsewhere, school and hospital work—begun almost everywhere by the clergy—is today passing more and more into lay hands. The mere pressure of numbers dictates this, so also do other pressures which we have already considered: those of increasing governmental control and africanization. A school controlled by a local parents' association, anxious to retain its particular character, can stand up to pressures far better than can a school controlled by a missionary bishop. This is indeed being widely realized.

Theologically, this is the age of the laity, an age in which we are coming to understand that a healthy Church depends in the end far less on the powers or even abilities of its clergy than upon the general sense of vocation and mission of the Christian people at large—a working laity: working in worship, in teaching and apostolate, in the shouldering of responsibilities within a secular society. The particular shortage of priests in Africa adds a peculiar edge to our need to recognize all this effectively, and in fact lay people already do play a very striking part in our church life. The catechist is a layman, but he not only regularly leads prayers in church but also preaches: a thing almost unheard of in Europe! Catechists and teachers have indeed borne the brunt of maintaining the Church's presence at grass roots level. Doubtless their training for the work involved has generally been very inadequate, and the approach often frighteningly authoritarian, their teaching the repetition of memorized formulas. Often, but not always. It would surely be difficult to say how much the Church owes to her African catechists—they have represented the first expression (and often a most devoted one) of a working laity. Today they need higher training and supplementation but not—I hope—clericalization.

The Y.C.S. and Y.C.W., Xaverians, the Legion of Mary, Parents' Associations, and especially Parish Councils are today offering more and more ways in which the laity can join actively in the living and mission of the Church. Almost always such associations cause a certain difficulty to priests, basically because priests often do not realize what their healthy existence is bound to involve: a real sharing of responsibility and policy-making. Unless the priest is prepared to let them have part in decision-making, and that means at least some of the time giving up his own view for theirs, such groups are bound to seem a mere collection of clerical lackeys and to shrivel up into insignificance. Where, however, Parish Councils and Parents' Associations are allowed to grow strong and effective, though they may seem sometimes in peace a thorn in the priest's side, they turn up trumps in moments of real difficulty. In the words of Donald Nicholl, "It is only those who are prepared to stand up to you who will in the end stand by you".[35]

We have always to remember that it is only a small part of the Christian activity of the laity which concerns the Church in an identifiable way: most of what most of them do, and that includes the whole activity of some of the very holiest and most active Church members, consists in their simply being the Church—the people of God—almost invisibly at work in office, field and factory, in club and political party, in the city of this world. That all this is part of the Church's own life is only formally provable from their Sunday Mass and communion: participation in the sacramental and liturgical centre. Here the liturgical movement is seen as basically one with that of ecclesial "laicization" for its great central point is exactly this: to make all Christians realize that the Mass is their common action, in which they have to participate fully and meaningfully, the necessary and adequate source for their Christian living, and their bond with the *ecclesia*. Everything else grows out from the experience of the liturgical community: financial support for the Church's needs, the determination to teach and spread the faith, social action based upon justice and charity.

It is quite clear that we have in Africa the extensive and loyal co-operation of many laymen; nevertheless there are some big gaps here, and the gaps are appearing exactly in those segments of society which are destined to be most influential upon the future thinking and behaving of society as a whole: the graduate section, the urban section, and even—quite largely—the post-school generation also in the countryside. As we sow, so do we reap. Our own pattern of missionary and pastoral work remains rural and school-minded. It is quite extraordinary how little care or interest we manifest in those who have once left our schools and in the quickly growing urban population. As regards the latter, Bishop Moynagh of Calabar has written: "If we consider that we are doing well enough when we concentrate on the older missions in rural areas, establish Christian families, foster vocations therein, and that we cannot just now give adequate care to these cosmopolitan townships, we are making a grave mistake. . . . We should

[35] *Search*, April 1966, p. 450.

try to staff the township parishes even at the expense of rural missions."[36]

Certainly in many countries there has been some real efforts to follow this advice in the last six years. Nevertheless the effort made seldom matches up to the scale of the situation involved in the larger towns (except perhaps in Kinshasa—Leopoldville). The following remark of a sociologist describing a township population could still be repeated for far too many places: "Organized religion plays a rather minor part in Kisenyi. Christian observance is low, though nominal adherence is high. There are no churches in the area, but there is a small mosque."[37] That is to say, most of the people there were Christians in the countryside, had been at mission primaries, and so on. On settling in the town, they entered a society hardly touched by the Church. Yet of such is Africa's future leadership.

In general neither the fully educated graduate class—admittedly only now becoming a group of sizeable dimensions—nor the townspeople provide the Church with committed lay leaders, and this follows inevitably from the fact that neither group has been much bothered about in missionary strategy, or easily finds itself at home in the Church as we have formed it up to now. This is not to deny that some priests have done, and are doing, most valuable work in urban areas and in the universities, but they are far too few, and their work remains largely unsupported within the general structure of the Church.

The preceding section already suggested some of the sort of institutions we need if the Church is to approach these new classes effectively. Through them, and through the building up of cells of active, committed lay Christians within the vast mass of nominal adherents, we must hope to arrive at a laity in whose hands the fortunes of the Church are as safe as within those of any clergy. In this era of stupendous growth the Church's life and ability to fulfil her mission in Africa depend above all upon the faith, loyalty, active commitment of lay people, and it is essential that those lay people be numbered not only among villagers and primary teachers, but also and especially among townsmen and graduates.

[36] "The Apostolate to the Townships", *AFER*, April 1961, p. 88.
[37] A. Southall, *Social Change in Modern Africa*, Oxford, 1961, p. 226.

11

At the heart of lay life lies marriage, and as it is marriage which seems to present the greatest of all obstacles to the growth of a Christian laity in Africa, it is to this topic that we must next turn.

6. MARRIAGE

Marriage presents problems in any Church and any society.[38] It is the nodal point of human life, the root from which all aspects of society grow. It creates but can also mar the most central human relationships. Precisely because it is at the root of a society, it is the most difficult thing to remould if members of that society enter into the light of the Gospel, but it is also the most important. It offers the greatest obstacles to the growth of Christian life, and yet equally it is the essential vehicle of that growth: Christian society without Christian marriage and family life is unthinkable. We have pagan patterns of marriage including polygamy, the consideration of woman as a possession rather than a person, wife-beating, divorce and so on, and we have a Christian pattern presenting fellowship, complementary mutual service, love, the mirror of Christ and his Church. The former provide the greatest abiding barrier to the growth of an effectively Christian society in mission lands; to stimulate the latter into being must be the object of our chief concern. Yet we must beware too of over-stressing this dichotomy, for Christian marriage itself is not simply a new thing, it is the old thing renewed. It is quite different from the other sacraments in that it is the uplifting and purifying of a given natural relationship, made effective, therefore, by the people themselves in entering upon it, not by any other minister of the Church. We should be very careful in practice not to betray this theology of marriage by so stressing the church ceremony as to suggest irremediably in the eyes of simple people that for us the essential thing in marriage is the priest's blessing or the giving of a ring in church rather than the basic consenting of two people. We have also to remember that if much was wrong in pagan marriage, much still could be right. It too could be the genuine expression of

[38] The basic works for a study of African marriage problems are the following: A. Phillips' *Survey of African Marriage and Family Life*, Oxford, 1953; *African Systems of Kinship and Marriage*, ed. A. Radcliffe-Brown and Daryll Forde, Oxford; A. Reuter, O.M.I., *Native Marriages in South Africa, according to Law and Custom*, Munster, 1963.

a real lifelong union of body and affection between man and woman.

In general, faced with a society full of polygamy and divorce, the missionary has obviously to concentrate above all on the simple witness of the monogamous Christian home. It is this that all our efforts must commend. The building up in a new land of the people of God means the building up of a people, marrying and giving in marriage. It is the frequency of the sacrament of marriage far more than the number of baptisms that really indicates the establishment of the Church. That and the imparting of orders are the marks of a living Church: men and women consciously living the consecration of their baptism in their adult lives. Marriage is then at the very heart of the missionary task, and it is truly extraordinary that the Conciliar decree on Missionary Activity, following the example of earlier papal encyclicals on the missions, has literally nothing to say on the subject. It is not mentioned once. This is terribly symptomatic of the clericalism that colours most missionary thinking, and is all the stranger as marriage problems surely present the chief cause of discouragement for working missionaries today.

Almost all missionaries feel that there is something deeply wrong with our approach to marriage in Africa, but when it comes to finding out just what is wrong, one is struck by the enormous complexity of the problems and variety of situations. The only agreement might be that control has been left far too much in the hands of canonists! Beyond that, it is striking how an analysis made by an experienced missionary in one area is found quite wide of the mark by equally experienced missionaries a few dioceses away. This arises from, firstly, the existence of vast differences between the traditional practices of different peoples (for example, in some places customary marriage was easily dissoluble; in others divorce was extremely rare); secondly, the degree to which new disruptive social pressures are being felt in a particular area; thirdly, the great variety in the practice of Church authority from diocese to diocese and society to society (for example, in one place dispensation for mixed marriage is almost unheard of; in another it is a routine matter); fourthly, the stage which missionary work has reached: in some areas the chief worry is the marriage of pagans who wish to be baptized, in others that of Christians. With all these differences missionary discussion of marriage problems seems often to go completely at cross purposes.

To take the last division first, the position with regard to pagan marriages may be described in the words of Fr Hochwalt, M.M., who works among the Sukuma people of western Tanzania. In his experience catechumens have on the average a history of 2–3 previous marriages.

The priest who instructs catechumens is bound to investigate the marital condition of each. The catechumen may be admitted to baptism only if his marital status is in accord with Christian teaching, or can be made to conform to it.

Every priest is familiar with the catechism of questions: Are you married now? To whom? Is this person your first husband or wife? Was the bridewealth paid? Is this accepted as a real marriage by the people? These are the simplest of the questions. If the present union is not the first, if there were other unions, then the probing continues and must continue until the often elusive "first spouse" is discovered. The probing does not stop with the first spouse, however. The priest and the catechumen now face the task of determining the marital status of the first spouse, since it is possible that the catechumen married a divorcee. If the "first spouse" was married before marrying with the catechumen, then the probing concerns "the first spouse of the first spouse", and if the "first spouse of the first spouse of the catechumen" was married before ... the probing becomes so confusing to the catechumen (to say nothing of the priest's confusion) that it becomes almost impossible to settle the matter.

The status taking has put the catechumen through an extraordinary, even upsetting, experience. It has impressed on him that marriage cannot be broken at will (a thing which he has in fact done!), that his true wife is still that woman whom he divorced years ago (a point which he can scarcely be expected to understand or believe!) only to practically deny the above points by allowing him to do what he wanted to do all along ... be married to his present wife, for example, or marry again as the case may be. Has such an investigation taught the catechumen anything? Has it really defended any essential Christian concepts?

The essential concepts or properties of marriage which we defend, and teach to all Christians and catechumens, are indissolubility and unicity. However, when treating of the marriage cases of converts we do not follow the consequences of the teaching that marriage is an indissoluble bond between one man and one woman to the exclusion of all others. To do so would be contrary to the good of souls, for it would prevent the baptism of many sincere persons. Moreover, the Church does not hold that all marriages are absolutely indissoluble and unique, because in practice the Church does dissolve the marriage of converts and does permit re-marriage.[39]

We teach catechumens that marriage is indissoluble and then proceed to dissolve their former marriages! ... Here our theoretical positions seem very doubtful and canon law fantastically complex, a maze which few missionaries can feel they understand, but the final solution is generally satisfactory. With those once Christian, however, the situation seems the other way round. Our Christians find themselves subject to marriage laws which have become stricter and stricter in the course of ages and which were certainly not devised with their sort of situation in mind. The result is that once the baptized come to marry, many of them fail to conform to some part of the Church's regulations, and drift into a permanent state of excommunication as a result.

This type of situation has been vividly described, as it appears in his part (the Tororo diocese of eastern Uganda), by another experienced missionary, Fr Lijding:

Two boys were presented to me as candidates for the Minor Seminary, John and Peter.

John's parents are both Catholic and I see them fairly regularly attending Holy Mass on Sundays, though they are "in a case", having contracted only a tribal marriage after baptism. And John has been an altarboy for several years, was baptized in infancy, attends our school, and receives the sacraments regularly. Altogether a good candidate, but ... he is illegitimate and for that reason cannot be presented as a candidate for the seminary.

[39] R. Hochwalt, "Are Customary Marriages Valid", *AFER*, July 1966, pp. 230–1.

Peter's parents are Protestants, who also contracted only a tribal marriage after their baptism, but being Protestants, that is a sacramental marriage. And Peter is a legitimate child. Peter, like John, has all the qualifications required to enter the minor seminary, without having John's stigma of being a bastard. Peter is now in the seminary, and if all goes well, will be a good priest one day, we hope.

Of course I did explain to John's parents why their son could not be accepted, but equally of course neither they nor the other parishioners could be expected to understand why the son of two Protestants is preferred to the son of two Catholics. In their eyes the Protestant parents are equally at fault in not having contracted their marriage in the Protestant church.

Two Catholics, living not far away from the church, were at last persuaded to get married in church, after having lived happily together for fifteen years or more. Both of them pretty regular churchgoers. All the children baptized. Altogether they had been quite a respectable Catholic family, and now they were straightening things out properly by getting married in church.

Just before the marriage, the woman comes to confession. Everything as regular as if she had never been away from the sacraments. But when I wanted to help her on, reminding her she had been living in a case for so long, all I got was "but he is my husband". And when I mentioned Easter duties, "but, Father, how could I, when you would never allow me". And when her husband came to make his confession, he could only give similar answers.

In their mind there is no question of sin at all; but it is just a matter of the Church forbidding them to receive the sacraments. And it certainly is not for not having heard it explained often enough in sermons and otherwise.

Now, the couples I spoke of above are some of the good ones. Happily there are many like that, and a number of them will eventually get married in church, before priest and two witnesses, *forma canonica*. But even for those pretty good families, the parents miss all the graces of the sacraments of penance and Eucharist all those years. And all those years their children miss the good example of seeing their parents receive the sacraments regularly.

Here in this parish, and in most other parishes in this diocese (Tororo, Uganda) and, from what I heard during the Pan-African Catechetical Study Week at Katigondo, in many more dioceses in Africa, it is quite the ordinary thing for most Catholics to get married, as they say, according to tribal custom.... We have also the proper marriages of Catholic teachers and the marriages of adult catechumens, mainly cases where a Catholic has lived with a pagan, who eventually also wants to "read". The pagan party cannot be baptized unless they also agree to marry in church. And even of those it is no exception that after all the "reading" the Catholic party refuses to marry in church, and the pagan party in consequence cannot be baptized. The general trend is: not to contract a church marriage.

We all know the consequences, that is *we* who are working in parishes of that type. A full investigation would most likely show that the greater majority of parishes in East Africa, in Central Africa and in West Africa are of that type.... We now have a very large percentage of adult Catholics who no longer take part in the *life of the Church*. They contract a tribal marriage, and have to stop receiving the sacraments. A number of them will continue to come to church or village chapel on Sundays, but very many stop even doing that after a while. They feel that they don't "belong".... They will usually bring their children for baptism, and send them to Catholic school, unless that in any way would involve a sacrifice.... When the time comes round for them to marry, what else can we expect than that they will follow the example of their parents, or rather that they will follow the general trend, and contract a tribal marriage only.... The main consequences of this trend not to marry in church is that the Church does not really get established as a living Catholic community. There is no real Catholic family life.[40]

The Catholics of whom Fr Lijding speaks have had a correct tribal marriage, including an official betrothal, the giving of a dowry, and the traditional ceremonies, and they have settled down to a monogamous married life, but they have had no church cere-

[40] "Tribal Marriage of Catholics", *AFER*, 1965, pp. 36–42. Fr Verheij, of Kisumu diocese, Kenya, confirms that the situation is quite the same there, *AFER*, April 1965, pp. 171–2.

mony. Let us note here, what is psychologically important, that in most areas marriage in church is not an alternative to tribal marriage: it is additional. The essential customs of tribal marriage, including the dowry, will be carried through in any case, whether or not there is also the church ceremony. Only with a few very urbanized or modern-minded Africans might that not be true— though there are a few fathers nowadays who refuse to accept any dowry at all.[41] In the eyes of the people there has been a real marriage, guaranteed by the dowry, and manifested by ceremonies signifying the consent of both parties and their families to the union. The ceremony in church is seen as a religious extra, a blessing upon the union; but if it is not added, then, in the eyes of the Church, they are not married but living in concubinage, they are excluded from the sacraments, maybe until death, and their children will be illegitimate and (in some dioceses) debarred from becoming priests.

Doubtless the proportions and the mentality behind them vary a good deal from place to place. Thus in some strongly Catholic areas such as Iboland in Eastern Nigeria,[42] Moshi in Tanzania or Masaka in Uganda there are a considerably higher number of church weddings than elsewhere, and a larger number of people also who really feel that marriage in church is the important thing, though even in such areas things may be getting worse rather than better. Elsewhere 40 per cent of Catholics may be married in church, 30 per cent, even less.[43] Examining the baptismal records of an old, large and flourishing parish in an area far from that of Fr Lijding, I found "illegitimate" marked beside some 65 per cent of all the children, in another 75 per cent, and that is still lower than many parishes, though evidently this does not indicate the permanent excommunication of all the parents of these children. A fair number may contract a valid marriage later on.

There is one important aspect of the matter that Fr Lijding does

[41] It seems that this can seldom be encouraged. The feeling that without a dowry there can be no true marriage is so deep that lack of it, even willingly agreed to at the time, may easily cause trouble later on.

[42] According to a recent social survey in some Ibo parishes 81 per cent of those making their first communion later marry in church. This is very good. Cf. B. Gogan, "Ibo Catholicism", *AFER*, Oct. 1966, p. 353.

[43] Miss Joan Dilworth refers to a sample survey taken in one East African diocese in which 75 per cent of the unions of Catholics were found to be irregular ("Marriage Education", *AFER*, July 1962, p. 233).

not touch upon: that of mixed marriages. In most places Catholics, Protestants and pagans live close together. Tribal regulations prohibiting marriage within the clan or the village have to be followed and already limit one's choice of partner considerably. It is absolutely inevitable in these circumstances that many mixed marriages occur: in an area like Buganda where most people are now Christians, between Catholic and Protestant; elsewhere still more between Catholics and pagans, or Catholics and Muslims. Nothing is going to stop this, as things are at present. However, in many dioceses dispensations for mixed marriages are seldom or never granted and the result again is that those entering this category are deprived of a church marriage, even if they should want one, and must join the ranks of the permanently excommunicated. Recently I passed by the home of an old couple just near a Catholic village chapel. They had lived happily together their whole life. He is a Protestant, she a Catholic, and she attends the service in the chapel every Sunday; but for all the thirty or more years of their married life she has been deprived of the help of the sacraments of her Church, and he of his.

One may note, paradoxically, the advantage of marrying while still a pagan. If a Catholic was married to a pagan before baptism, the marriage is all right and she or he can go on living with the pagan husband or wife and come to the sacraments. If, however, the marriage took place after baptism, the poor lady may have to spend the rest of her life excommunicated. To quote Fr Verheij (of Kenya): "Half of our Catholic women consists of those who are married to non-Catholics, and who devoutly receive the sacraments, because it just happened that their marriage preceded baptism by a few months, and the other half consists of women who are married in the same way but who will never again be allowed to the sacraments because, unfortunately, their baptism preceded their marriage by a few months".[44]

Throughout Africa the picture seems roughly the same: a large proportion of Christians for one reason or another never marry in church. For them active sacramental Christian life is limited to the years from baptism to adulthood; with adulthood comes excommunication. The bigger the Church becomes, the more is

[44] *AFER*, April 1965, p. 171.

this getting out of control. Even in some old Christian areas where a tradition of church marriage has been established, there has been a marked decline in the number of marriages in comparison with the number of Catholics. The vast swelling of the latter, characteristic of the last decade, is too often only the swelling of the excommunicate and of a Church whose whole pattern of life must be judged gravely unhealthy.

For Protestants the situation is similar, indeed probably worse. Canon Taylor has made a very careful study of the position in one area: in the Anglican Church in Buganda some 87 per cent of married men and 80 per cent of married women are permanently excommunicated.[45] His comment is as follows: "A Church in which the majority of adult members are permanently excommunicated is a monstrosity which demands the most serious reappraisal of basic assumptions".[46] Much the same picture is true for the Protestant Churches in many other parts of Africa.[47]

There are five different groups of Catholics, excommunicated on account of their marital condition, that one ought to distinguish. First, there are couples living together who have not been married even according to native custom, but have simply eloped. These unions are sometimes permanent, sometimes temporary. Secondly, couples married according to native custom or civil law but in circumstances that cannot be accepted, e.g., because one has been married in church already—customary law admitting polygamy and divorce. Thirdly, a Catholic married by native custom to a non-Christian. Fourthly, a Catholic married by native custom to a Protestant. Fifthly, two Catholics married by native custom when there was no objective reason against their being married in church.

In different parts of Africa the chief marriage problem arises with a different one of these groups. Thus in some areas polygamy or some other basically unacceptable traditional marriage pattern may

---

[45] John V. Taylor, *The Growth of the Church in Buganda*, 1958, S.C.M. Press, p. 244; see also p. 176.
[46] *Ibid.*, p. 182.
[47] Cf. *Report of the All-African Seminar on the Christian Home and Family Life, Mindolo, Zambia*, Feb.-April 1963. F. G. Welch can even write in *Training for the Ministry in East Africa*, Limuru, 1963, p. 216, "Less than 5 per cent of baptized men and women marry in church" in most areas of East Africa.

still be the chief obstacle to the development of Christian family life. For the most part, however, simultaneous polygamy is on the way out, except as a luxury for the rich. Lack of a surplus of women, the education and emancipation of girls, and the stated policy of most African governments are against it. Nevertheless there is still time and need for missionaries to reconsider what is the best attitude to take towards the pagan polygamist who wishes to become a Christian. Doubtless the answer often depends on particular circumstances, but in general one may question whether the breaking up of sincere human marital contracts and the repudiation of the obligations a person had taken on towards other human beings in accordance with the respected customs of his country are really a suitable pre-condition for entry into the life of the Church. In a pagan society a polygamous family unit is not necessarily an expression of sin but it represents the stable environment of many people's lives and the framework of mutual obligations. To break it up because the husband and father wishes to be baptized may involve the smashing of the whole pattern of many lives and the destruction of the home in which children are being brought up. Yet if polygamy is not sinful, it is certainly un-Christian and expresses a view of society incompatible with the Christian way of life. Full conversion to Christianity *does* involve destruction—of beliefs, customs, a whole shape of society. It is worth it if accepted with real comprehension and carried through with compassion, a sign for the individual of Christian death and rebirth. Where that cannot be obtained it is surely better to leave the would-be convert in his polygamy, inscribing him as a permanent catechumen and deferring baptism until old age or the approach of death.

Polygamy is not by any means the only aspect of traditional African marriage that presents problems for christianization, and not nearly enough serious thought has been given to the relating of Christian living to particular patterns of tribal and marital life. My impression is that missionary work in fact succeeds chiefly among tribes whose marriage patterns are not too dissimilar from those of Western Europe, but is either rejected or tends to remain superficial in its effect among other groups. Here a central division is between "patrilineal" tribes, most of which had in the past considerable marriage stability, a fairly high bride price and a pattern of family life fairly comprehensible for Westerners, and "matrilineal" tribes, which tended to have frequent divorce, trial marriages, a low bride price, and a pattern of family obligations very different from those customarily associated with the Christian home.[48] Doubtless the majority of peoples in black Africa are patrilineal, the matrilineal being prevalent especially from the central Congo across northern Zambia to some peoples of Malawi; and the latter also vary among themselves, some tribes having a strong patrilineal element as well. It would be important to examine what success missionaries have had among matrilineal peoples, and what attempt they have made to adapt Christian family attitudes to the customs of such peoples (e.g., to the placing of authority over children in the hands of the senior maternal uncle rather than in those of the father). But probably most large Christian groups in Africa have grown up inside patrilineal societies whose structure was more easily understood by missionaries and more easily accommodated to the traditional Christian pattern; as these are the societies in which the dowry is of central importance, Christian marriage problems have inevitably become closely connected with it.

From the viewpoint of Christian society today a greater problem than polygamy may be presented by the first group of people mentioned above: those living together but not married in accordance with native custom. Many of these unions are, of course, mere temporary liaisons, with no character of marriage about them, but others are intended to be permanent. Such situations are becoming more and more common, as the hold of traditional tribal morality upon the young weakens, and immigration mixes people of different tribes and customs together, not only in towns, but also in the countryside. But besides these general reasons, there is the further very important one of lack of money to pay the dowry required for a proper customary wedding. This is specially true in areas where the amount demanded in dowry has risen of recent years. It is difficult to generalize but it seems clear that in very

---

[48] Cf. the vast amount of information and discussion in *African Systems of Kinship and Marriage*, ed. A. Radcliffe-Brown and Daryll Forde, especially the chapters by Max Gluckman and A. I. Richards. One may note that in modern conditions matrilineal groups seem to be moving in a patrilineal direction, doubtless in part under missionary influence.

many areas the dowry has become one of the greatest obstacles
to the growth of Christian married life. Its amount varies enormously, from three or four hundred shillings in one country to
(almost unbelievably) as much as three hundred pounds in another.[49] Nevertheless many young men may be quite unable to
find even the lowest amount; instead with mere trifling gifts they
persuade the girl to come away and live with them, and an
irregular but often quite permanent union is formed in this way.
Alternatively, a heavy dowry may simply prevent many young
people from marrying at all, while the rich are encouraged to buy
several wives. The bride price had its own justification within the
traditional pattern of African clan life. Today, with the growth
of a different sort of society—a freer, more personal one—it is
becoming too much a matter of money: the exploitation of the
young by the old. In the words of Archbishop Zoa of the Cameroons: " When a system is recognized to be anachronistic and
outmoded or has become evil to the core, why keep it with the
excuse that it was better in another time? As it is practised today
in the southern Cameroons and in certain other territories, the
bride price is a plague, an obstacle to the development of Africa.
It is illusory to try to correct the system with odds and ends."[50] It
is not everywhere as bad as that; but in too many places it is becoming a pointless burden, a real obstacle to the formation of young
Christian homes, and a denial of the dignity and freedom of
women. Nevertheless for most Africans the giving of a dowry is
still seen as the outward sign and guaranty of marital stability,
and girls themselves often like a big dowry—the bigger the dowry,
the greater their prestige. Its rapid abolition appears psychologically impossible, but it is surely for the local Church, and very
especially for responsible lay Christians, to take a lead in this
matter—at least by their own example in asking for their daughters
a dowry which is only symbolic, not oppressive. As a serious social

---

[49] Archbishop Zoa writes that in the Cameroons it may range as high as
$1,000 plus livestock. In different parts of Uganda it varies from about
400 shillings to as much as 2,000. Among different tribes of South Africa it
varies mostly between about £30 and £100, but can be as much as £200, being still paid most often in cattle. Cf. Reuter, *Native Marriage in South
Africa*, pp. 248–9. Among matrilineal peoples it may be much lower, e.g.
a mere 5–10 shillings among the Bemba of Zambia (cf. *African Systems of
Kinship and Marriage*, p. 225).
[50] "The Problem of the Bride Price," *AFER*, July 1962, p. 181.

evil the high dowry is certainly a matter for government control. It is certainly not something the Church can hope to solve alone.

It may be asked why, in some areas, fathers seem often so complacent about their daughters going off, dowryless, to cohabit with a man, but so furious if an attempt be made to validate the union when the full dowry has not been paid. Certainly, such attitudes of mind encourage a great number of illicit relationships. In places, however, there is a sort of half-way house. The young man makes some gifts to the father at the start but is unable to pay the full dowry. The father hopes to extract more from him as time goes on and lets his daughter go on this basis, but he does not want his "loss" of her to be sealed by the Church until the full amount has been paid up.[51] Hence years—maybe a lifetime—of waiting. Cases like this cannot be simply classed as "abduction" and are to be more or less assimilated to those of "customary marriage": they represent permanent monogamous unions.

This, of course, is even more so with the other three of our five types listed above. Each represents a stable monogamous union into which a Catholic has entered, and where there is no certain natural impediment to a true marriage and—where both are Christians—a sacramental marriage; the impediment is a canonical one. Here, many would argue, canon law—far from backing up the struggle for monogamy in a traditionally polygamous environment, which is surely by far the most important struggle in this field that the Church can undertake—seems instead to be confusing the matter by bringing its full weight to bear on what are in fact relatively secondary issues (and generally in the circumstances unobtainable ones) in such a way that it is literally impeding the main campaign.

Before examining this question further, it may be noted in terms of the general picture of exclusion from the sacraments which all this is causing, that a dowry is very often not paid by the young man himself. He is helped by his father, uncles and other relatives. If that dowry is for the customary marriage of a Catholic, all those contributing may be held to be taking part in his sin and there are areas where the whole lot will fall under excommunication (if they have not already done so on account of their own marriages!).

---

[51] In other places it is quite normal for the marriage to be solemnized when only part of the dowry has been paid, but the rest has been promised.

Equally, anyone who receives part of that dowry will be judged the same. Hence one customary marriage in these circumstances may land not two but a dozen or more people in a state of lasting excommunication (especially in the case where the bride is a Protestant). And so the snowball goes on!

To complete this picture one may add that, again in some dioceses, a fair number of Catholics who have escaped permanent excommunication for marital reasons incur it for failure to pay up their church tax, though this is now the case in fewer and fewer places. We have seen the importance of supporting the Church financially and the reluctance of many to do so. Here we simply note again that the means taken to overcome that reluctance (often with a fair degree of success) further swell the ranks of the excommunicate.

To get back to the heart of the question: Why do many Christians not want to marry in church? There are, without doubt, a number of reasons. The first cause we should cite is that of general indifference, and this springs in part from lack of pastoral care on the part of the Church—an inevitable consequence of our shortage of priests. To return for a moment to Canon Taylor's study of the Protestant Church in eastern Buganda. The marriage situation among Anglicans in south Kyagwe, where he made his detailed research, is very bad indeed: of 26 Anglicans in a village studied, 19 had married their first wife by African custom, 4 had abducted her ignoring tribal custom, and only 3 had had the Christian rite.[52] But then a study of his book shows that pastoral work in the area had largely broken down too and only some 20 per cent of the baptized go to any service on a Sunday. Clearly, if village people are not in any regular contact with the Church or a priest, they will see no point in incurring the extra expense of having part of their wedding ceremonies some miles away from their home.

There are plenty of Catholics who were married in church, or are unmarried, but do not practise their religion. The reason is only too obvious: they were baptized as children in large groups without any personal instruction or they were baptized in infancy, being children of those who had been through a mass catechumenate; religious instruction at school may have consisted of little more than

[52] *The Growth of the Church in Buganda*, p. 123.

learning some things by heart and compulsory attendance at Mass (if their primary happened to be in a central parish) about which they understood almost nothing. Once they left school they quickly ceased to go to church, especially if it was some miles away. They are not known or cared for personally by any priest. How can they be? There are far too many people in the parish for that. When a priest does manage to make a pastoral visit to an outlying village, really visiting the homes, he will inevitably be concerned with trying to put marriage cases formally right, giving the sacraments to the sick and dying, trying to get those who have slipped baptism to come along. But the basic problem of the completely uncommitted state of so many of the baptized can hardly concern him (though doubtless it worries him); in the circumstances of the rare visit to the village what can he possibly do about it? When such people come to marry, they will obviously not undertake the extra obligation and expense of a church ceremony.

One basic cause of so many of our Christians not being married in church is then simply lack of a real commitment on their part, and lack of the intense pastoral care which is the only way the Church can set about turning nominal religious allegiance into a genuine commitment. As in the field of orders, so in that of matrimony, we are suffering the consequences of an over-extended condition of the Church. (By that I mean a condition in which structure is not keeping up with numbers.) Such a condition tends of itself to become worse. Miss Dilworth cites the example of a whole diocese with a rapidly growing population which has suffered an actual decrease in the number of church marriages.[53] Most parishes whose registers I have checked show a relative decrease, while one with an annual average of 53 marriages about fifteen years ago has since sunk (with a rapidly rising population: infant baptisms almost doubled meantime) to an average of 23. With priests so overworked, these little things may not even be noticed! The fact is that we give baptism very easily, especially to the young, but our complex matrimonial legislation (like our complex seminary regulations) causes a blockage further along the road. The marriage situation in fact should carry us back to re-examine our basic policies, not only with regard to marriage itself, but also with regard to Church

---

[53] "Marriage Education," *AFER*, July 1962, p. 233.

membership and the ministry. Thus, the excommunicated state of many Christians who have not been married in church has its real cause, not in something specifically matrimonial, but in the policy of extensive baptizing coupled with the subsequent impossibility of providing an adequate follow-up; it is in part simply an expression of general lapsation.

However, that is not the whole story. There are plenty of people for whom religion does mean something and who nevertheless fail to contract a valid marriage. Fr Lijding provides examples: people who continue to come to church regularly for years when they are excommunicate. This is not an expression of sheer indifference, whatever else it may be. As we have seen, one big reason is that of the mixed marriage but—where that does not apply—there are others. One is the additional expense of a church wedding: transport to a distance, European wedding clothes and so on—much of it very ridiculous and unnecessary no doubt, but we have allowed a lot of social frills to become an almost indispensable part of a church wedding and many people cannot afford it on top of the "tribal" expenses of dowry, etc. In the words of a recent Protestant report: "A second reason why church marriages are shunned does us no more credit. It is that weddings have become so expensive; demanding such costly special clothes, and such odd ones, sometimes; such expensive entertainment of so many guests—a heavy burden when added to all the expense that has gone before, in the traditional exchanges between the families."[54] The church wedding, in fact, has become in some places the mark of europeanized people with extra money to spare. Those with fewer pretensions rest content with a traditional marriage and—excommunication.

Do we need to continue in our present attitude to tribal marriage? It was only Trent with the *Tametsi* decree of 1563 which ended the Church's traditional recognition of the validity for Christians of non-church marriage and in some countries this was not applied until as late as 1908 (the *Ne Temere* decree). Only, then, in the last fifty years has it been universally obligatory for a Catholic to marry in church, but the Tridentine decree has been applied in the African missions all through the modern period. Is it wise? Doubtless this insistence on clerical witnesses has its reasons. It ensures that

[54] *Report of the All-Africa Seminar on the Christian Home and Family Life*, p. 10.

marriages are properly registered, that the Church's marriage laws are taken note of, and it makes matters easier for the Church's courts if the marriage subsequently lands up in them. The general insistence on the marriage of Christians taking place in church is, of course, completely traditional and very suitable. But it is also quite clear that for hundreds and hundreds of years a vast number of Christian marriages were in fact not celebrated in church, despite the remonstrances of preachers and canonists. Certainly it would have been better if they all had been—better, not only from the viewpoint of ecclesiastical bureaucracy, but also spiritually—nevertheless the Church realized, through the greater part of her history, that sociologically her children were not ready for the imposition of this. The present state of the law is the conclusion to a long evolution, not only of the law but also of society in western Europe. The imposition of an evolved law upon an unevolved society can be disastrous and marriage laws require missionary adaptation as much as any other side of ecclesial life.

Will a change help? Fr Lijding holds that it would indeed and that "were it not for the legalism of the Church, all those marriages would be valid",[55] and many other missionaries feel the same. Others[56] hold, on the contrary, that it is not a question of law but of basic intention, that the reason why many Christians do not marry in church is simply that they don't want a true indissoluble marriage at all, but a temporary or "trial marriage", and that consequently, quite apart from the prescriptions of canon law, their marriages are invalid from defect of intention; moreover, that the traditional tribal approach to marriage is in most places so utterly different from the Christian one that the only possibility of getting the Christian ideal across is to insist absolutely upon the church ceremony.[57]

It has to be recognized that the chief reason behind the widespread reluctance to marry in church is indeed the desire not to tie oneself too absolutely, at least at first. People have heard it stressed

[55] *AFER*, Jan. 1965, p. 40.
[56] Fr Francis Mpomulekule, *AFER*, July 1965, pp. 263–7; Fr E. de Bekker, W.F., "Consent Makes Marriage", *AFER*, Oct. 1965, pp. 299–306.
[57] Many, though by no means all, non-Catholic missionaries have come in the past to the same conclusion. Cf. the discussion in *Survey of African Marriage and Family Life*, pp. xxx–xxxii, 403–10, which is not, however, entirely satisfactory.

so much that a church marriage is indissoluble and this may actually strengthen them in the conclusion that a tribal marriage is not. Faced by a choice between the two, some deliberately opt for the second, either because they want to be sure of having children before tying themselves for ever, or because part of the dowry has not yet been paid, or simply because they do not want to be bound at all. Now it is clear that where people have a deliberate intention *not* to enter an indissoluble union and because of that intention reject a church ceremony, their marriage is invalid not just because of canon law but also because of natural law: nothing the Church can do can make the union of two people a true marriage if they intend only a temporary alliance. Surely at present this is the case with many, and the removal of the obligation for Catholics to be married in church could not change that.

Nevertheless, the question is considerably more complicated than this. Firstly, because in areas where the great majority of Catholics permanently contract only a tribal marriage, it is probable—as Fr Lijding asserts to be the case—that this attitude towards indissolubility is at the origin of a general practice, rather than a universal cause of individual motivation. Having become a general practice, Catholics—unless they are very fervent—simply continue it, though an individual couple may often have adequate matrimonial intention; but they practise the custom of the village and look on church marriage as an expensive "posh" affair for the élite. Even in present circumstances, in fact, it seems clear that while some of these unions are naturally invalid marriages, a great many others are not. There is confusion of mind and tepidity of Christian life rather than a wholly inadequate intention. What is indeed needed is "a change of mentality in the people themselves",[58] but the question is whether the enforcement of canonical regulations which effect, in many places, the permanent excommunication of 60 to 80 per cent of adult Christians is really the way to bring about the growth of a more Christian view of life.

What is still more important is to see how intentions flow from situations, and if many Christians today do intend to enter into a dissoluble marriage by going through a tribal, but not a church, ceremony, it is partly we who have created the situation in which a

[58] E. de Bekker, *art. cit.*, p. 304.

choice between dissoluble and indissoluble marriage came clearly to exist for them. Both for them are marriage, and are still called so by Christian and non-Christian alike. Asking a catechist, "Is this a child born in marriage?", he may answer, "Yes, he is born in marriage, but not in *matrimonio*". We teach that marriage is a natural institution, but effectively our practice denies this with our Christians. Instead of saying, "Yes, you have always had marriage given you by God, even if you did not understand it very well; for Christians this natural union has been made a sacrament, but it is exactly the natural union which is that sign for Christians", we have—while teaching the validity of pagan marriage in itself— effectively separated the two in the minds of Christians. By declaring the customary ceremony, when performed by Catholics, of itself invalid we have made it for them something which is still a real, respectable marriage union in the eyes of their neighbours, and yet which is dissoluble—the Church herself will countenance its dissolution and the remarriage of one of its partners with someone else.

Behind all this, and indeed behind the whole development of canonical regulations about marriage, one detects a subtle "clericalization" of marriage akin to so much other clericalization of Church life. Practically speaking, despite the theory, the stress has been more and more on what the priest does in the marriage ceremony rather than on what the bride and bridegroom do, so that we can even arrive at what a distinguished canonist describes only as "a popular simplification", the assertion that "the blessing of the priest is the marriage".[59] In the popular conception in Africa the Church is seen as concerned, not with the human consent of two people, but rather with the giving of a ring, the payment of a church fee, the blessing of the priest. In a land of few priests and tenacious local marriage customs the result is a sheer disaster for Church life. What we need desperately to do is to re-stress that Christian marriage is made by consent and that if that is manifested in a recognized public way, known and acknowledged within the local society, then it is enough for validity.

The perfection of Christian life requires far more, but that perfection is to be obtained by exhortation, the influence of the sacraments, the slow effect of example, not by excommunication. It is

[59] A. Reuter, *Native Marriages in South Africa*, p. 252.

claimed that a change of law and the recognition of the validity of customary marriage would result in "great confusion and very serious harm to the good of souls and the common good. Customs and civil law may change at any time."[60] Such arguments seem too reminiscent of those employed in the past against the use of the vernacular! In fact it is perfectly feasible for each diocese, or group of dioceses, to state the civil or customary forms recognized within it, and for parish priests to continue to register valid marriages of Catholics as completely as hitherto. As to the good of souls and the common good, it is difficult to think that anything could be worse than the present situation in many dioceses, to say the least. It is very easy to think that a legally clear situation is necessarily for the common good; in fact, if the law is not adapted to the human condition of its subjects, it can make—as surely in Africa at present— for destruction rather than edification.

If modern canon law, developed in accordance with the ecclesiastical history of Europe, is surely not adapted to an infant Christian community within an entirely different social milieu (and surely a mere look at the Church's own principles of missionary adaptation could show us that that is bound to be so), one can even further doubt whether it is fully suited to Europe or America either. Has the historical direction of marriage legislation really been wholly dictated by the good of souls, or has it not rather been influenced by the subconscious urge to make clerical control of every aspect of Christian life ever more effective? One knows today how marriage cases have piled up in the Church's courts, and one wonders whether the whole thing is not just another example of the application of a "governmental" type of ecclesiology, of trying to see the Church as a "perfect society" comparable, in Bellarmine's words, with the kingdom of France or the Republic of Venice.

In practice, what is to be done? Firstly, it is clear that in some places certain things can be fairly easily corrected with no change of principle involved. Dispensations should be easily given for mixed marriages both with separated Christians and with pagans, or at the very least such marriages should be validated at the birth of the first child. Illegitimate boys should be admitted to seminaries

---

[60] E. de Bekker, *art. cit.*, p. 306.

(as they are in many places) on exactly the same conditions as the legitimate.

Such reforms are rather easy. Far more difficult is the general problem that modern matrimonial canon law is totally unadapted to our African situation. Yet it is not easy, seeing the great variety of situations with which we are faced, to say on what great lines it should be amended. Something must be done and something drastic. Here and now what we need is a high-powered commission of theologians, sociologists, lay people and missionaries, with a canonist or two as well, to examine the situation of Christian marriage in Africa extensively and analytically and then propose their recommendations to Church authority. Certainly the last things to hold untouchable are *Tametsi* and *Ne Temere*.[61] The problem is too big to tackle in a small way, and far too serious not to tackle at all.

In general our aim must surely be to cut down law to the necessary minimum. Church discipline must be accommodated to weakness; one senses in this field the same mentality that refused to allow people to communicate without an intense and extensive preparation. It is the sacraments themselves and the round of Christian life that must build up the Church. In circumstances like ours, to make laws beyond what is absolutely necessary and to enforce them by excommunication is simply to render the Church's work impossible.

Thirdly, if we simplify our laws we must renew our pastoral practice to communicate better the ideal of Christian marriage and draw our people to want to have their marriages blessed by the Church. There can, of course, be no wavering as to the value of this, though it should be able to be done in village chapels or, maybe far better, at the home of one or the other, and not only at the often distant central mission church. Revised and more significant rites should be drawn up, as the Vatican Council has itself declared,[62] based upon what is meaningful in particular areas, though again we should beware of trying to incorporate customary ceremonies

---

[61] It is worth noting that the Council has already breached the wall requiring the canonical form for the validity of marriage in the decree on the Catholic Oriental Churches, art. 18.

[62] Constitution on the Sacred Liturgy, art. 77. For a proposed African type of wedding rite, see B. van Amelsvoort, W.F., "Suggestions for an Adapted Marriage Ceremony", *AFER*, April 1959, pp. 111–15.

which will be repeated elsewhere: the church ceremony can then appear as simply a rather silly imitation of the real thing. At least what prayers we do say should concern the bridegroom quite as much as the bride: the one-sidedness in the present nuptial blessings matches only too well the traditional imbalance between husband and wife in Africa.

Sunday marriage within the parish Mass can add greatly to the dignity of the sacrament in the eyes of the people, especially if communion be given to bride and bridegroom under both kinds. Its social character—a building of the parish community—like the social character of baptism, will then be brought out.[63] Marriage anniversary celebrations should also be encouraged and celebrated in church, again with the giving of the chalice. One may feel too that our universal missionary practice of separating husbands and wives in church, and both from their children, is hardly a way of manifesting the importance of the family as constituting the unit out of which the parish is made. Marriage and the family need, in fact, to be built into the church's local liturgy, and that we have not tried to do: we have commanded much, but our practice has hardly *commended* the greatness and beauty of marriage among people who had not previously sensed it.

Fewer marriage laws but more marriage liturgy and more marriage apostolate. Certainly celibate missionaries, priests and nuns, have not from every viewpoint been the best of people to understand the problems and put across a really positive approach both to Christian marriage and to the whole mystery of sex. Fear of social contact between boys and girls and a stress on large families often seem the sum total of the clergy's positive contribution in this matter. Today that is very certainly not enough. The intimate human co-operation of husband and wife, the spirit of a united family, the need for family planning (so necessary in countries of great poverty and a rapidly rising population[64])—all these things can best be taught by lay people through movements like the Catholic Marriage Advisory Council, the Christian Family Movement and such like.[65] The vigour and strength of a Christian com-

---

[63] See C. Van Berkel, M.H.M., "How can we invigorate African Parish Life? The Sacrament of Matrimony", *AFER*, July 1961, pp. 203–11.
[64] See the Constitution on the Church in the Modern World, art. 87.
[65] Cf. John M. Robinson, W.F., *The Family Apostolate and Africa*, Helicon, 1964, for much information about this field of work.

munity depends upon the health of its marriages and family life. The anaemia from which too much of the Church in Africa is clearly suffering cannot but be largely due to our failure to communicate at the level of marriage. It is, as we have said, the most difficult—because the most central—thing in society to christianize; it is also the thing which the Catholic missionary army has been least equipped to tackle. There can be no doubt today that on the possibility of a really new and successful approach in this field will depend, more than on anything else, the health of the young Church in Africa.

7. CONCLUSION

There is an enormous vitality in the Church's life in Africa today. This vitality comes from the natural religious sense of simple people freed and canalized by the preaching of the Gospel; it comes from the breath of the Spirit in a world not dried up by a subtle materialism; it comes from the vigour and example of the missionaries, many of whom have made an enormous personal impression upon the peoples they have evangelized by their self-sacrifice and devotion; and it comes again from the universal desire for education which brings youth into the schools where they are still in most places receptive to the influence of the Church.

Nevertheless behind this very real vitality and the constant new initiatives from outside, the Church is in many places already fighting for her very life. She has grown so fast and all concerned have been so busy with one thing and another, that there has been little time even to notice the things that are going wrong. Yet behind the rapidly mounting statistics, behind the great schools and seminaries and hospitals, erected either with government money or with funds collected in Europe and America, most serious diseases there already are. The first is the europeanness of most of our religious practice, the failure to adapt and the consequent lack of relationship with the deepest moods and ways of expression of African peoples; the second is a failure at the marriage level which includes the application of a crippling legislation; the third, failure to cater— except with schools—for the quickly growing numbers who in towns or elsewhere have got outside the traditional pattern of village life, which almost exclusively the missionary Church has attempted to tackle. Again, there is the misplaced authoritarian tone which is so characteristic of Catholic life in "mission countries". In the past missionaries have often called Africans children, and they have certainly tended to treat them as such, even to the extent of disregarding their natural rights. At times missionaries have taken too much advantage of their comparatively defenceless, clueless condition to carry them *en masse* into the Church. The intentions were excellent, the sacrifices made heroic, but one may question whether the human dignity of those involved was always sufficiently respected. Today our very greatest need in Africa is to treat people as adults, even if they seem to be very simple people. The disregarding of the natural rights of pagan parents to decide the religion of their children, excommunication for failure to pay church tax, the use of public and humiliating penances, of confessional cards, and so on, is all a failure to treat people as adults, with their full human rights and natural dignity. A stress on submissiveness will never produce a strong, outgoing Church. We have educated for docility, rather than for leadership.

In one way or another we fail widely both with the élite and with the masses. Too often we ignore the needs of the former once they leave school and they find the Church unsympathetic and unenlightened; while for a variety of reasons an increasing number of the latter drift into a condition of more or less permanent excommunication. How can it be otherwise with newly converted Christians living in a society where the pressures of traditional pagan ways can be almost overwhelming, coming as they do from the elders of the family, the people one has always been taught to listen to, and where they can only see a priest, and be fortified by his teaching, on rare occasions? Parishes with two priests and twenty or thirty village out-stations, many of them even a hundred miles away on shocking roads, are simply normal in many dioceses. Villages may be visited no more than twice a year in some instances. How can poor, hardly educated people grow up into Christian life in such circumstances? Yet as things stand now we will never be able to provide a priestly presence for them. Inevitably such people drift back into polygamy or what have you. Then a new religious influence arrives in the village—Islam, the Pentecostals, a separatist African Church—and our Catholics only too easily pass into this new allegiance. In Africa today conversions away from the Church are already a rapidly growing phenomenon.

Lack of priests makes it more and more difficult to get to grips with half our problems, even when we see them, and it almost completely precludes many sides of pastoral work. The majority of Catholics can never receive the last sacraments, priests are present at almost no funerals, the frequent visiting of homes is an impossibility. Priests in Africa have to concentrate on providing the essentials of a completely economy church: Mass in the bigger villages every two or three months, confessions, some teaching and supervision in the primary schools (or perhaps only in those closest to the central mission), some part of the instruction of catechumens, a care for the catechists and the school teachers—there is no time for more. The personal knowledge and care of his sheep which is hoped for from a pastor in Europe is impossible in Africa, and without it the situation can grow only worse. Above all, the post-school generation in town or country largely fails to practise at all. It easily falls away from church-going, once compulsory school attendance ceases, it marries away and then it stays away. The children will be baptized, come to school and then do the same. The numbers go ever up; the vocations inevitably fail to materialize, and the disease of the Church grows steadily worse.

Coupled with all this, as we have seen, is a partly uncomprehended liturgy and the neglect of Scripture. People do indeed pray devotedly and loudly in an African church at Mass, but the full sense of it all and a real sharing in the action has often not been communicated. Nor has Scripture. On these two points, however, there is a very real progress going on today.

Certainly some areas are far better than others,[66] but in far too many it looks as if a dinosaur type of system, which might pass muster when the only rival was traditional religion, will certainly not be able to stand up to the rapidly growing pressure from more flexible religious movements. It seems only too obvious that if we do not want Pentecostalism to replace Catholicism among millions we will have to change our own approach most radically.

Again, our continuing concentration on big institutions, whose scale makes them wholly dependent upon foreign sources of income, both distracts us from the real problems of development of

---

[66] See, for instance, an encouraging account of the situation in some of the most Catholic parts of Eastern Nigeria: B. Gogan, "Ibo Catholicism, A Tentative Survey", *AFER*, Oct. 1966, pp. 346–58.

the young Churches and actually cuts away the possibility of stressing self-help convincingly and the growth of a really self-reliant local Church.

In structural terms our trouble lies in an over-extended Church. Despite the severity of early regulations about the catechumenate and baptism, we have in fact—especially since about 1920—baptized fairly easily. The fear of the spread of Islam has driven missionaries on. At the same time severe post-Tridentine regulations about the sacraments of marriage and holy orders have prevented the development of a rounded Church. Time and the population explosion have made the situation steadily worse. I do not believe that the answer is, or could be, a refusal to baptize. In practice we have gone far too far already and could not pull back if we would; in theory, how could the Church limit the obedience she owes to the command given at her foundation? What does have to be done is a drastic readjustment of her human pattern of life—worship and canon law and ministry—to the real conditions of the society she is trying to inform.

To save the Church in Africa today we have, more than anything else, to declericalize her. We have to declericalize the liturgy: to make it again a genuine common action, a parish communion, not a Latin ritual, performed silently and unintelligibly by the clergy. We have to declericalize Scripture: caring that it is read not only by priests in their Latin breviaries, but to the people and even by them in their homes. We have to declericalize parish organization, giving real responsibility for the Church of God to all the members of the people of God in the area. We have to declericalize the apostolate, making the layman realize that the mission to bear the light of Christ, to convince the world, belongs equally to every baptized and confirmed child of God. We have to declericalize marriage, recognizing it again as essentially a human contract between two people to be manifested according to the customs of human society. Finally, and most difficult of all, we have to declericalize the ministry.

VI

The Ministry

1

No RELIGIOUS BODY can ever have had a missionary force as numerous, as disciplined, as zealous as the great missionary army which the Catholic Church deploys in Africa today. It has brought in from outside some 12,000 priests and still more nuns, teaching brothers and devoted laymen to join with Africa's own native workers. Behind each one of these is an individual choice, a deliberate vocation, and yet they are all harnessed together by the great missionary societies and the diocesan organization into a unified team, finally directed by the Congregation of Propaganda in Rome.

It is clear that the total missionary achievement owes quite as much to the brothers, nuns and lay people, who have staffed schools and hospitals and in a hundred different ways have placed flesh upon the skeleton which priests have formed, as to priests themselves. Nevertheless the life of the Catholic Church, as we believe it to be, does require the ministry of an ordained priesthood in a unique way, and it is that ministry about which we must speak here. Surely the human tradition of the priesthood, already established in Africa, is a very great one. The faith, self-sacrifice, obedience and zeal of countless missionaries, both of past generations and of today, must be plain for every objective observer to see. As one who belongs to no missionary society, I can say how overwhelmed and humbled one is by the spirit of so many, the faith, the determination in overcoming obstacles and continuing despite reverses, the cheerfulness, the love of Africa.

They have now been joined by a quickly growing body of African clergy. Their training was, indeed, more than slow in getting under way. Only twenty-five in all were ordained in the century preceding 1910, and half of those were in Senegal. In 1939 there were still only 257 African Catholic priests through the whole continent, and 148 of those were within the three territories of Uganda, Rwanda-Urundi and Tanganyika. Only in the last thirty years has this work really been accorded in most parts of Africa the importance it deserves, but today there are over 2,500 African priests, and they are increasing by about 150 a year. Great seminaries like Katigondo,[1] Mayidi, Kipalapala, Ouidah, Enugu, Nyakibanda and Kumi, have been the most decisive institutions in the establishment of the African Church. Though their facilities may at times be inadequate in comparison with the highest standards of the universal Church, it is clear how much care and effort has been put into them since the 1930s.

From this point of view a comparison between Catholic and Protestant work is interesting. As has been pointed out, in the early years of African missionary work, Protestant missionaries were nearly everywhere far ahead of Catholics in their real appreciation of the importance of preparing an African clergy. But in the last thirty years, it has often been quite the other way round. The recent judgment of a Protestant missiologist is as follows:

> With notable exceptions, seminaries have long been the weakest link in the entire chain of educational work in Protestant missionary outreach.... By and large the seminaries are small, ill-equipped, under-staffed "stepchildren" of the churches. I can recall a period of several years when the only training school for the entire ordained ministry of a large and rapidly growing church in Cameroon was taught by *one* missionary who also had other duties....
> Whatever may be the deficiencies of the Catholic seminary curriculum, it is generally well taught and adequately staffed. This has been the case for many years and may indeed provide a more marked contrast than any other aspect of the Catholic-Protestant missionary endeavour. To return to my illustration from Cameroon, when the Protestant seminary to which I re-

---

[1] Katigondo, in Uganda, has full right to first place: it was the first African seminary to provide a regular stream of priests. The first African bishop of modern times—Joseph Kiwanuka—was trained there, and so was the first African cardinal, Laurean Rugambwa.

ferred was taught by one man who had only general theological preparation himself, the Benedictines sent three doctors of philosophy, all of them experienced teachers, to staff their seminary from its inception. In less than a year that faculty was reinforced by two others with comparable qualifications.[2]

The Catholic effort in this field does not everywhere go back as far as the above writer seems to suggest, but there can be no doubt that since the Second World War seminary training with relatively high academic standards has everywhere had a high priority, and that the Protestant failure to do the same is having a considerable effect on the balance of influence of the Churches. But we must surely be glad that in the last few years there have been very notable efforts also on the part of non-Catholic Churches to raise the standard of their clergy training, especially through the Inter-denominational Theological Education Fund.

No one can question the quality and loyalty of the Catholic clergy of Africa. Having lived with them—with seminarists, with young priests and with old ones—I may be permitted to say that the friendship of many, of every generation, has been one of the most cherished things in my life. Such complete commitment to the priestly vocation, such unaffected kindness, such a simple acceptance of material difficulties: all this must strike one. Nobody can doubt that the Church is as safe in their hands as she is in that of any group of priests anywhere. Only, in comparison with the needs of the Church, they remain so far too few.

One of the most urgent tasks facing the Church in Africa is vastly to increase her strength in local priests. The present rate of ordination—some 150 a year—though very valuable in itself, is utterly inadequate to the needs of this great and rapidly growing Church: indeed it does no more than maintain the present rough ratio of one African priest for every 10,000 African Catholics.

Nevertheless in approaching the problems of the ministry and of priest formation at the present day, neither in Africa nor elsewhere is it possible to be concerned only with numbers. Equally important is the deep adjustment of the clergy to the mentality and requirements of the age. The reform of seminaries, so much talked

[2] Norman Horner, *Cross and Crucifix in Mission*, Abingdon, New York, 1965, pp. 105, 114–15. Cf. F. G. Welch, *Training for the Ministry in East Africa*, Limuru, 1963, pp. 86–7.

of today, is needed not chiefly because priests are not numerous enough, nor because they are not holy enough, but because it is becoming clear that their collective mind and approach to the laity and the world is somehow antiquated and at times ineffective, and that this is due not to the personal defects of priests but to a seminary training which has not been sufficiently adapted to the circumstances of today. Faith and the essentials of Church order cannot change, nor the need for service, but the temporal structures of the Church, her pattern of ministry, the type of knowledge and concrete disciplines her priests need to possess do change, and it is generally realized today that after a long rather static period both the ministry and the training for it need to undergo a very considerable re-shaping. It is not, then, enough to ask, How can we get enough priests? We have also to ask, What sort of a priesthood do we need today? And the two questions go together, for in so far as the pattern of priestly formation and life is unadapted to the present time, so is it likely to be difficult to obtain sufficient recruits, and recruits of the right calibre.

Such questions are in no way special to Africa, but one cannot approach the problems of one part of the Church without some recognition of problems that face the Church as a whole. It is absolutely necessary to place an examination of the problems of the ministry in Africa within a wider setting. Clearly the key to the mind and work of the clergy lies in the major seminary. Doubtless the major seminary is not an absolutely necessary part of the Church's life: it is instead one of the most valuable contributions of the post-Reformation period. Its development enormously raised the general standards—both intellectual and moral—of the mass of the clergy at the time, and all over the world it has continued ever since as the great bulwark of ecclesial life. To say, what is now widely recognized, that in many and serious ways the major seminary régime, as it has long existed, is no longer fully suited to the needs of the Church, is not at all to say that the major seminary has not been of vital importance in the past, nor that, with serious adaptations, it will not remain essential for the future. It is just because the seminary is so utterly vital to the Church that it is necessary to examine whether its traditional structure is suited to the situation of today.

The two central defects now widely recognized as existing in our seminary system are, firstly, a certain remoteness and ineffectiveness in the general life; secondly, the matter and method of study. At present a major seminary is too often a distant rural institution, as far removed as possible from all the storms and interests of the current world, in which the future ministers of the Church are segregated for six or seven years of their life. Its atmosphere and discipline have tended to be semi-monastic, too much concern for what is actually happening in the world is practically—if not theoretically—discouraged, very few visitors come to speak to or meet the students, and rather little responsibility or freedom is accorded them. The atmosphere of benevolent paternalism is almost akin to that of a prep school. And this régime is for fully grown men in their twenties, whose contemporaries are not only treated as independent adults, but hold down positions of responsibility and importance. No wonder that some vocations fall victim to nothing else than boredom. Doubtless some of these characteristics are almost inevitable in any institution providing such a lengthy course of adult studies, while others derive from the inherent purpose of the seminary which has necessarily to form people in a way of life as well as impart a quantity of knowledge. The discipline of regularity in prayer, study and work still needs to be imparted. Nevertheless these points are compatible with a life more responsible, more involved, more genuinely adult, than most major seminarists are still permitted.

Here, as everywhere, changes are on the way. In some seminaries of Europe and America the whole picture of the closed institution has already gone, and the students are free to maintain an active life outside its walls. When large and expensive buildings have been erected they cannot easily be abandoned even if their location is unfortunate. Nevertheless even in Africa there is a movement of seminaries from countryside to town: in South Africa the African national seminary has moved from Pevensey in the mountains of Natal to a spot not too far distant from Pretoria. The new national seminary of Kenya is on the outskirts of Nairobi, and that of Uganda is to be close to Kampala.

As far as possible—especially in a Theologicum—it is obviously desirable to escape from a feeling of domination by rules and bells. Details of régime can vary from seminary to seminary and are not very important. What is important everywhere is a spirit of deep mutual confidence and openness between staff and students. The former needs to inspire rather than govern, while every effort should be made to break down the hiatus between seminary and post-seminary life, to give the students some sort of serious pastoral experience in the course of their training and before their definitive commitment. The institution of a special "pastoral year" at the close of the seminary course, which has been advocated and even introduced in some quarters, does not seem the best solution. An advanced and intensive pastoral course can better be undertaken after some years in the full-time ministry; on the other hand the whole study of theology, not just a final polish, needs to be related to the apostolate. This is not at all an easy matter to work out in practice, but at least it should involve the seminary itself and its staff in activities which are going on outside it, and in a way planned by the seminary. A mere leaving of seminarists free to help their parish priests for a month or two is a quite ineffective way of providing pastoral training.

The restrictions on the use of freedom and responsibility that the seminary course does involve over a long period of adult life make it all the more necessary that its own internal content should be really worth while. That content is surely not just one of study; nevertheless study is its most extensive component and it does desperately need to be such as to hold the student's interest and to appear as genuinely relevant to the life that will follow ordination and to the mental preoccupations of our own age. Much can be improved in this line, following the indications of the Vatican Council.[3]

Most people have come to realize today that a very great deal of the scholastic theology and philosophy customarily taught in seminaries is irrelevant to anything that 90 per cent of our priests will say or do from the moment they leave the seminary. Many priests are unable themselves to make the terminological translation necessary in order to teach the theology which they learnt in scholastic terms to people whose knowledge of scholasticism is nil, and the result too often is that they practically avoid teaching theology at all. It is still often tragic to compare the length of a priest's training with his real unpreparedness to cope with many of the actual tasks he has to face when he comes out of it all. Too

[3] Cf. the valuable directives in par. 16 of the Decree on Missionary Activity, as well of course as the Decree on Seminary Formation.

13

much speculative matter has been given him—much of it frankly unusable—while a lot of what he really needed has not been provided: practical parish administration, accountancy, voice production, even adequate liturgical preparedness.

Today, with the directives of the Vatican Council firmly behind us, we have to re-shape the seminary course in an integral fashion according to the stresses of modern theology. This is easy to say, but far less easy to do. For years extra bits and pieces have been brought into the theology course, now things must be dropped out as well. It is surely not possible to draw up an ideal course *a priori*, nor desirable that all seminaries should follow the same pattern anyway. What is needed is vigorous experimentation, and a refusal to allow each professor to maintain his own accustomed teaching area as untouchable. The general stress has surely to be more centrally scriptural than are the old text-books, with regular liturgical, pastoral and ecumenical openings. At the same time it would surely be great loss to abandon everything with a trace of the scholastic about it: our whole belief in theological and doctrinal development means that theology is not just scriptural interpretation in a narrow sense. It would not be progress at all if able seminarists ceased to want to buy and to read the *Summa Theologica*. Indeed it does not seem that the scholastic should be replaced as such by the scriptural principle as providing the all-inclusive scheme of study; what is required is rather the historical principle as such. It is history more than anything else which can give unity both to modern studies outside the Church and to the new theological approach. Scripture is indeed the history of salvation, but neither history nor salvation stop short in A.D. 100. Only a grasp of history can make sense alike of the revelational development of Scripture and the ecclesial development of the Christian era, and can then relate them to global and human development within a vision of the one creative Word, Christ, Alpha and Omega.

There has been a lack of adjustment in the major seminary course not only for the great majority of seminarists who are not destined for an academic life, but also for the minority who will be engaged in teaching, writing and scholarly work. They are doubtless enabled to pass on what they have themselves learnt, but after so many years of training they still remain ill-equipped to enter the intellectual life of the modern world. Seminary-trained priests often sense this and demonstrate an attitude of inferiority which is both unfortunate and quite unnecessary. The trouble arises from the way—a medieval way—in which studies both in major seminaries and in the Roman clerical universities are still largely conducted. Teaching is geared far too exclusively to a lecture system and the study of a fixed text-book. Libraries tend to be poor, written work almost non-existent or—when given—not seriously criticized, discussion largely avoided. Today, almost everywhere, efforts are being made to modernize teaching methods from these points of view, though one often feels that such efforts are not sufficiently far-reaching: they involve the fringes of a system rather than its core. And it is, of course, true that teachers who have themselves been brought up in one system can abandon it only with the greatest difficulty: someone accustomed only to a pattern of lectures, mercurials, and an examination based rather exactly upon the matter actually "seen", can hardly imagine how a system continually using seminars, essay-writing and an extensive library really works.

It has to be remembered that the necessarily very wide range of intellectual ability to be found in a seminary makes the teaching problem in some ways different from that of a university, and more difficult. The seminary has to cope with a majority of students who do not attain university standard, and its studies cannot be geared to the needs of its most intellectual minority. Nevertheless weaker students can benefit—within their own range of achievement— from discussion and the opportunity of personal work almost as much as the ablest ones, so long as the matters treated are seen as relevant. And almost everybody nowadays resents the *Ipse dixit* approach. Doubtless there has got to be a core of material which must be taught and accepted in a fairly straightforward way, but it would seem perfectly possible to cut down the common lecture course very considerably on what it tends to be at present, and so to leave far more room for group discussion, essay-writing, serious private reading and specialization. Specialization can be in the Gospel of St John for some seminarists, in practical religious sociology or in plumbing for others.[4]

[4] The English university system has always balanced the "outline" paper against the "special subject". The seminary curriculum needs to find space for the latter.

Obviously all this depends on the capabilities of a seminary staff. It is no use expecting the impossible, and often blame rests much more with those who are not in a place than with those who are there and do the best job they can. In Africa especially it is extremely difficult to provide a really adequate staff for large numbers of important seminaries in countries where there is a great shortage of clergy. Those who have made most effort to advance this work may be those who now find it most difficult to develop it effectively. The Society of the White Fathers, in particular, who have led the way in training an African clergy and are today responsible for a number of important seminaries in Africa as well as their own training houses in Europe and America, cannot but feel the strain of so many commitments. It is not always easy to see what can be done to improve this, yet a certain lethargy and fear of experimentation and innovation surely make it worse than need be. What would seem to be most necessary is a greater diversification within the seminary teaching body. Apart from those academically qualified it is most necessary to have others who have had extensive practical pastoral experience, and to make provision too for serious courses in manual skills. More too could be done in the way of providing short but intensive courses by outside lecturers, including lay people. The odd talk from the passing visitor can be useful but its value is obviously limited; what is needed and with some trouble could be provided in many places is a planned contribution from outsiders to the regular teaching. This could well include visiting lecturers from Europe and America. Is it too much to hope that distinguished theologians could be found willing to give a term's teaching in an important African seminary? Have theologians so little sense of responsibility for the young Churches that this should be unthinkable? I prefer to believe that they have simply not been asked.

If the seminary staff needs to be more diversified, so does the curriculum of studies in order to suit the abilities of different students. All over the world I have been struck in seminaries by the failure to cater seriously for those whose intellectual ability is definitely above average. The general course has inevitably to be geared to a fairly commonplace level; this fails to place any serious intellectual demands upon the able who are left to direct their own private studies as best they can. Most have not yet come to a stage of maturity in which they can do this effectively. They need real direction from the staff, that is to say individual or group tuition. Nothing would be more helpful for the general sense of purpose than some serious specialization within the seminary curriculum, and in a six-year course this must obviously be possible. But it must not be felt that everyone has to specialize in the same sort of way or to the same extent; the general course can be more than enough to hold the minds of some students. In an African seminary nothing could be better than to have a group seriously studying Greek and then setting itself to the practice of Bible translation, while another group works away at some aspect of ethnology, and a third undertakes a detailed pastoral survey in the neighbourhood. Yet others may prefer to tackle Rahner or to master practical electricity, plumbing and gardening. Each one of these things needs serious direction if they are to get very far, and it is surely for the seminary staff to do its best to provide this specialized direction as well as the matter of the basic courses.

One must plead, too, for a serious approach within the major seminary to non-theological subjects. Theology in a vacuum is never a healthy thing, and a great value of placing a major seminary in or near a large town or university is precisely to bring it into contact with other disciplines. But these disciplines need to be appreciated, and to some extent practised, within the major seminary itself. The library, at least, should cater seriously for non-theological subjects, and the reason is clear. It is only across these other subjects that a priest can subsequently bring his theology into contact with the thinking of the educated laity. Otherwise—and in practice this is so often the case—there is a breakdown in communication. Doubtless for the most part the priest must acquire his knowledge of other subjects either before or after the theology course, but there also needs to be a serious cross-fertilization during the seminary period. Today a priest's theologizing needs to be done in some way within the circumference of such other fields of thought as literature, politics, sociology, ethnology and secular history. *Macbeth* or the *Kinsey Report* and for that matter Ekwensi's *People of the City* or Dr Nkrumah's *I Speak of Freedom*, can be as useful texts for the study of budding theologians as the *Quodlibetales* or *Rerum Novarum*. Theology, in fact, as it needs to be grasped by the individual seminarist, is not a detached, unchanging discipline; its value for the priest who has to minister to the wide world depends upon the degree in which, while remaining true to itself, it has been shown as relevant to what man today outside the seminary walls is thinking and doing.

Young men who have studied theology in this way will not have been somehow separated by it from their fellow men, and they will neither fear the science of the rest of the world nor be indifferent to it: their mental formation will have been truly ministerial.

To be biblical, pastoral, ecumenical, open to contact with secular disciplines, diversified, and practical—these surely are the needs of major seminary teaching today. A grip on Romans at one end and on accountancy at the other with a dose of Karl Marx and Pan-Africanism in between. These are high requirements, not easily fulfilled, but at least let us put them forward as standards to be aimed at, as a pattern of teaching which may frighten some, but should challenge all.

At least 95 per cent of African major seminarists have previously spent four to six years in a minor seminary. Perhaps there is no other institution in the contemporary Church which is as difficult to evaluate as the minor seminary, and in which there can be such a full-scale clash between old and new forms of approach. Basically, the minor seminary is an anachronism, for it aims at providing a vocational and professional training for children at an age when in the past such training was given but today is not. Up to some fifty years ago, a trade or profession could be chosen in one's early teens, and an apprenticeship would follow. Even the students in universities were—until the nineteenth century—boys rather than men. In such a context the minor seminary was entirely understandable. Today with the world-wide extension of non-specialized secondary education, the situation in which a minor seminary really made sense is ceasing to exist. It is an anachronism, and as a result its continuation inevitably produces tension with contemporary attitudes and patterns of education; every effort should be made to draw vocations increasingly from post-secondary school boys. Nevertheless *hic et nunc* we obtain extremely few vocations this way in Africa, and to scrap the minor seminary system could only lead to disaster, but it can and must be overhauled.

The minor seminary, as it has traditionally existed, has had the following chief characteristics to set it apart from other secondary schools: firstly, a strong stress on vocation; signs of "no vocation" could produce expulsions at any stage of the course. Secondly, a régime of spiritual exercise and a type of discipline (including the *magnum silentium*) closely modelled upon the major seminary. Thirdly, a pattern of other studies strongly weighted on the "ecclesiastical" side, and generally deficient in much that any good modern school is expected to provide: science courses, an extensive library, openness to current events, the reading of newspapers, the teaching of art.

With regard to these three aspects it is realized today that, for the first point, boys in their teens are normally not able to make a serious judgment on what it means to be a priest or whether they want to be one. At the same time the staff also cannot normally decide suitability at this age. A very few boys may be clearly unsuitable, but for most one cannot judge. Boys who are very troublesome at 17 may be excellent priests at 26; boys who are meek and docile at 17 may either be so because they are weak, passive characters, not truly suited to be priests, or they may explode into total rebellion later on. On the whole minor seminaries tend to eject strong characters and to retain conformist ones. Training for the priesthood cannot really begin until a normal human and Christian formation has been obtained; the former is the task of the major seminary, while it is with the latter that any pre-seminary course should be chiefly concerned: not then with the training of a priest but with the training of a man.

As regards the second point, the round of spiritual exercise evolved for a major seminary is clearly unsuitable for young boys. It has to be compulsory, and for most becomes a matter of mere routine, cast aside wherever possible in the holidays. Judgment on the suitability of seminarists (and hence on their continued presence in the seminary) comes to be based chiefly on signs of (1) piety, (2) obedience, and (3) no observed lapse from continence. Fear of being cast out, and having all their secondary studies upset as a consequence, can result in the first producing hypocrisy, the second a cowed attitude towards superiors. The régime does not encourage openness and courage, but the giving of a good appearance, reserve, etc. The result is the frequent "surprise" caused by apparently excellent seminarists packing up without warning once they have passed their final examinations.

As regards the third point, the inadequacy of studies in many minor seminaries when compared with neighbouring secondary schools creates a sense of grievance on the part of the older seminarists, and adds extra problems for the large majority who will leave the road to the priesthood sooner or later. But it must be added here that a great many minor seminaries in Africa have notably raised their academic standards in the last few years, just as some have given much thought too to the modernizing of the other aspects of seminary life. Here as elsewhere criticism is of a system which as such is no longer suitable; it is not one of individual institutions. Those operating them are often only too conscious of their limitations, but do not see how to escape from the basic pattern which they have inherited.

It is curious how it is still taken for granted today in Africa that for a diocese to be complete it has got to possess its own minor seminary. Of course there was a time when each diocese in the world was encouraged to have its own major seminary. Today that is recognized as being a mistake in modern circumstances: the large regional seminary is a far more effective institution than the small diocesan one. Lack of qualified personnel, of money to be spent on adequate libraries, and so on, are all considerations which dictate a pooling of resources. Exactly the same is true today for at least the senior part of the minor seminary. The disadvantages in their multiplication should be obvious. Firstly, the standards of staff and equipment are bound to suffer. Seminaries receive no government grants and the Church cannot provide adequate science and library facilities or qualified staff even for "O" level work, let alone "A" level, if this has to be done for every separate diocese. Secondly, there is a wastage of staff, and this is extremely serious in a Church which is gravely short of priests. In the small seminary the upper classes become very small, but require the same number of teachers. Three seminaries quite near each other have today 8, 4 and 15 boys in their top class. Together they would make one decent class of 27 with 35 periods a week, requiring less than $1\frac{1}{2}$ priests to teach them. Separately, they involve 105 periods and 4 priest teachers. Furthermore, small groups easily grow dispirited, and so do their teachers, especially if they lack clever students. It is far easier to be really interested, and so generate interest, if you are teaching a class of 27 including several bright boys, than if you are teaching a class of 8, with perhaps only one above average. Again, that one—lacking competition—easily grows bored and wants to go elsewhere.

As a matter of fact the small diocesan seminary tends to remain geared to the needs of the youngest boys in the large, bottom forms. Only in the larger seminary can the older boys be properly catered for and really feel at home. But it is essential for the successful running of any school that it be geared to its top, not to its bottom. In this most minor seminaries seem to fail badly. Every educationalist knows that the small secondary school is inefficient and wasteful, and it is extraordinary that the Church should keep on multiplying them. We would save staff, raise standards and greatly improve the general spirit of the seminarists by aiming at regional minor seminaries of at least 200 boys (distributed over a maximum of six standards). If it is thought helpful for recruitment to have some sort of vocational institute in every district or diocese, this might perhaps be realized by having a greater number of "pre-minor-seminaries", providing a single year's course, in which a basic training could be given and some weeding out done.

The general needs of the minor seminary in Africa today would seem to be: firstly, to concentrate upon the human virtues— honesty, courage, initiative, generosity—rather than on the specifically priestly ones. Secondly, to diminish compulsory spiritual exercises, give much more room for freedom and responsibility, and get rid of the constant fear of dismissal which haunts seminaries. The foundation of the work must be a spirit of confidence between staff and seminarists. To obtain this, it is most necessary that the seminarists feel that the staff is really interested in them as boys, and not only as future priests. The Christian vocation has to be presented as primary, its sacerdotal canalization as secondary. Thirdly, educational efficiency needs to be greatly improved, that is to say, library and science facilities, provision for "A" level courses[5] and the general range of education offered. What minor seminary at present teaches art? Yet that is a field in which at least some

---

[5] That is, the "Higher Certificate".

priests need to be proficient, quite apart from its general human value. Fourthly, the last point does not imply that dull boys who may fail even their "O" level examinations cannot be retained. On the contrary, if they have strong character and good judgment, I think they certainly should be. They can become excellent priests. At this level, as elsewhere, room should be left for diversity.

At the same time as overhauling our minor seminary system, we do need to make a serious effort to find future priests in other secondary schools and among young men who have been at work for a few years. To achieve something in this line, two or three priests could be charged as a full-time concern (on an inter-diocesan basis) to work from a national centre where late vocations are prepared in a congenial way for rapid entry to a major seminary.

Priest formation cannot be discussed today only in seminary terms. Neither the seminary nor the Roman clerical university is today sufficient to provide us with priests able to hold their own in the intellectual conflict of modern plural society or to occupy positions in non-ecclesiastical centres of higher education. For this it is increasingly necessary to have a large number of priests who have graduated in a variety of disciplines in the secular university.[6] This applies to African priests quite as much as to missionaries. It is in fact highly desirable in Africa as elsewhere that some priests should be recruited from the ranks of university students, so that they enter the seminary with a B.A. behind them. For others, who come from a minor seminary or secondary school, it may often be more appropriate to send them for secular university studies before completing theology and receiving ordination. A genuine vocation must surely be able to stand up to that test.

Finally, let it be remembered that it is not sufficient to have some priests with a B.A. or M.A. That is all right for secondary-school teaching or as a form of general educational broadening, but it is not enough for priests who have to operate at super-graduate level, that is to say as members of the professional staff of a university. It is most necessary to allow a certain number of the ablest priests to add a Ph.D. to their M.A. Their subsequent

---

[6] I do not intend to exclude from this category universities like Louvain or Lovanium in the Congo which, though in some way Church controlled, have a full range of faculties and a large proportion of lay staff and students.

usefulness will far outweigh the extra two years involved, but all the same some way should be found of shortening the basic major seminary course for those for whom a long training in a secular university is envisaged: two years in the major seminary could be followed by entry into the university for a three-year B.A. course, after which two or three more years of theology in the seminary would lead to ordination; university studies for a doctorate could then be resumed.

Behind all the variety of possible patterns of ministry and priestly training there must remain the unchanging sense of a consecrated sharing in Christ's service and uplifting of man, a work whose whole point is to be found in divine faith and love, whose qualities must be humility, obedience, compassion, gentleness. These virtues are equally necessary for the village catechist and for the Ph.D. who is a senior member of a university academic board, but they neither militate for nor against wanting to be a village catechist or a Ph.D. The role one fulfils in life, the sort of man one is, depends upon one's abilities, the circumstances of one's upbringing, and the whole range of values which are presented before one. The priestly ministry has to be related both to the needs of contemporary society—in our case a society increasingly graduate-controlled—and to the psychology and abilities of the aspirant to the priesthood; and the calling to the priesthood is only part—a possible apex—to the wider calling to human integrity and Christian holiness, which is offered to every one of the baptized. If it is presented to a young man in terms which deeply conflict with his own sense of contemporary society and his place within that society, he will either abandon the priestly calling, perhaps after much struggle, or make the sort of act of faith and rejection of the natural which sometimes turns out fine but at others creates in after years a psychological wreck or an embittered man.

If one once allows a young man to receive the impression that his love of literature, or science, or knowledge of any kind, is in some way in natural opposition to his desire for the priesthood rather than, for him, a proper part of it, the battle has been half lost. The Catholic priesthood should be the perfect expression of the human ideal of the twentieth century at its best—the apex of the human vocation in this as in every age; if it seems in practice to be, on the contrary, a turning aside from the great contemporary struggle for truth and the service of humanity to floating in an educational backwater and then entering into a rather self-satisfied little society of clerical dignitaries, we are sure not to obtain the cream of our youth for the priestly service of God, his people and the world.

2

Year after year we rejoice at the very rapid increase of Catholics in Africa: today they are over 28 million,[7] the glorious fruit of the great modern missionary effort. Nevertheless millions of Catholics who are not living or having the chance of living a proper Christian life are hardly a blessing. To create a Church consisting of millions of lapsed Catholics is not a matter for rejoicing. In the words of Pope John, "There is no virtue in numbers alone if the quality is lacking" (*Princeps Pastorum*, 26). There are many reasons why people do not practise their faith, but a basic one is lack of priests. If they are lacking, the people, especially people still very new to Christianity, are almost bound to fall away. To baptize thousands, but not to provide them afterwards with pastoral care and the chance to share regularly in the Eucharist, is inevitably to create nominal Catholics only, and to develop in Africa the sort of situation that exists so deplorably in South America and which it is now so difficult to remedy. Now it is clear as day that the Church and her missionaries are today perfectly well aware of the need for an adequate African clergy and have made enormous efforts to develop one. The intention is there, but intentions are not enough. Their effect is negatived if the attempts to give them substance are not adequately adapted to circumstances, or if the system within which people are working somehow blocks their initiatives, without their even realizing what is the matter; and this often happens. Intentions have to be measured up to facts and if the facts indicate that the system being operated is simply not achieving the required results, then the only rational course is to change the system. Faith and good intentions are not enough. This has been shown many times in the past history of the missions, and it remains equally true today.

---

[7] If recognized catechumens be included (as they should be, for they are also the object of regular priestly care), the figure should certainly be over 30 million.

A key point in this question, enabling us to make some sort of an objective judgment about the pastoral possibilities of the Church in a given situation, is the priest-Catholics ratio in any country, and that is a matter of statistics. In general it is estimated that 1 : 1,000 is a fair ratio; in fact it will probably leave little time for non-pastoral work, and the management by a single priest of a parish of 1,000 requires considerable energy and efficiency.[8] Accurate religious statistics are not easy to obtain, African statistics especially so. I have struggled with as many as I could get hold of, but the figures that I present are certainly not entirely accurate. Anyone who has tried to correlate the figures given in the *Annuario Pontificio* with those in other such works will fully realize what I mean. Nevertheless I do not think that any figures I use are, for my purposes, seriously wrong; that is to say, more exact ones would not alter the picture in any substantial way.

The 1965 British *Catholic Directory* gives an estimated Catholic population for England and Wales of 3,827,000, and a total of 7,714 priests (4,959 seculars, 2,755 regulars). That gives a ratio of 1 : 497. It is generally agreed that this population figure is a serious under-estimate but— in the words of the *Directory*—"it gives a good indication of the numbers known to the parish clergy", that is to say, the number of those actually subject in some way to pastoral care, which is really what interests us here. If, however, we estimated that there was a total of 5 million Catholics in England and Wales, we would still have a ratio of 1 : 644. It is true, of course, here as everywhere, that not all these priests are engaged in any sort of pastoral care. However, even if we were able to set aside contemplatives, the old, the retired, the sick, England would still have a ratio far below 1 : 1,000. This is certainly a very good one, although many feel that the Church is still very far from over-staffed. Anyway, it should leave the clergy at least a fair amount of freedom for concern with non-Catholics who form the great majority of the population.

These figures offer some sort of yardstick for examining the African situation. The total number of Catholics in Africa in

---

[8] Evidently the number a priest can effectively care for depends greatly on geographical and other circumstances. It will be far higher in, say, southern Holland where distances are small and the Catholic population dense; much lower in most of Africa where populations are scattered and roads appalling.

1966 was at least 27 million, the total number of priests about 15,000, of whom about 2,800 were Africans.[9] So we can make the following comparison:

	Catholics	Priests	Ratio
ENGLAND AND WALES	5,000,000	7,714	1:644
AFRICA	27,000,000	15,000	1:1,800

Fr Masson found the ratio in black Africa to have fallen from 1:1,506 in 1949 to 1:1,740 in 1961. Our ratio of 1:1,800 for 1966 would be roughly in line with this. However, the general situation is already more serious than this suggests. The reason is that the total includes some fringe areas with a good priest:Catholics ratio. The Republic of South Africa is one example. It has 1,100 priests and some 800,000 Catholics; hence a ratio of about 1:720. Many of these priests are, of course, working among the comparatively small white Catholic community. Again, in the northern part of Africa, especially old French Africa, there are a number of territories with few Catholics but a fair number of priests. These areas are largely Muslim. Thus Gambia, Guinea, Upper Volta, Niger, Mali, Senegal, Sierra Leone, Somalia and Chad have between them about 900 priests and hardly more than 500,000 Catholics. Obviously it is very important that these priests (not in all a very large number) should work in these areas, presenting the Gospel in far more difficult circumstances. If we cut out these special areas we will be left with a general ratio of 1:2,000 for the great missionary Churches from Ivory Coast to Mozambique.

To see the position clearly, however, one must study individual territories and even dioceses. Here is the 1965 position for three important countries:

	Catholics	Priests	Ratio
KENYA	1,171,000	544	1:2,152
UGANDA	2,547,000	764	1:3,333
NIGERIA	2,870,000	943	1:3,043

[9] The diversity of ecclesiastical jurisdictions in Africa makes it most difficult to arrive at total figures. The *Annuario Pontificio* for 1965 gives about 13,000 priests for the territories under Propaganda, and 1,014 for those in Portuguese Africa. The C.I.P.A. (no. 219, 8 May 1964) also gives a

The figure for Nigeria includes catechumens. Notice how bad Uganda's position is despite having been for long the most forward country from the viewpoint of native vocations.

These figures represent a situation which is already near breaking point. Priests cannot cope with a pastoral situation of 1 : 2,500 or 1 : 3,000 Catholics, especially when distances are large and roads bad. Obviously the sheep are just not being fed, despite the heroic exertions of their shepherds. Let us remember too that the ratios given are not the real pastoral ratios. A considerable number of these priests are full-time teachers in mission schools, able to give no more than a helping hand on the strictly pastoral side. According to Mgr Mullin, "Parishes of 40,000 Christians, staffed by two priests, are by no means unknown".[10] The inevitable effect is that a very large proportion of our Catholics do not go to church, even when they can, and a very much larger proportion of them live permanently without the sacraments. Certainly there are other important causes for this, but the point is that nothing can be taken properly in hand while the priest : people ratio is so bad.

But of course the situation is far worse than this, for work in Africa is not merely pastoral but missionary. There are all the millions of pagans beyond and so many of them are ripe to enter the Church. A great deal of our time and energy ought to be devoted to them, while those already in remain even more untended.

I suppose that everyone would agree that that is the general position today, but I think they would feel that, though bad, it has not yet become impossible. The Church, after all, is in its early stages in Africa, and there are bound to be difficulties at the beginning. There are African seminarists on the way. We are building for the future. The question is, Are we?

If the pastoral situation remains for long as it is at present, or if it gets seriously worse, our new Church is just going to fall apart from the inside. There will be no chance for most of our Chris-

---

total of rather over 14,000 priests. According to Fr Masson, S.J. (*Nouvelle Revue Théologique*, March 1963), there were 11,860 priests in all for black Africa in 1961 as against 11,323 in 1960. The same rate of increase would bring the total for 1966 to less than 14,000. The booklet *Ready Information about Africa* (St Edward's College, Totteridge Lane, London, N.20, 1965) gives a total of 28 million Catholics in Africa and a general ratio of 1 : 1,850.
[10] *The Catholic Church in Modern Africa*, Chapman, 1965, p. 63.

tians to live a eucharistic life, to receive pastoral care, to hear the word of God regularly expounded; the early fervour of the majority will pass clean away, as in many places it is already passing, and we will be faced with an ever-growing multitude of those who have passed in and then, effectively, out. If that is the real conclusion to the Church's great missionary effort in Africa, it will have been a vast disaster.

The point to examine, then, is the direction in which we are moving. What is the position going to be like in the future? We might first of all consider briefly what has been happening in the last fifteen years. These have been years of tremendous missionary endeavour. Since the Second World War an enormous effort has been made to bring more missionaries out, and the number of African priests has also risen very considerably. At the same time the number of Catholics has shot up. Missionary personnel has doubled, and even more than doubled in some areas, yet it has seldom kept even level with the number of Catholics. The division of dioceses and other factors make it difficult to get exact figures for the relative positions over the years, but here are a couple of examples (figures taken from the *Annuario Pontificio*):

Onitsha, Eastern Nigeria

	Cath. pop.	Afr. priests	Miss.	Gen. ratio
1950	122,538	7	47	1:2,279
1955	211,478	5	81	1:2,453
1960	380,893	12	102	1:3,342
1965	302,664	14	63	1:3,940

Notice that part of the diocese was removed before 1965; this should not greatly affect the ratio. What we see here is that despite an enormous increase in missionaries—the force has more than doubled in fifteen years—the priest:people ratio has steadily worsened, and now looks as if it is about to get completely out of hand.

Mbarara, Western Uganda

	Cath. pop.	Afr. priests	Miss.	Gen. ratio
1950	196,948	16	52	1:2,897
1955	236,164	24	65	1:2,651
1960	306,821	32	57	1:3,449
1965	494,527	38	90	1:3,859

Before 1965 the new diocese of Fort Portal was erected out of part of Mbarara; our 1965 figures add the two together. Here again we see a great increase in priests, but a very serious worsening in the always bad priest:people ratio. Certainly for most dioceses the ratio has not become as bad in these fifteen years as in these two examples, but almost everywhere it will have worsened noticeably. For East Africa as a whole (i.e. Kenya, Uganda, Tanzania) there were, according to the 1965 *Catholic Directory of Eastern Africa*, 1,842[11] Catholics per priest in June 1959, but 2,039 only four years later.

That is the situation to date. What does the future hold in store? How many Catholics will we have? What new priests can we throw into the breach? There are two possible sources—expatriate and African. Now today the missionary societies seem almost everywhere to be feeling a pinch in vocations,[13] a pinch which in fact is pretty general throughout Europe and North America and which is affecting non-missionary orders even more than the missionary ones. Only in a few countries such as Spain are vocations increasing, while in some countries they have very greatly diminished. There is no likelihood then of any significant increase in the total missionary output per year. That does not mean there will be no further increase in the total number working in Africa, because for many societies if the ordinations of the 1960s are no more, or even slightly less, than those of the 1950s, they are still far more than those of the 1920s; and it is missionaries of that vintage that they are mostly replacing. However, no increase in the missionary army comparable with that of the 1950s can be looked for. Let us remember that there was a considerable flood of vocations in the post-war years and that did much to back the great expansion of the 'fifties. It is true that more non-missionary societies are sending men to Africa; this is an excellent thing, but most often these are sent out to run a single house or some relatively small work. That is rather obvious: it is unlikely that a society would have a large

---

[11] It may be noted that Tanzania, with over 1,200 priests, has by far the best ratio of any country in Africa with a large Catholic population. In 1963 it was still only 1:1,460. It is, however, alas, deteriorating rather rapidly.

[12] Fr Beckmann, S.M.B., speaks of "the marked decline in the number of people responding to the missionary call" as priests (*The International Review of Missions*, Jan. 1965, p. 80).

14

labour force free to dispose of in some, for them, quite new work. There are also secular priests coming out as volunteers under the inspiration of *Fidei Donum*. These again are most useful, but their numbers are far from revolutionary. All in all it is not easy to see where any very great addition to the present missionary force is going to come from, unless there is some really drastic change in the whole shape of mission work. The possibility of this I will consider a little later.

On the side of the African clergy the position is different. The number of those ordained by 1939 was only 257 (CIPA, no. 254, 5 March 1965). In the last twenty years there has been a big increase and this is continuing. By 1964 there were 2,551 (*ibid.*). That is to say, there is a big increase in comparison with what came before; but if we compare the numbers coming through at present with ordinations in other Christian Churches, then it is a very different matter. In a number of countries the coming of independence has had a serious, if possibly temporary, bad effect on the number of ordinations. In general very large numbers enter the lower classes of minor seminaries, but very few indeed persevere to the end of the long course in the major seminary and reach ordination. The *Status Seminariorum Indigenarum* for 1963–1964, issued in Rome by the Work of St Peter the Apostle, gave a total of 80 major seminarists for Kenya, 172 for Uganda, 197 for Nigeria, 23 for Malawi. The total for Africa was 1,980.[13] Certainly not all of these will arrive at ordination; 75 per cent would, I expect, be a more than generous estimate, and they arrive there only across seven years.

Kenya had, in 1965, 66 African priests and 478 missionaries. This means that, if she is lucky, she may by 1972 have as many as 120 African priests. If in the same period the missionary force increases by 130 she will then have a total of 725 priests. It is difficult to expect more. But what will the Catholic population be? According to the 1965 *Catholic Directory of East Africa* the figure for June 1959 was 764,258 and that for June 1963 was 1,027,614. This would give a growth rate of about 8 per cent. We shall surely not be exaggerating if we forecast 2,100,000 as a minimum figure for

---

[13] Compare this with the 2,025 for India, which has only some 6 million Catholics as against Africa's 27 million. And the Indian Church will not be expanding in the same way. Yet she, too, is short.

Kenya Catholics in 1972. If that is roughly correct, the position will be as follows (a very serious worsening in the pastoral situation):

	Catholics in Kenya	Priests	Ratio
1959	764,258	400	1:1,910
1965	1,171,000	544	1:2,152
1972	2,100,000	725	1:2,924

Nigeria, the giant of Africa, has also the most rapidly increasing Catholic population. An analysis of her statistics would probably reveal the most frightening situation of all. In some countries the present rate of Catholic growth is not as high as it is in Kenya or Nigeria, but almost everywhere it is very great, and the reasons are obvious. The first is the population explosion, a factor to which we do not pay nearly enough attention; the second is the continued rapid spread of education and the general desire of pagans, once the traditional pattern of life begins to dissolve, to have a respectable religious allegiance—Catholic, Protestant or Muslim.

In 1966 the total population of Africa, as given by United Nations statistics, was over 310 million. Of these at least 27 million were Catholic. According to the same authority one can expect 450 million people in the continent by 1980 and 768 million by the year 2000. How many of these will be Catholic? According to Bishop Fulton Sheen,[14] while the present general population increase in Africa is 2·6 per cent a year, the general Catholic increase is 12·5 per cent. This is, however, a considerable exaggeration. For the years since 1949 7–8 per cent would seem about right. If, however, the percentage rise should continue at an average of no more than 5 per cent a year,[15] we would still have 53 million Catholics by 1980 and over 120 million by the year 2000. These figures are vast, and if to some they sound very wonderful, they are also frankly terrifying when one considers the mechanism of pastoral care they must entail. If it is unrealistic to shrug our shoulders about what may happen in the year 2000, it is sheer madness not to look ahead to

---

[14] *Missions and the World Crisis*, 1964, p. 170.
[15] It can hardly go below that, seeing (1) that the general rate of population increase guarantees us a rise of 2·5 per cent per year without any conversions at all, and (2) it is at present far higher than 5 per cent in many important countries and cannot possibly fall down at once, such changes being always gradual.

the year 1980. The boys we are admitting now into our minor seminaries will hardly be ordained by that date. It is not far away.

How many priests can we hope to have by 1980? Only in the years 1951–3 did the total annual increase of priests in sub-Saharan Africa come to more than 450. It has gone down since then. According to the *East African Catholic Directory* the average annual increase in the years 1959–63 for Kenya, Uganda, Tanzania, Malawi and Zambia, all added together, was just 108. In the coming years it seems next to impossible that the total figure for Africa should continue to rise by 450, or perhaps by anything near that. Yet if, *per impossibile*, we managed to keep up such a rate of increase for the next fourteen years, the general ratio would still have fallen from the present one of 1:1,800 to 1:2,400, which means of course that many territories would be far worse off than that.

What the position may be like by the year 2000 hardly bears thinking about. On the present system one can envisage there being, with great good fortune, 12,000 African and 20,000 missionary priests to cope with a Church of up to 120,000,000 Catholics. The average ratio will be about 1:3,500, but many dioceses will have one of 1:7,000 or worse. In fact by that time there will have been a widespread breakdown of the Church in Africa, simply clogged by numbers. To summarize:

	Catholics in Africa	Priests	Ratio
1966	27,000,000	15,000	1:1,800
1980	52,000,000	21,000	1:2,400
2000	112,000,000	32,000	1:3,500

Please note again that these forecasts are based on the most favourable assumptions; actually future ratios may well be far worse. Remember also that throughout this study we speak only of *absolute* ratios, not of the real pastoral ratios. To find out the latter, one must first subtract the number of all those priests who are too old to work much, ill, contemplative, or engaged in full-time teaching or administrative work. Evidently, the pastoral ratios are considerably worse than those given.[16]

---

[16] The general priest:Catholic ratio for Latin America is said to be 1:4,928 for 1965. It may be thought that Africa has still a long way to go to reach that dreadful figure, but of course the work of priests in Africa is not

What is to be done?

Three solutions have been proposed. The first is to get far more African vocations in the traditional way—through the regular minor and major seminary course, adding some who have not been to minor seminaries but have studied at other secondary schools. This is Fr Masson's solution: an immense vocations campaign in black Africa.[17] But in fact an enormous effort is already being made to achieve this today. A vast amount of seminary building has gone up at great expense in the last years and a large number of priests are occupied full time in seminary teaching. There are certainly some results to show for these efforts. What is striking, however, and anyone with experience in this field would agree, is how constantly the numbers—very high in the lower classes of the minor seminary—fade away until a mere handful is left at ordination. As for obtaining vocations that have not gone through the minor seminary, almost nothing has been achieved in this line hitherto. Personally, I am convinced that quite a lot could be done to better the position if there was both a really radical change of approach to the function of a minor seminary, and if one or two priests were appointed in each country to full-time vocations work outside seminary walls on an inter-diocesan basis linked with special centres (not minor seminaries) for preparing late vocations in a hurry for major seminary entrance (on the Osterley model). Nevertheless it cannot be imagined that our present system, even with such overdue modifications, is going to produce in the foreseeable future a number of priests in the least sufficient for our needs. In this context missionaries often speak of the need for generations to pass. The point is that we cannot wait. If the situation does not quickly improve, it will become infinitely worse: and the worse lay practice grows, the fewer vocations there will be. The trickle of priests coming through in the next ten or fifteen years is not going to begin to save us from the consequences of our population explosion.

The second solution proposed is what may be called the appeal to the Universal Church. The argument has been stated a number

---

only pastoral but missionary. Moreover, the pastoral ratios alone of some important territories, such as Uganda, may well have attained South American standards long before 1980.

[17] *Nouvelle Revue Théologique*, March 1963.

of times; for instance, Mgr Mullin, in the epilogue of his book *The Catholic Church in Modern Africa* (pp. 241–2) writes: "What world evangelization most needs is the sending of priests to those parts of the world where they are most needed. At present, some 80 per cent of the world is mission territory; yet only 12 per cent of the priests of the world are working there. Eighty-eight per cent of all Catholic priests are concentrated in that one-fifth of the world where the Church has long been planted. In round figures, of the 392,000 Catholic priests in the world, 359,000 are working in the older Christian countries, while only 33,000 are working in the remaining four-fifths of the world . . . a just apportionment of the priests of the world to those places which need them most is the first contribution which it is hoped the General Council will make to the work of evangelizing mankind." This sounds very nice, though the General Council has, inevitably, failed to make any such apportionment. We have in fact to ask ourselves whether this could offer a feasible solution to the Church's problem. What seems to be proposed is a really massive dispatch of priests from Europe and North America to do missionary and pastoral work in Africa, Asia and South America—priests who do not belong to missionary societies and have never up till now felt a vocation to go. Doubtless a larger number of secular clergy than have come hitherto could be recruited to help in Africa and Asia for some years, and there are still orders which could take on new missionary responsibilities. Every effort should be made to encourage this; nevertheless to envisage a redeployment of priestly personnel on a sufficient scale really to affect the pattern of the pastoral situation in Africa and elsewhere in the course of the next fifteen years seems unrealistic. Were it to happen it might indeed create new problems rather than solve existing ones, for the following reasons.

Firstly, the Churches of Europe and America for the most part cannot spare them. This may sound strange, but it is really quite obvious. Everywhere priests are already busily occupied with activities and responsibilities of every kind. Those who are not thus occupied, on account of age or for some other reason, would be quite unsuitable to send abroad. To send a really substantial number of priests away from most places would mean, at the very least, an administrative revolution of the first order—for instance, the wholesale turning over of teaching responsibilities to the laity: such as, in England, the laicization of Ampleforth, Downside, Stony-hurst, Ratcliffe and other schools. Would either the clergy or the laity of England be prepared to accept such a revolution? Would it in fact be administratively or psychologically possible? Is it reasonable to strip some Churches to the perhaps doubtful advantage of others? Let it be remembered that at present nearly every country is facing both a decrease in vocations and a rise in population. In these circumstances the margin of help in personnel that can be sent abroad is not likely to be very large.

Secondly, can we really believe that it would be good for the Churches of Africa to receive a vast new influx of foreign personnel to help them, not with extraordinary and specialist work, but with their ordinary needs? These Churches need, more than anything else, to stand upon their own feet, and to plan that for years and years the quite simple functions of the pastoral ministry should be carried out by foreigners is surely to condemn African Christianity outright.

Thirdly, it is extremely doubtful whether any African or Asian governments would allow into their countries a vast increase of missionary personnel. Already in some countries entry permits are being limited to people with qualifications to undertake educational or other specialized work. But what we are looking for is exactly people to do the basic pastoral work. To imagine that thousands of Europeans and North Americans will be allowed in to do this is probably idle day-dreaming.

It may be answered in Mgr Mullin's defence that, in the passage quoted above, he is thinking as others who have said much the same have thought, of the needs of missionary work to the tens of millions of non-Christian Africans and Asians rather than of pastoral work among Christians. To this it may be answered: first, that the existing pastoral work already presents us with conditions of crisis, and that to set about a vast new programme of world evangelization without first dealing with this is merely to exacerbate the already almost insolvable problem; secondly, that foreign priests drafted to help in Africa and Asia would in fact be far more easily usable in pastoral work, doing reasonably familiar things, than in strictly missionary work—as can be seen already by the use made of most of the secular priests who come out for a few years on loan—very few indeed do real missionary work in the narrow sense of evangelizing non-Christians; thirdly, it is even more unlikely that hundreds of foreigners would be allowed entry by local governments in order to open up new missionary work among non-Christians than that they would be allowed in to minister to existing Christians.

At this point it becomes necessary to realize that far from being able vastly to increase the number of foreigners engaged in the pastoral ministry in Africa, it may well happen that within a few years even the present numbers will not be allowed. Warnings to indigenize the ministry have already come from politicians. It is theoretically unsound and in practice crazy to leave these Churches utterly dependent for their continued existence upon the unimpeded entry of foreign personnel, as they are at present. In the southern Sudan, when the missionaries were expelled, just 26 priests were left to look after half a million Catholics. Humanly speaking, the result could only be an ecclesial collapse. Just the same would be bound to happen if missionaries were expelled from, say, Kenya. The existing clergy could not begin to cope and the Church would simply crumble away, to remain a shadow of its former size.

I have concentrated attention hitherto chiefly upon the total existing ratio of priests and people. But it is plain that what is almost more important is to consider the position of the African priests alone, 1:16,500 in Kenya; 1:9,000 in Uganda, and so on; and most of these ratios too are becoming steadily worse. The most alarming thing here is the present state of vocations as evidenced by the numbers in major seminaries. The 44 dioceses of the Congo have at present (according to the *Status Seminariorum Indigenarum*) just 250 major seminarists. That is to say, over the next seven years these dioceses, on the average, will not obtain even five new priests each. As the number of Catholics swells, that of seminarists may even decrease. Take the example of Burundi (data from *Annuario Pontificio*):

	Catholics	Major Seminarists
1950	609,000	41
1955	847,000	52
1960	1,169,000	87
1965	1,560,000	53

Only in a very few areas, such as Tanzania and Eastern Nigeria, is there any appreciable improvement in the position of vocations. Elsewhere diocese after diocese has the same story to tell: either the rise in the number of seminarists is not commensurate with that of Catholics, or there is actually a decline. In a few places, such as Rwanda, the fall in numbers has been quite disastrous. This general picture is true both of areas in which the Church is comparatively old and well established, and ones in which she is still very new. Dahomey, for instance, is a territory where the Church has been for a long time. It is one of the oldest evangelized lands of Africa, and there is a sound tradition of the native priesthood with a Dahomean archbishop. Yet, though the number of Catholics is steadily rising, that of seminarists has definitely fallen: there are 23 seminarists today as against 28 ten years ago.

Here again are some figures for the important archiepiscopal see of Yaounde in the Cameroons (from *Annuario Pontificio*):

	Catholics	Major Seminarists
1950	234,223	30
1955	263,000	40
1965	337,859	15

Even in such a diocese as Masaka, Uganda, where the first African priest was ordained over fifty years ago, and which has had its own local bishop and clergy for over twenty-five years, the ratio between African priests and African Catholics is getting steadily worse. Fifteen years ago it was about 1:2,500; now it has passed the 3,000 mark. The figures for the diocese of Kisii, entrusted to an African bishop in 1961, are particularly frightening. It is one of the most Catholic parts of Kenya. In 1962 there were 116,553 Catholics with 14 diocesan priests, 12 missionaries and 3 major seminarists. The priest:people ratio was 1:4,480. By 1965 there were 162,800 Catholics, 16 diocesan priests, 20 missionaries and 4 seminarists. The ratio, appalling when the diocese was formed, is already somewhat worse, and if a lot more missionaries are not found from somewhere, the pastoral situation there is bound to become a hopeless one. Finally, to give one reference to Central Africa: Zambia, with 550,000 Catholics, has just 37 diocesan priests and 28 major seminarists.

We have an absolute duty to face up to these facts. The system is just not working. The situation, far from slowly improving, is getting worse almost everywhere. Only in a few places has the number of major seminarists notably risen, and even then not in proportion to the Church's needs. In some cases the immediate worsening of the situation is due to political circumstances, which may be temporary. But it would be a great mistake to see that as the primary cause. The fact is that the position we are getting into now is a vicious circle. A small Church really living the sacramental life will produce many vocations, and out of them the Church could grow in a healthy manner, but a large Church with a very bad priest:people ratio is almost bound to produce few vocations, because the people cannot receive the regular pastoral care out of which new vocations will spring. This may not be true in the early years of a conversion movement, but it will quickly become true as the new Church settles down. One does not want to exaggerate, but it is reasonable to see the failure to obtain vocations precisely in terms of our over-extended church life. We can end up with the situation of South America where 98 per cent of the population is said to be baptized, yet thousands of missionaries have still to be poured in, and almost unavailingly.

On one side, then, we have to recognize that the urgent needs of the African Church cannot be solved by a vast new blood transfusion from without; on the other side, the present system cannot save her either. It will certainly not be able even to preserve, let alone improve, the present very bad priest:people ratio. The statistics are going to soar in the next ten years, and at the end of it—if we have not done something drastic—we shall be lost. The third solution is to change the system. Without some new way of getting priests, local priests, who can provide a simple ministry for the millions of the baptized, we cannot begin to remedy the situation. The mistake seems to lie in a basic lack of missionary adaptation in the character of the ministry we have tried to develop in Africa, as elsewhere. The pattern of the ministry must be adapted to the needs of a society, and a new and quickly growing Church may be quite unable to provide the sort of ministry which can be taken for granted in an old and somewhat static one.

The essential starting-point for a sound line of thought is that a community which can provide baptized men must also, in a few years at the most, be able to provide a sufficient number of ordained men to minister to them. If this does not happen, it is because we are trying to impose a pattern of ministry worked out in different circumstances in such a way as to stifle the life of the young Church. If our present system of clerical training and subsequent pattern of ministry are in fact preventing the baptized from participating in the Church's eucharistic life, for which they were baptized, then it must be that our system is partially wrong for this time and place, and needs to be adapted. The ministry has varied enormously in the history of the Church from the tent-making of St Paul to the intricate organization and fifteen years' training of the Society of Jesus. To consecrate a single form regardless of the contemporary needs of the lay Church is clericalism: the subordination of the Church to the ministry and the spirituality of the clergy, instead of the ordination of clergy and ministry to Church. It is that from which we must free ourselves today.

3

A chief trouble in the last few centuries has been a growing rigidity in the shape of the ministry, coupled with the increasing segregation of clergy from laity. These two factors are behind both the failure of the Church's ministry in older Christian countries to respond adequately to new needs and the failure of the same ministry to grow satisfactorily in new lands. Despite the very fruitful multiplication of religious orders destined for particular purposes, our general pattern of ministry has become from some points of view increasingly monolithic. On the one hand the diaconate and all the minor orders were reduced to frills of seminary life. On the other hand the pattern of priestly life became more and more uniform. Some of the chief characteristics of that pattern have been: (1) it is a vocation for life, entered upon in youth, the earlier the better; (2) it is a full-time occupation, incompatible with other employment; although, in fact, this has often been modified both in some European rural areas where priests continue to do a good deal of cultivation and as regards the profession of school-teaching, which has always been accepted as suitable work for a priest; (3) it requires a professional training of some six years, which must have been preceded by quite a few other years of schooling; (4) it involves celibacy; (5) it is differentiated as far as possible from the rest of the community by the type of education and cast of mind the clergy have received, by dress, modes of address, etc. Fluency in Latin, the cassock, the segregated upbringing of a minor seminary, the celibate life—these are the four most normative characteristics of the Catholic clergy as it developed, on Dark Age and medieval foundations, in the post-Tridentine period. Much of this pattern derived from a specifically monastic, rather than priestly, approach to life. For each element of it there has been good reason in its time, and there is obviously no question of abandoning all these points wholesale; nevertheless seen together they have brought about a deep "apartness" of the clergy from the laity, and they constitute the core of clericalism.

Today we are beginning to realize how seriously this one particular pattern can impede both the work of the Church's ministry and its extension. It was perfected according to the needs of southern Europe in the sixteenth and seventeenth centuries, but much about it is worse than irrelevant to the twentieth century, either in Europe or in Africa.

In fact all over the world the pattern is being considerably modified in one way or another. In countries like Britain cassocks are never worn out of doors and often not inside; the minor seminary is becoming almost obsolete; most priests have shared a common secondary schooling with other boys and a fair number—so-called "late vocations"—common employment with other men. Latin is becoming less and less the characteristic core of the culture of most priests. There are many other moves in one country or another to vary the pattern of priestly existence, introducing a new diversity. In France the priest-worker experiment, recently resumed with official approval, has sought to break down the concept of the ministry as necessarily an exclusive occupation. In Germany and elsewhere a number of married men have been ordained, indicating that insistence on celibacy may at times be an obstacle to bringing into the ministry all who can usefully participate in it. Again, the Vatican Council's restoration of an independent diaconate, even for married men, again makes for greater diversity both as to the actual division of the ministry and as to the sort of people who can be called to it.

Apart from such particular initiatives, there has been in this century a growing diversity in the pattern of priestly work as it is

actually carried out, and this derives from the necessity of specialization in modern society. Already in the remote past the creation of
missionary societies and other orders was a practical recognition
of the fact that the Church's ministerial work has a complexity
about it which requires not only temporary *ad hoc*, but permanent
diversification within the ranks of the clergy. Today youth work,
the apostolate of the sea, the universities, radio and television, are
all more and more requiring men permanently involved in a particular field and mentally prepared for it. The traditional territorial,
parochial ministry cannot be abandoned, but it can provide only
part of the service which the Church needs to offer in our complex
modern society.

The real need of the Church today is simply to take this already
existent diversification of the ministry further still: to develop the
Beda system, the priest-worker system, the married deacon system,
and other ways too that her ministers may both be rightly trained
and rightly placed to help their fellow men both within and without
the Church. What is needed everywhere is flexibility within the
ministry. Clearly all this requires the abandonment of many aspects
of the traditional clerical pattern and especially of that stress on
apartness which had become so marked a characteristic of the
post-Reformation Church. What is wanted is not one wholesale
alteration, but a willingness to adapt and experiment according to
the needs of the Church in different circumstances and countries—a
flexible ministry. When one calls for radical adjustments to the
ministry in Africa, one is not then calling for something quite
different from what is needed or is even being provided elsewhere,
but one is recognizing that in Africa the priestly ministry, as it has
developed up to now, is even more mono-form than that of Europe
and is proving, because of the strikingly different social and
religious situation, unadapted to some of our immediate needs.
Today so much is talked, with strong official approval, about the
adaptation of Church life to Africa, it would be strange indeed if
this one element of the ministry should not require any such
adjustment.

It is striking that the missions, recognizing this situation but
accepting too the immutability of pattern of the Church's official
ministry, created a new and very effective, unofficial one: the order
of catechists. Without the catechist the Church in mission territories,

and especially in Africa, could never have developed very far. He has been the missionary's "right hand man" (Pope John, *Princeps Pastorum*, 39), his essential auxiliary; interpreter, assistant, substitute; little by little the local Church came to be built up more and more around a chain of catechists, and the greater the catechist's responsibility became the stranger it grew that this person who led the regular prayer of the people of God and taught them in the name of the Church was a mere layman. The clericalism which simply ruled out the possibility that such men should be given Catholic orders of any kind drove the Church as a consequence into a pattern of local church life which was really very Protestant, and which we have now come to take for granted.

As a matter of practice, while priests are so few, it is obviously necessary to have a less well-trained but far more numerous group of people able in some way to maintain the presence of the Church in the villages, to baptize at need, gather the people together for prayer, provide at least some simple instruction and be a guide for the priest when he does occasionally manage to visit the individual village.

Roughly speaking, there have been three stages in the history of the catechist in Africa. The first stage, going from the last century up to the 1930s, was the period when the catechist was really regarded as the corner-stone in mission work. He was trained and cared for by missionaries accordingly. A second type of catechist dates from the time when missionaries became chiefly concerned, instead, with the development of a schools system which could be recognized and aided by the government. Catechist training centres were closed or transformed into Teacher Training Colleges. For many years, until recently, for instance, there was not a single catechists' training centre in Uganda. The mission Church was concentrating upon teachers, but as the catechists' work could not just be dropped almost anyone willing was co-opted without much training to fill their ranks. Quite clearly this second type, who is still with us today, has often lacked the quality of his predecessor. Today in a few places a third type is just beginning to appear, in far smaller numbers, from reopened catechists' schools. This pattern in the history of catechists is common to most parts of Africa. Fr Willekens, a missionary in Zambia, has described it for his area:

Some twenty-five years ago we had a great number of catechists, rather low in academic attainment, but fervent Christians. Under the educational and social conditions then prevailing they did excellent work. By now they have either died or become too old to adapt themselves to new ways of thinking or working. To these succeeded an intermediate group of about equal academic ability but less well trained and, which was more unfortunate, less fervent than the older catechists. Many of these have left of their own accord or have been dismissed. During the last ten or twelve years a new group of catechists has come out from the training school or is at present in training. They have a much higher academic standard, are catechetically as fully trained as possible, and the greatest stress is laid on their personal conviction and fervent Christian life.[18]

Naturally this process of change has not been precisely the same everywhere. It has depended in part upon local circumstances of social progress and the policy of the particular missionary society, but the general picture Fr Willekens presents seems to be a true one, though requiring local modifications. In Masaka diocese, Uganda, where there was almost no catechist training for years, catechists are now often chosen by the villagers themselves. This system has its own advantages. Having his home already in the village, the catechist is not dependent upon the Church for his plot of land and will not lose it when he has to retire. He is respected by his neighbours, and should be a reliable and influential church member. What he does not have is any training to help him preach Sunday after Sunday to his fellow Catholics. Nevertheless, it would be a great pity to lose entirely a system like this, in favour of one in which we have only catechists who have been trained as such while young. The two should rather be combined.

In most places Fr Willekens' new, third group does not as yet exist, and there are no training centres for them. The only one existing at present in Uganda, I believe, and that of very recent

[18] *AFER*, Oct. 1964, p. 396. For a very interesting account of the decline of the catechist in an old-established Protestant Church, see J. V. Taylor, *The Growth of the Church in Buganda*, S.C.M., 1958, pp. 124–41. In general Protestant mission policy since about 1950 has attempted "to dispense with catechists in favour of a combination of ordained men and voluntary lay workers" according to Dr Sundkler, *The Christian Ministry in Africa*, S.C.M., 1960, p. 65.

origin, is the school at Ibanda, Mbarara diocese. In Tanzania there are more, notably the important training centre of Bukumbi, Mwanza. In South Africa there is the well-known centre of Lumku, Queenstown. There are others elsewhere, opened as people at last rediscover the urgency of training serious ministers of the Church in a simpler and more extensive way than that offered by the seminary system.

As we see, the second group of catechists tended to be less capable and less fervent, not as a result of their own fault, but because in the social development of Africa missionaries turned their attention elsewhere. Many of the later catechists have had no proper training at all; they were simply co-opted from among their fellow villagers, gathered together for an occasional retreat and given some elementary duties to perform. The catechist's social status has fallen as a result. In the old days it was very high, but his education, pay and sense of confidence failed to rise with those of others. A person with initiative would no longer wish to take on the job, and people with some education would expect a better salary. All this rebounded on the catechist's ability to do his job well. He might even be regarded no longer as the church leader in his local community; teachers and others were taking this place. The time has come when some have asked whether the Church really needs catechists any more. Can we not make do with teachers instead? The answer to that seems in principle to be a decided no. The teacher is a government servant, more and more slipping away from any necessary Church commitment. He may or he may not be a fervent Christian. In some circumstances a teacher could be appointed also catechist of the place, but as such the two functions are different: one concerns children and schools and is basically secular, the other the whole church community and is basically religious.

With the shortage of fully trained priests it is absolutely necessary to supplement the ministry with lower orders and to maintain at least some full-time catechists, but the haphazard system of past years should no longer be tolerated. Little of real value can be expected from those to whom almost nothing is given. To be of use catechists, like everyone else, require a proper training, an adequate salary and the renewed prestige which these bring with them. Evidently these conditions will entail a diminution in the total number of the catechist force. The training centre at Bukumbi provides a fine example of the new approach.[19] The course lasts two years and only people with at least seven years of formal education behind them should be admitted. Our catechists must be properly literate. They should also be married and come to the training centre with their wives, as at Bukumbi, so that the whole family can receive a suitable training for its apostolate. It is to be an apostolate of life, and it is very much better that it be the life and work and example of a married couple that is in question. The course has to provide solid spiritual, liturgical, biblical, doctrinal material which can really make of our catechist a man qualified to teach people in church. This can be done in two years.

These catechists are to be considered as full-time workers and paid accordingly, even though they have also to spend quite a few hours during the week working on their plantation. Something like a hundred shillings a month is at present a reasonable minimum wage. Of course payment presents, or is thought to present, the great problem: where is the catechist's salary to come from? The obvious and correct answer is "from the local community", but it may not be a very palatable one in places where Christians have not yet come to take their duty to support the Church very seriously. Yet economic self-sufficiency is an essential attribute of a real Church, and the low salary of a catechist is the least that a Christian community can be asked to provide. Failure to do so, except in the very poorest areas or ones where evangelization is only beginning, is simply an indication that there is something utterly wrong in the Christianity which is being built up. To fall back, as the Pan-African Catechetical Conference and the Vatican Council itself[20] have done, upon an appeal to Europe to pay, not only for the training of catechists but also their low regular monthly wage seems to me to be a betrayal of the essential character of our work, which is the building up of a strong Church, not of an extensive range of services. Money can rightly be provided from outside for special, non-recurrent needs, but what is required for the regular running of the local Church must be provided locally: acceptance of the economic burden is part of a human community's accept-

[19] See Fr Koenen, *AFER*, Jan. 1962, pp. 69–70; Fr Vulkers, *AFER*, Oct. 1964, pp. 399–405.
[20] Decree on the Missions, n. 17.

15

ance, in this world of buying and selling, of the truth of Church and Gospel. The missionary who cushions his Christians from this is impeding them from fully sharing in Church life. Moreover, if something is first maintained with foreign money, it is far more difficult afterwards to persuade people to give locally. This indeed is one of the key weaknesses to Christian life in Africa: entry into the Church is seen as giving one a right to sharing in a perpetual hand-out by generous missionaries. The endless appeal today by bishops and priests, both missionary and African, for financial help from America and Europe may be very good for the apostolic spirit in those lands but it can be very bad for the sense of stewardship and financial responsibility in the young Churches.

On account of the standard required and the salary provided there will be far fewer of the new kind of catechist than of the old. There cannot be one for every village. But they will do far more, and their work can be supplemented by other entirely voluntary lay workers, able and committed people who are prepared to sacrifice a few hours to helping the Church's ministry. Such work would, of course, in no way be paid. It is simply an aspect of the active laity and its apostolate on which the Church is coming to depend more and more.

At the end of the two-year course at Bukumbi the new catechists at present receive a "canonical mission" in a para-liturgical ceremony. The ecclesial status and true ministry of these essential men has got to be brought home more clearly than that. Let them be given the minor orders of acolyte and lector at the close of their course.[21] These give a solemnity to their calling and manifest that what they have to do really is a sharing in the Church's ministry. As acolytes they are called to look after the church and lead prayers, as lectors to read and explain Scripture to their people. But that too is not enough. The Vatican Council has now agreed in the Constitution on the Church to revive the order of a permanent diaconate for married men and it is quite obvious—as the Conciliar decree on Missionary Activity indicates (n. 16)—that if we can look anywhere for such people it should be first of all among the ranks of our trained catechists. The deacon can do far more than the lector. He is the regular minister of baptism and

[21] Cf. the suggestion of Mgr Te Riele, M.H.M., in *AFER*, July 1963, pp. 278–9, and Fr Loire, W.F., *AFER*, Jan. 1965, pp. 55–7.

witness of marriage; can distribute communion both to the sick and at a Sunday service where there is no priest, can officiate at funerals and give sacramental blessings. If some of our catechists can do such things, they will be taking a real burden of work off the priest.[22] I would not suggest that the full-time catechist should be ordained a deacon immediately after his course. This should come later, after some years of conscientious work in the ministry as an acolyte; he would then return for a further period of training—six months or a year—before receiving the diaconate and a rise in pay. Doubtless some catechists would never be called to this; it would depend on a number of factors, but for many it would be the natural ascent within the ministry of the Church which they are called upon to share.

The road of the trained catechist should not be the only one to the ministry of the diaconate.[23] Besides the full-time salaried deacon there is room for the part-time unpaid one. This type of deacon would be chosen chiefly from the professional classes, well-educated and respected members of the local church—secondary school masters, doctors, and the like. The middle-aged villager who has been elected a part-time catechist should also not necessarily be excluded. Evidently such people, with employment of their own, could not have even a one-year training course. Their usually higher education would enable them to do more study on their own, supplementing short but well-planned courses. Especially in towns such men could be of the very greatest use, and not only in Africa, of course: this is doubtless the type of deacon who will also appear in Europe and America. It will enable laymen to teach regularly from the pulpit, and in general will help to keep priests and laity in close touch. For all such deacons, whether full-time or part-time, it seems important to retain and stress their lay character. We must not try to "clericalize" them. They should not wear a special dress, they should normally be married, combining in their different ways a major commitment to the Church's ministry with the intuitions and responsibilities of the layman.

A third type of deacon—this time a clerical deacon—could very

---

[22] Cf. F. Murray, M.M., "The Diaconate In East Africa", *AFER*, Oct. 1965, pp. 346–50.
[23] Cf. Bishop de Reeper, "Restoration of the Diaconate", *AFER*, Oct. 1962, pp. 292–9.

well come from our orders of brothers, where they exist. In Uganda, for instance, the *Bannakaroli* often already fulfil in country parishes very much of the role of a deacon. They live, three or four together, near the priests, sharing in their prayers, kneeling in the sanctuary, joining in all the parochial activities and, of course, especially, teaching in the primary school. It would be eminently suitable for their senior members, say ten years after profession, to be ordained deacon.

At this immediate moment the most important thing as regards the ministry in Africa is to go ahead really vigorously with the development of a permanent diaconate: the choice of men, their training and their integration into the existing pastoral ministry. Such a move forward, if it is to be of any real value in helping our pastoral problems, has to be carried out at once on a very considerable scale. This requires imagination, courage, readiness to experiment. It is the thing to do at once because the way is not barred to it, but it cannot be the complete or final solution. Valuable as the diaconate may be, it remains a subsidiary part of the ministry. Within a Catholic ecclesiology there can be no substitute for the priesthood. As we have always said: It is the Mass that matters.

It is difficult not to come to the conclusion that, in a land where there is a terrible shortage of priests, some of the men, of the various sorts described above, who have been conscientiously fulfilling the work of a deacon, could and should be promoted the further step to the priesthood. If the Church can really trust a man so far as to ordain him a deacon, to distribute communion, baptize and preach the word of God, she can surely trust him so far as to ordain him a priest. And the difference in his usefulness will be, of course, enormous. There should be no question of promoting all deacons to the priesthood. It would depend on utility in particular circumstances and the general qualities of the man. Some well-educated professional people might well be called to the priesthood within a part-time ("tent-making") ministry in towns where there is a great shortage of full-time priests. But the deacon who, in Africa, is most obviously eligible to be made a priest is the "full-time" catechist who lives on his own and practically presides over a Christian community which can at present only occasionally be visited by a priest from a central station. His ordination would not, of course, mean his becoming an independent parish priest. He would be the curate of a sub-parish.

The great objections to giving the priesthood in such circumstances relate to celibacy, the standard of education expected by the Church of any and every priest, and thirdly, the possible troubles that could result. Fr Murray, M.M., in an article strongly urging the development of the diaconate in Africa, has recently written:

> Lately there has been talk about having a married clergy in East Africa in order to solve the problem of the critical shortage of priests. It is true that it was only towards the end of the eleventh century that Pope Gregory VII enforced the obligation of celibacy upon all the clergy of the Western Church and that very strong monastic influence can be detected here. . . . But the path followed by the Western Church for almost a thousand years cannot be lightly abandoned. Even before Gregory VII practice of celibacy by the clergy was quite common. Moreover, clerical celibacy has its origins in the Apostolic Church and is a powerful witness to the sublime nature of the Gospel of Christ. To opt for a married priesthood before attempting to solve our pastoral difficulties through a diaconate seems unreasonable.[24]

Certainly we cannot lightly abandon a practice which has been followed, and fruitfully followed, for so long. However, there are other patterns of ministry which have existed historically, and also with fruit. The appeal to history and experience can be conclusive neither way. In fact a married clergy continued to exist, illicitly, in the Western Catholic Church for hundreds of years after Gregory VII; medieval society could have been served in no other way. It has always existed in the East. Moreover, there is the Protestant experience which we should not neglect. There is no reason to think that marriage has destroyed the fruitfulness of the Anglican ministry, for instance, although it may well have inconveniences which we would be equally unwise not to examine very carefully. On the whole a married clergy makes for enrootedness, but not for evangelical dynamism. It may well be that a combination of the two is the ideal for a Church, the difficulty being how, if marriage is allowed, to maintain a sufficiently numerous celibate group! Let

[24] *AFER*, Oct. 1965, p. 350.

it be stated clearly that I am not arguing here for any general abandonment of clerical celibacy. To allow the ordination of older married men is quite another thing to allowing fully trained priests to marry after ordination. It may be that the admission of the one would make more difficult the refusal of the other. I do not know. If one step is needed, let us take it, and then see in the light of this new experience what else we should or should not do.

Fr Murray, arguing rightly for the value of a deacon's work, writes again:

> I have heard some say that if a deacon can't hear confessions and absolve, he is useless. This is certainly extreme depreciation of the very noble functions of the deacon as defined in "De Ecclesia". It should also be mentioned that the thinking of many of us is coloured by our having been taught in the seminary a somewhat exaggerated notion of the importance of the sacrament of Penance, while at the same time we were not taught the full significance of the Sunday celebration of the triumph of Christ (p. 349).

Surely this is indeed the point. The priest may perhaps not be needed to hear more confessions, but he is needed to celebrate the triumph of Christ on a Sunday. A deacon cannot do that; but it is that celebration which is the essential heart of the Church's life, and it needs to be the heart too of every local church.[25]

Another missionary, Fr Slaats, C.S.Sp., has also recently been tackling this problem.

> One of the headaches of the Church at present [he writes] is the shortage of priests. It is not that there are not enough people to fulfil the priestly function within the local Christian community, but the requirements demanded of a priest are so very high and rigidly insisted upon without respect to the community, that few people can cope with it. Celibacy is one of them. The intellectual standard, practically uniform for the whole Church and often not in proportion to the intellectual standard of the local community, is another one. The intellectual standards required in the Anglican Church at least in mission countries seem

---

[25] Thus, to start distributing communion extensively outside Mass because we have deacons but not priests would certainly not be a healthy development.

more realistic. If somebody becomes the priest in a community which hardly has the most elementary education, why should he have an education of a European university level?... To go an almost impossible step further: if we find in an African community a natural religious leader, even if as yet only a catechumen, why not get this man to become a priest?[26]

Surely Fr Slaats's general line is the true one. Non-essential requirements for the priesthood must be related to the needs and standards of a given community. What is principally important is to find someone who can really lead and influence a given type of community, rather than someone who conforms to certain standards which have grown up in quite other circumstances.

Of course there are many different sides to the problem. In Africa the Church is not everywhere "a community which hardly has the most elementary education"; it is a community made up of extremes. The far lower academic standards required by the Anglican Church in Africa have also very serious drawbacks: the local clergy can get out of touch with the new leadership in society, which in its turn will despise and ignore the Church's ministry. The result could be a "Peasant Church", closed in on itself, out of touch both with new movements of thought in other parts of the Church and with the upper strata of the new African society. It was against this that Roland Oliver warned us in the closing pages of *The Missionary Factor in East Africa*[27] and it is a danger which particularly confronts some of the Protestant Churches in East and Central Africa. There are Protestant leaders in Africa today who look as enviously towards the Catholic system as Fr Slaats does towards the Protestant.[28] The Roman insistence upon a rather highly educated local clergy is intended to escape this danger, and in part really does so, but it is leading us into others. The two approaches need to be combined. The answer is always the same: we must be willing to diversify.

It would be a complete mistake to concentrate simply upon the one point of celibacy. Merely allowing marriage to priests trained

---

[26] *AFER*, Oct. 1965, pp. 345–6. Both Fr Murray and Fr Slaats are missionaries in Tanzania.
[27] Pp. 291–2.
[28] For instance, J. Taylor, *The Growth of the Church in Buganda*, p. 139; F. G. Welch, *Training for the Ministry in East Africa*, pp. 86–9.

as at present would solve few problems if any; on the contrary it could be utterly disastrous. One of the chief problems facing the ministry in Africa is that of basic economics: there is very little money to support the clergy. This difficulty would be enormously aggravated if Catholic priests were married, as a suitable salary would depend on one's general standard of education, and our priests are well educated. This is one of the chief obstacles in the way of the Protestant Churches raising the educational standards of their (married) clergy: they can only afford a handful. We have the educational standards, but celibate priests can live together and cheaply. If we were to marry, our bills would go up vastly and there would be no one to meet them. No, our present pattern of ministry in Africa, as elsewhere, does indeed seem to require celibacy, but if—within an altered pattern of ministry—it does present an insuperable obstacle to certain valuable types of people becoming priests, then we do need to ask ourselves very searchingly what sufficient reasons there are for maintaining an unbreakable rule of celibacy when enough candidates for a celibate type of priesthood are simply not coming forward, and when there is plenty of precedent, within the Catholic Church, for a married priesthood.

The second great objection is that of standards of education. Here we have come to a very strange position, and a very untraditional one. We have argued that the priest must be highly trained to fulfil his functions, yet we have allowed his most difficult function—that of preaching—to be exercised by almost untrained catechists, and it will of course now be carried out also by deacons. It is what they are for.

To preach and explain the word of God requires more training and skill than to celebrate the Eucharist. In the Middle Ages the local clergy said Mass but seldom preached; they were not thought able to do so. That has often been true in the Eastern Church as well. In modern times we have exactly reversed the position, allowing the Church's village representative to preach, but not allowing him to celebrate. Surely there is something wrong here. Doubtless there was often a reasonable fear of confiding permanent sacramental powers to people who might later on fail one, and one would not want to suggest a return to the medieval situation. The comparison does, however, show how arbitrary one's sense of the fitting can be. What should be clear is that if well-trained catechists and deacons can be relied on to explain the Gospel Sunday after Sunday in the village church, they can be relied on also to say Mass and to absolve. In questions of penance they can receive clear instructions as to passing on the more difficult cases to a more highly trained priest. In fact there is now some important new thinking going on about the sacrament of penance, and our practice in this regard may very well have changed considerably within a few years time. It would indeed be lamentable to refuse to ordain suitable, godly men simply because they have not passed through (and then largely forgotten!) all the intricacies of moral theology.

One deep reason why preaching was allowed to catechists, but saying Mass withheld from them, has of course been the question of Latin. Latin has been the mark of the priest. His text-books are in Latin and he says Mass and breviary in Latin. Hence only someone with years of Latin study could be allowed into this field. Here again much is changing. Now that a great deal of the Mass, including all the variable parts, can already be said in the vernacular, as also all the breviary, this obstacle to ordaining men who have not had many years of seminary training has also fallen to the ground.

The third sort of objection to the ordination of such people as mature catechists concerns possible unfortunate eventualities which it is thought might arise. Will they persevere? Undoubtedly up to now quite a few catechists have had to be dismissed after some years for reasons of morality. Others, even men who have been through a period of training, decide to give up the work of cate-chists after a time for some other occupation—though they may remain excellent Christians. Is it safe to give permanent orders to such people? It seems to me that the first answer to this is that the status of ordained catechists would be quite different from the present one, hence also attitudes towards it. No one is suggesting ordaining men in a hurry, without years of preparation, years in which both they and their superiors can decide whether they really intend to persevere in this work. At present many of the better men leave just because of the unsatisfactory status of the catechist in the world today. Ordination would change that and give them quite a new sense of dignity and vocation. Moreover, if some deacons or priests wish to retire from activity after years of work, one does not see the great harm in that. Defections doubtless there will be; but they are there already with the present system and we survive them.

It may be true again that one reason why there have been so few schismatic Churches breaking away from the Catholic Church in Africa compared with the many that have broken away from Protestant missions could be our reluctance to give orders to any but highly trained men. May we not find ourselves victims of schisms, if we ordain men with a limited training who may come to quarrel with their superiors and then, conscious of the possession of orders, break away to found Churches of their own? A possibility of this cannot be denied. On the other hand it must be borne in mind, first, that our present pastoral position is certainly opening the way wide to breakaway Churches—that is to say communities of thousands of Christians lacking priests to care for them are obvious prey both for new schismatic sects and for extreme Pentecostal groups, whose activities are everywhere spreading in Africa. At present the Pentecostal Churches in South America are the most fast growing Churches in the world, and they are feeding entirely on nominal Catholics; they can do this because the Catholic ministry in South America is limited and ponderous while their own is so flexible. The Catholic Church in Africa, following in the wake of the Catholic Church in South America, with an increasingly dinosaur-like condition, will soon be their obvious victim.

Secondly, there are other things which tend to free us from the internal fissiparous tendencies of many Protestant Churches. The lack of internal schisms within the Catholic Church in Africa is due especially to the whole sense of order and obedience which Catholics acquire so much more deeply than Protestants. Again, many of the breakaway sects are in part a reaction from the non-ritualistic character of Protestant missionary religion, they have often quickly incorporated elements of Catholic liturgy into their services. This suggests that an important reason why we have not yet succumbed to schisms in the same way as Protestants is that the religious pattern of Catholic life has appealed to Africans more than that presented by Protestant missionaries. We need not fear that the ordination of more priests, rather less well trained, will produce a proliferation of serious schisms. Much more likely that a lack of pastors will do so.[29]

This is not a plea for all deacons to be ordained priests, nor for all those engaged in the ministry of the Church to be ordained at all; the determining factor must be local need. There is much ministry work—its pastoral care, its teaching—which does not require ordination, and women too can and do take an active part in it. Theologically, in fact, it is far from easy to make a clear division between ministry and mission. The latter concerns all Christians, the former only some, but one merges into the other or provides a central core for it. In the past clericalization has affected not only the ministry but also, even more obviously, mission and apostolate; today the full breadth of the lay apostolate has again been realized, and it would be a profound mistake to give the impression that it in some way requires ordination—though it may for some require more religious knowledge than ordination (thus a lay teacher of theology in a teacher training college or university may need to have studied deeper than a village priest). If, as urged here, it is vital to bring some of those active in the mission within the narrower field of the ministry, it is because the life of the Church has to be fully structured sacramentally, not because there is no mission which is not sacramental. Moreover, diversity within the ministry will help to close the gap between clergy and laity, both a lay diaconate and a worker priesthood demonstrating something of the continuity between ministry and mission.

Where it seems to me we have unconsciously gone wrong has been in working from the assumption that all priests must have approximately the same amount of training and the same background. In practice there may have been extremely good reasons for that in the post-Reformation period when the medieval ministry had proved inadequate and it was absolutely necessary to raise the general standards required of the priesthood. It was also important when starting with the priesthood in mission lands to make sure that at least some native priests had an education equivalent to that of their missionaries and could, therefore, stand on a level

---

[29] The first serious breakaway from the Catholic Church in Africa—the "Legio Maria" in Kenya—has happened in the dioceses of Kisumu and Kisii which have a large Catholic population and a very bad pastoral ratio (1 : 4,000).

of psychological equality with them. Today, however, our aim should rather be a very diversified ministry, bound together by charity but not by uniformity. It will correspond to the diversity of the society it has to serve. We will continue to need priests with a middle sort of education, of the type that almost all receive now; we need even more really well educated priests with a full university training—and that means a genuine university training, not only an "athenaeum"—and we need men, too, whose background and cast of mind enables them to speak to and understand a rural peasantry. Our clerical caste has tended on the whole in modern times to be a middle-class one, whereas the ministry needs to belong to all classes, and this belonging is one not only of family origin but of educational formation and even way of life. To see the ministry as a collegiate affair, in which different people are given different gifts and tasks, is an entirely New Testament way of approach: "There are diversities of ministries, but the same Lord. ... Are all apostles? Are all prophets? Are all doctors? Are all workers of miracles? Have all the grace of healing? Do all speak with tongues? Do all interpret?" (1 Cor. 12. 5 and 29–30). St Paul tells us that there are a variety of ministerial charismata, of jobs to be done, and no one should have a monopoly of them. In the ministry of the future, a ministry which in Africa we must set about inaugurating at once if we are to avoid disaster, we must reconcile apostolic leadership and mutual help and respect with great diversity of function. The university graduate, the young man with a competent secondary education, the married doctor, the trade unionist, the village elder, so many people can co-operate together within the ordained ministry of the Church, each doing work of his own. Certainly the fully trained theologian—even more highly trained than the normal priest today—will be urgently required as adviser, special preacher, supervisor; but if the others will certainly need his help, so will he theirs. It will be for him to provide an intensity of understanding of the message of revelation within the life of the Church and the world; but it is for them to carry it effectively through their ministry into all the varied conditions of our world-wide communion.[30]

---

[30] Canon Douglas Webster and I have shared our ideas about the ministry in our separate communions and have found the widest measure of agreement. My treatment of the subject here owes much to him, both through

A diversity of ministry with a flexibility which can enable it to be adapted to a variety of circumstances and to be multiplied far more quickly and easily than is possible at present: that is our crying need in this field today. It is a real need even in Europe and North America, but in Africa and South America it is a need of such an order that—if it is denied and ignored by those who find personal satisfaction in the present system and refuse to break out from their accustomed attitudes or to face up to the need for institutional change—it can bring an almost unprecedented disaster upon extensive Churches. If, however, we should boldly accept the urgency of change, and that means empowering individual bishops and local hierarchies to go ahead on their own with vigorous experimentation, then not only our pastoral but also our missionary potentialities could be revolutionized. The machine of world evangelization, at present creaking to a halt from the sheer complexity of institutionalism which our existing ministry requires, could be so rejuvenated that it would again become possible for young and enthusiastic Churches to send out missionaries of their own. Something of that spontaneous expansion which marked the first centuries of Christianity, and which Roland Allen quite rightly sensed to be of the nature of the Church yet rendered next to impossible by our present system, might again become a reality. We stand at the parting of the ways. Courage upon the one hand; convention upon the other. In fifteen years it may be too late, and in fifty Church historians will lament the great opportunity for ever missed.

conversation and through his writings; I would refer particularly to a paper entitled "The Theory and Practice of Ministry in the Anglican Communion" (1965).

VII

Ecumenism

NOTHING HAS weakened and confused Christian life more in Africa than the divisions and rivalries it has been subjected to from the beginning,[1] and nothing could strengthen it more today than ecumenical reunion. It would be strange, then, to speak of the needs of Christian life and to say nothing of ecumenism, the most crying need of all. Indeed, in the non-Catholic world, it grew out of missionary activity, for the modern ecumenical movement really dates from the World Missionary Conference at Edinburgh in 1910. Ecumenical attitudes, having grown quickest in "mission" territories, have then spread back to the home countries. Among Catholics this unfortunately has not proved true: in Africa and Asia on the whole Catholics have been and remain lagging behind their brothers at home from the ecumenical viewpoint. The ecumenical spirit has developed far more in Europe and North America, in fact in large parts of Africa it has made almost no impact at all within the Roman communion and even forward-looking priests can still set it aside as "inopportune".

This provides an obvious paradox: the revolution in inter-denominational attitudes, especially those relating to the Rome-Protestant divide, has been probably the most effectively important thing in Church life in the last five years, and yet the "new Churches"—those where traditions are least long and where the ecclesial mind should still be most fresh and adaptable—have

[1] What a wealth of light is shed by the following matter-of-fact missionary report (dated 1929): "Church work seems to progress slowly. The opposition of the Roman Catholics, the Seventh-Day Adventists, the Church of England, the Wesleyans, and the Independents, not to speak of the Ethiopians, seems to have taken much of the vigour out of the remaining workers in the L.M.S. Church"; quoted in B. A. Pauw, *Religion in a Tswana Chiefdom*, Oxford, 1960, p. 229.

proved rather impervious to this mental revolution, and even consciously resistant; the same thing is true in places with regard to the liturgical and catechetical revolutions. In all these fields attitudes have changed almost unbelievably in five years in Western Europe and the United States; they have changed far less in Africa. In Africa our experience of the new dynamic wind which has been blowing through the Catholic Church as a whole is still only beginning. Nevertheless in the past two years (since 1965) a very real advance has been made in many places in the ecumenical field, just as it has been made in the liturgical and catechetical fields.

If something has already been done, much more will doubtless come soon. Our purpose here is to examine the existing situation from the ecumenical standpoint, point out initiatives where they have already been made, and indicate the most practical lines for future development. Most of what has been done so far is more in the nature of a pre-ecumenical phase than a real expression of ecumenism. That is to say, ecumenical activity strictly so-called is aimed at bringing Christian disunion to an end, while the purpose of pre-ecumenism is to replace attitudes of social hostility between the denominations by a good-neighbour attitude and co-operation on the social level.

It is quite evident that such activity is most important and where there are old traditions of bitterness and mistrust it is an essential prerequisite for true ecumenical advance. Such is the case over much of Africa. It has to be admitted that in many places Catholics and Protestants were taught to see each other as open enemies, and far more than in most European countries they have presented two rival social groupings struggling for every position of power and influence. Evidently such groupings are often linked as much by school connections as by loyalty to a faith. All this stems from the initial missionary situation at the close of the nineteenth century. It is a pity that, in spite of some striking individual exceptions, the early missionaries were unfriendly to one another, but it was largely inevitable seeing the religious climate of the time. Both sides saw Africa as a rather easy religious prey that they might capture entire if it were not for the irritating interferences of other denominations. Both Catholic and Protestant missionaries were even up to recent times extremely doubtful as to whether the other side could really be said to be preaching Christ at all.

Such missionary attitudes inevitably passed across to the new Christians and feelings of hostility, often even stronger than those to be found on a wide scale in Europe, developed among them. Such feelings, reinforced by loyalties to a particular school, became focused in a struggle for social and governmental domination. Inevitably much depended on the religious sympathies of the colonizing power. In Belgian Africa Protestants developed very justifiably a deep sense of grievance, while in British Africa Catholics could generally feel that they were carefully kept out of the inner circles of political power, though not so directly discriminated against in an easily provable way; wherever the Union Jack flew Anglican missionaries managed to carry with them the status of a quasi-Establishment. The bitterness engendered among people who knew nothing of the historical and national background to all this was very great, and remains so with the older generation.

That is the background against which modern ecumenical activity needs must grow. It has, however, already been changed to a considerable extent, not so much by the changing tempo within the Christian Churches themselves as by the modern spirit of nationalism, taken in its widest sense, that has swept across Africa the spirit of national co-operation required for State building in new independent countries. The stress on a unified non-tribal, non-religious society that is common today almost throughout Africa can of course tend towards the complete substitution of the political for the religious kingdom in the loyalties of politically minded Africans, but it does at least bring with it a diminution of the futile denominational rivalries of the past.

Today, then, Africa may be said to stand on the verge of great ecumenical developments. The old delusion that one missionary group or another might easily succeed in converting the lot has passed away: the Churches stand mostly overwhelmed with the burden of pastoral work among those already converted while the non-Christians remain as ever a vast majority. The feeling of being rivals in a race where the prize could be but for one is changing to that of fellow bearers of an overwhelming mutual burden. Nowhere is ecumenism more called for from a strictly ecclesial viewpoint— the need for bearing a unified witness to the One Lord; nowhere would ecumenism respond better to the general pattern of social change. Yet hitherto, though much has been accomplished between various Protestant Churches, very little between Rome and non-Rome. If the old bitter hostilities are to a large extent dying away, the general objections to ecumenism which have been encountered everywhere (that it breeds indifferentism, that the common people are bewildered and do not understand, that when ecumenism begins conversions decrease, etc.) are at present to be frequently heard where discussion of ecumenical possibilities arises among Catholics.

To turn now to these practical possibilities, it is easiest to examine them after a brief survey of already existing Protestant ecumenical activity with which the Catholic effort has inevitably to try and dovetail if it is to involve a true dialogue and not just a soliloquy. If non-Roman ecumenism originated from the mission situation, this is nevertheless truer of Asia than it is of Africa. Apart from the at that time unsuccessful "Kikuyu Movement" in Kenya, it is only during the last decade that the Protestant Churches in Africa have really been coming closer together, though the major Churches in a number of countries have been in consultative relationship with one another through a National Christian Council for a longer period. Their first All-Africa Christian Conference was held at Ibadan, Nigeria, in 1958, their second at Makerere, Uganda, in 1963. It was clear at the latter especially that many of the African Church leaders are growing increasingly impatient with the existing denominational divisions, but only Nigeria has hitherto put forward a scheme for a corporate reunion, to embrace Anglicans, Methodists and Presbyterians. In Kenya (at Limuru), in South Africa (at Alice), in Nigeria and Ghana, there are interdenominational institutions for the training of ministers.

It must be remembered that in Africa as elsewhere Protestant Christians may be very roughly divided into two chief groups; the more traditional and "orthodox" on the one hand—Anglicans, Lutherans, Presbyterians, Congregationalists and Methodists—and many more extreme and diversified bodies—some very fundamentalist, others Pentecostal—on the other. The first group entered Africa at the same time as the Catholic missionaries, they are therefore old-established and certainly more easy for us to understand. They belong to the World Council of Churches and take a leading part in the ecumenical activity already spoken of. The others, sects of every type including many of indigenous African

16

origin, have arrived more recently, are often much more active in proselytism but far from ecumenical. It was the influence of such groups that forced the Congo Protestant Council to withdraw from the International Missionary Council when the latter integrated with the World Council of Churches at Delhi in 1961. This division is important in practice in the development of Catholic-Protestant relations. In Uganda, for instance, where the vast majority of Protestants are members of the National Anglican Church, or in the Bukoba area of Tanzania where they are Lutherans, evangelized from Sweden, ecumenical relations should be far more easy to develop than, for example, in the Lake province of Kenya, where there is an enormous proliferation of independent sects.

Into the world of ecumenical thinking Catholics have now to enter. The Decree on Ecumenism published in the third session of the Vatican Council (1964) leaves them no alternative; nor should the example of Pope John; nor should the urgent need among Christians of a new attitude towards one another—that of manifested charity—and of a new single-minded and single-voiced witness before the ends of the earth. The time is ripe and if hitherto Catholics have done little to enter into friendship with their separated brethren, to discover and make real their common brotherhood and then to work earnestly towards nothing less than full ecclesial unity, they have now to start in earnest. The Decree on Ecumenism clearly indicates what it is that has to be done:

> The term "ecumenical movement" indicates the initiatives and activities planned and undertaken, according to the various needs of the Church and as opportunities offer, to promote Christian unity. There are: first, every effort to avoid expressions, judgments and actions which do not represent the condition of our separated brethren with truth and fairness and so make mutual relations with them more difficult; then, "dialogue" between competent experts from different churches and communities. At these meetings, which are organized in a religious spirit, each explains the teaching of his communion in greater depth ... and wherever this is allowed, there is prayer in common. This is the way that, when the obstacles to perfect ecclesiastical communion have been gradually overcome, all Christians will at

last, in a common celebration of the Eucharist, be gathered into a single church in that unity which Christ bestowed on His Church from the beginning.

Catholics need to understand quite clearly that they have no option but to be ecumenically minded, and they need to understand further just what that means in practice. As we see from the text above, ecumenism does not mean simply co-operating with non-Catholics in the social and civil sphere, substituting friendliness for the old hostility; it means beyond all that working deliberately and together for the complete ecclesiastical unity of eucharistic communion.

Where there unfortunately remains an active state of bitterness and conflict, it is high time for both sides to examine what positive steps they have taken or can take to escape from so un-Christian a situation.

Ecumenical initiatives can best begin at the level of personal contact and friendship. Without this, other activities can break down only too easily and formal meetings can develop into a diplomatic impasse. As a matter of fact it is extraordinary how out of touch with each other Catholic and Protestant missionaries have generally been; even though there may have been a mere handful of Europeans in a district all told and they have been there for years and years, each group may remain unaware even of the names of their opposite numbers. Personal friendships can make all the difference. It is pleasant to remember what the Anglican missionary Philip O'Flaherty wrote from Kampala on Christmas Day, 1881, of his White Father opposite number: "Livinhac I love, he and I have many long walks, talking of the deep things of God—those delightful things that refresh the spirit. And oh, the spirit needs to be refreshed in this dry parched land. We take mutual pleasure in each other's company." There is plenty of precedent for friendly help and contact from those early days, even if there was also plenty of undisguised and embittered rivalry, but the helpful contact at least grew less and less as the various missionary organizations spread and established themselves in Africa, becoming almost entirely self-supporting. Of late for practical reasons contact has grown again, brought on by common educational and medical responsibilities and also by a renewed feeling of Christian fellowship. Today friendly contacts need to be sought and strengthened at every level without too many *arrière-pensées* as to where they may or may not lead.

Next to that we may place social co-operation; in some shape or form this has gone on for years, at least in former British territories in educational and medical matters, but it has seldom spread beyond the sphere of central administration. Today it requires effective application in a wider sphere, one recent and excellent example of this being Uganda's Joint Christian Council. At its first meeting this Joint Council set up sub-committees for the fields of education, social services and communications; its meetings end with a common prayer. The entirely new circumstances which the Christian Churches are now entering in a continent of independent states anxious to be masters in their own house, and often resentful of the great privileges which the old colonial governments accorded to the missions, make co-operation particularly opportune and valuable, not of course in order to "gang-up" against a new government, but in order to negotiate terms which are both acceptable to the modern nationalist and maybe "socialist" order and guarantee a continuing effective influence of the Churches in the social field. In some territories the schools system has been in the past very drastically divided on a denominational basis, which does not appeal at all to the present government. The Churches have now to learn how to co-operate not only within a national schools system but also very often within individual schools. Failure to do this, and insistence instead on the one-denominational school formula could in fact result in unnecessarily secular State schools.

Beside the problem of schools is that of marriage. In many parts of Africa mixed marriages are entirely inevitable. Failure to admit this and the lifelong excommunication which often follows on both sides as a result may simply drive newly converted Christians back to a state of near-paganism. It is an urgent ecumenical need to recognize that it would be immoral to break up such unions and that, in an imperfect world, living with a Protestant partner is at least no more dangerous than living with a drunkard or a ne'er-do-well! The Christian response is to offer the help of the sacraments, not to issue forth excommunications which do no one any good at all.

A further level of ecumenical activity may be found in the field of strictly biblical co-operation. As Stephen Neill has remarked: "What has brought Protestant missions together more than anything else has been fellowship in the work of the translation of the Bible."[2] Throughout Africa today Protestants are far ahead of Catholics in this field. Doubtless some translations leave a good deal to be desired, but at least they have them in numerous languages in which Catholics have nothing or next to nothing. Practically speaking, it would be impossible for Catholics to catch up in the foreseeable future. Moreover, there is no point in trying to do so independently. Europe and America are already providing the example of co-operation in this field. The fact is that everywhere Catholics are realizing today that Christian life does require Bible reading; this requirement is particularly exacting in Africa where there are so many different languages. So whatever the reason for biblical co-operation in Europe and America, it is enormously strengthened in Africa.

There are two alternatives open to Catholics. One is simply to adopt a satisfactory Protestant translation of the Bible, and this the Hierarchy of Tanzania has recently done for the Swahili version. The other is to co-operate with Protestants in a new common version, or a common revision of one already existing. This is being done at present in more than one place in the Congo. For these reasons the resolution of the Pan-African Catechetical Study Week, opened by His Eminence Cardinal Rugambwa, at Katigondo, September 1964, is very welcome:

> Having in view the common love for Holy Scripture which unites all Christians, the needs of the Ecumenical Movement, and the absolute need for Scripture in the vernacular, the Pan-African Catechetical Study Week earnestly requests the Hierarchies in all African territories where deemed advisable, to contact the Protestant Authorities in order to work together for the early publication of both the Old and New Testaments in versions adequate both exegetically and linguistically.
>
> We recommend that where Hierarchies judge it advisable, permission be sought for Catholics to make use of Protestant editions in the meantime.

[2] *A History of Christian Missions*, p. 540.

Here as everywhere, what is most important, and also most difficult, is to take the first step. Once that is done, we should get along
fine. It is certainly true that it is the sincerity which Catholics are
now showing in Bible study that, more than almost anything else,
is breaking down Protestant suspiciousness towards them. The
Word of God will unite us more and more.

The next level to be reached is that of direct theological discussion—the "dialogue" spoken of above in the Decree on Ecumenism. Hitherto there has been very little of this in Africa, and of
course lack of qualified personnel and the distances often involved
can also be effective deterrents. But I know of various mixed theological discussion groups which have met regularly: two Catholic-
Lutheran, in Tanzania;[3] another, Catholic-Anglican, in Uganda.
The latter has a membership of about twelve, it meets about once
a month for a couple of hours over tea and discusses theological
topics in a friendly, informal way. Nobody expects any immediate,
startling results from such meetings, but the growth in understanding, mutual openness and interdenominational friendship after
even a year of meetings was very marked. It is much to be desired
that such groups should be prudently multiplied.

These meetings, as those of the Joint Christian Council, end in
common prayer. Hitherto there have not been many other opportunities for this, though common Independence anniversary celebrations, for example, provide a very suitable occasion. Nor has
the Octave for Christian Unity yet been celebrated with great *élan*
in many parts of Africa, so far as I know. Positive ecumenical
attitudes have not in fact as yet penetrated through to the common
man or even to many of the clergy. The encouragement of prayer
and thinking on ecumenical lines needs very much to come from
above: positive guidance aimed at making of the Ecumenical
Decree a reality in the African setting. This must work its way
down through conferences and lectures in schools and seminaries.
As a matter of fact the younger generation of African Christians
are very ready indeed to take up a more ecumenical attitude if this
is put to them rightly; it links up, as said above, with the whole
work of positive nation-building, and also with the desire to be

---

[3] For one of these, in the Moshi area, and its method of approach, see
V. Donovan, C.S.Sp., "A Protestant-Catholic Dialogue", *AFER*, Jan. 1962,
pp. 41–9.

"with it" from the viewpoint of developments in the world Church as a whole. Personal contact between Catholic seminaries and Protestant theological colleagues, not only at the staff but also at the student level, is much to be desired. And could we not make a special effort throughout Africa to observe the January Octave of Christian Unity by prayer and meetings?

There are many fields of work where ecumenical activity is both possible and highly desirable in Africa today. What is important is to make a start and that in as many different places and ways as possible; it is for the Holy Spirit to lead us on and direct our purposes but He can do nothing if we obstinately refuse to move. Here as elsewhere "superficial and imprudent zeal" must, as the Decree says, be avoided, but the danger at present is still all in the other direction. Let us hope and pray that the Catholic bishops of Africa will quickly be able to put into practice their own Conciliar recommendation that "everywhere in the world ecumenical work should be vigorously stimulated and guided with prudence".[4]

It is good to remember that the Catholic proto-martyr of modern Africa, St Joseph Mukasa Balikuddembe, was killed in 1885 because he had bravely spoken up against the murder of the Protestant Bishop Hannington; that the last night the body of David Livingstone spent in Africa was in a Catholic chapel, of the Holy Ghost Fathers at Bagamoyo; that it was a Protestant minister who presided over the funeral and prayed at the grave of Bishop de Marion Brésillac in Freetown in 1859. Best of all, our martyrs died together. Catholic and non-Catholic were burnt side by side at Namugongo for their common belief in Christ, the Protestant Alexander Kadoko as well as his uncle the Catholic Bruno Sserunkuma. It seems sad that in canonization they should be divided. We have indeed always shared a common brotherhood, but brothers must come together around the same table and go out from it to work in harmony. It seems to me that between Catholics and many Protestants there is less and less substantial to divide us. In the sixteenth century the greatest break was over Mass and worship, but today we are coming to agree again over the chief liturgical principles and the meaning of the Eucharist. Thus one can find

---

[4] An excellent example has been set here by Bishop Van Cauwelaert of Inongo, in the Congo, with a fine pastoral entitled "The Apostolate of Christian Unity", reprinted in *AFER*, Jan. 1965, pp. 1–8.

only praise for the New Liturgy for Africa, drawn up recently for Anglican use.[5] Doubtless today we are far from ready upon either side for corporate reunion, but we must work with full deliberation towards no less than that: the coming unity of a single communion. Schism was a chief cause in the decline and extinction of the great African Churches of the early centuries. Let their fate warn us so that we turn in time from our divisions to unity of communion and common witness to the Lord in whom we all believe.

[5] See Archbishop Leslie Brown's *Relevant Liturgy*, S.P.C.K., 1965.

VIII

The Needs of Today

AT THE END of this survey it seems sensible to attempt a brief summary of the Church's greatest immediate needs in modern Africa, as I have tried to uncover them in the preceding pages. They have slowly grown upon me during years of work in Africa, but have become clearer and more explicit in the course of writing this book. I would list twelve.

1. To put first things first, that is to say Eucharist and Gospel, not as a matter of lip-service but of real preoccupation. Until now we have not been so preoccupied; every diocese has its full-time school administrators, but almost none its Bible translators. What has been done in that line has been achieved by individual priests in their spare time. As for the Eucharist, its centrality has not been denied, but it has not sufficiently appeared. For too many of our Christians the rosary, the Ten Commandments, the rule of catechist and the sending of children to school seem the real cornerstones of our religion. Again, we seem to have presented Christianity too much in the spirit of the Old Testament rather than of the New,[1] in the form of law rather than in that of Gospel. It is not enough to express our faith in Jesus and the Trinity, Eucharist and Scripture, we have to communicate a life that is consciously centred upon them.

2. A Church of freedom. If it is the Gospel not the Law that we are sent to preach, it is a life of freedom not of compulsion that we must build up. Almost everywhere in the past the Church has tended to be over-authoritarian, but this is particularly true in the

---

[1] Many Protestant missionaries have fallen down from this point of view even more than Catholics have done, indeed a regression to Old Testament attitudes seems deeply characteristic of a part of Protestant tradition.

17

missions. Examples could be multiplied indefinitely, and they make church life very irksome for young people, now less than ever willing to be dragooned either in tribe or church. Long lists of tribal practices, rigorously and often uncomprehendingly forbidden to Christians,[2] the imposition of punishments, fines, a whole régime ruled over dictatorially by priests and (often worse) their representatives, the catechists—all this expresses an attitude which must go. Everywhere in the Church today there is a new discovery of freedom balanced by personal responsibility, and there certainly cannot be some special régime for erstwhile mission lands. Freedom is the greatest natural gift God has given to men and it is for us to show by our deeds that we recognize it as such in the spirit of the Council's Declaration on Religious Liberty: the freedom of man both without and within the Church. This in no way weakens the primacy of truth and the authority of the teaching Church, but concerns the proper way in which truth and authority are communicated to and accepted by men. Freedom of the mind to read and think widely, freedom not to be bludgeoned and intimidated in one's religious observance, intellectual openness and the collaboration of mutual trust between clergy and laity—all this is implied here. There is no group to which this can be applied more generously and more profitably than to that of seminarists.

3. Laicization. The liturgy, the apostolate, every side of the Church's life belongs fully to the whole people of God; yet in almost every field there has been in the course of ages—and for very understandable reasons—clericalization, either blatant or subtle. Today we are called to move in just the opposite direction, and especially so in Africa where, as a mere matter of practical politics, we are and shall remain fantastically short of clergy. To the laity in this age can best belong the control of schools, through boards of governors, parents' and teachers' associations; to the laity too belongs most fittingly much of the running of the parish, but also the obligation of making the church self-supporting. Above all, there belongs to them the Church's service of society and the

---

[2] In the words of a Tanzanian priest, James Komba, now a bishop, "What a burden it is to a young Ngoni Christian when he does not know what attitude to take in this or that pagan environment. In every pagan rite he spies an occasion of sin. He is pulled in opposite directions by two powerful forces, the authority of the parents and the authority of the Church. It seems to him that the Church has nothing else to offer than a 'Thou shalt not'". Quoted by W. Bühlmann, O.F.M.Cap., *Concilium*, March 1966, p. 27.

clear presentation of the message of Christ and the love of Christ in every social, political, human context to Africa as a whole.

The problem of institutions is today very specially a problem of the right kind of laicization. The Church's fecundity and social concern are absolutely rightly manifested in the founding and running of institutions such as schools and hospitals, and the clergy are particularly adapted for the work of foundation. This being done, and right values having been built into the institution, it seems most natural for the clergy to recede little by little, leaving things in the hands of the laity. Everywhere in the social sphere the role of the clergy appears most fittingly as one of initiation—their greater mobility helps them here—rather than one of continued control.

As should be obvious, laicization need in no way be synonymous with secularization, for all the faithful share in the priesthood of Christ. It relates to a structural change within the Church, not to a diminution of her influence or of the sphere of religion.

4. Africanization: of Church structures, of liturgy and art and music, of leadership. This does not mean a policy of archaization, of insisting on the imitation of some practically disused folk art. Nor does it mean doing the same everywhere. It means using terms and forms which are suitable here and now. To the africanization of Church structures—that is to say the adaptation of the institutions and shape of Church life to the society and needs of today's Africa—almost every other point is an illustration. As regards liturgy, it is clear that types of ceremony which are appropriate among one people may be quite unmeaningful only a short distance away. There can be no question of general sweeping liturgical changes even within a single country; moreover, what is needed is not so much changes in the central prayers and actions of the liturgy as in extra prayers, blessings, processions, and in the manner of popular liturgical response.

The revision of Church music and hymn singing, however, is urgent, but it too requires the expert hand if countless pitfalls are to be avoided.[3] The use of drums is not identical throughout Africa,

---

[3] On this subject cf. K. Carroll, S.M.A., "African Music", *AFER*, Oct. 1961, pp. 301–12; P. Van Thiel, W.F., "Divine Worship and African Church Music", *AFER*, April 1961, pp. 144–7; "Text, Tone and Tune in African Sacred Music", *AFER*, July 1964, pp. 250–7, and Jan. 1966, pp. 53–62; "For a Genuine African Liturgical Music", *AFER*, April 1966, pp. 130–3; "Church Music in Tanzania", by S. Mbunga, *Concilium*, Feb. 1966, pp. 57–60.

indeed among pastoral peoples they may not be used at all. Different tribes put words to music with quite different tone patterns; to understand that, together with the sort of word patterns that can be effectively sung with a particular music, already requires great musical skill, but to get that far is by no means the end of the matter. Every existing tune will conjure up its own particular words or occasion for its hearers: if they are religious they carry the minds of their hearers back to ceremonies or sacrifices they have now rejected, if secular their whole ethos will seem unsuitable. New tunes suited to the new circumstances and the new words but possessing the intrinsic musical genius and technique of the old songs have to be created, and that requires not only the will but also men with the gift. Such things must take time, though the progress made recently in some places is most encouraging.

As regards visual art, in South and East Africa we have no developed past tradition to look back to, but we can at least make use of the work of the enthusiastic young people trained in places like the Makerere School of Fine Art instead of continuing to import Burns and Oates plaster statues. West Africa and parts of the Congo are in better plight; the pioneering Christian art centre of Oye Ekiti in Western Nigeria would seem to be a model of what can be done.[4]

Only in the africanization of leadership is the Church indeed going ahead as fast as she reasonably can. The necessity for this is obvious. Nevertheless it is not synonymous with africanization as a whole. For African priests, trained in the traditional Western clerical pattern, the readjustment of Church life and structures required today may involve at least as painful and thoughtful an effort as it requires for missionaries. It is upon their effort—force-fulness linked with imagination and a deep ecclesial sense—that almost everything will now depend.

5. The Outward Mission. The Church's purpose in life is not to build up her own snug watertight compartment but to convince and serve the world. Our African Church must be outward-going, far more so than she is at present. She must be prepared to serve the hungry, even when her own members are not too well fed. She must be prepared to stand up to the totalitarian claims of Caesar even though she may thus lose the comfortable subsidies of the State. She

---

[4] Cf. articles by Fr K. Carroll, S.M.A., in *AFER*, April and July 1961.

must be ready to send missionaries out of their own tribe to less-developed areas. She must be ready, not only to teach her own children, but to offer a disinterested service to less-educated Muslim communities, and to enter into intellectual dialogue on neutral ground with those whose ideology is different. How much is being done to train her, not for survival, but for service?

6. Ecumenism. Nothing is more important in Africa than a massive new approach to other Christians of all denominations. This has been dealt with in Chapter VII. There is nothing to add here.

7. Relations with Islam. Sub-Saharan Africa is the one great area of the world where Christians and Muslims can meet with a rough numerical equality and where they are really mixed together in common societies. It is a wonderful opportunity for Christian-Islamic relations to take a new turn. Hitherto almost nothing has been done in this line and for very obvious reasons. What is required initially is the establishment of two institutes for Christian-Islamic studies, one in West Africa and one in the East, as centres for the development of a positive approach towards Islam on the part of Christians and the beginning of a dialogue in the spirit of Louis Massignon, Abd-el-Jalil and Canon Cragg.[6]

8. Marriage. A reassessment of marriage legislation and of the pastoral approach in this field is urgently needed. In a continent of great poverty and a very rapidly increasing population this must obviously include a positive approach to family planning. There is nothing to add here to what was said in Chapter V.

9. The Ministry. The position here too has been adequately surveyed in Chapter VI. The central need is greater diversification both that individual tasks may be better fulfilled and that numbers may increase. A general overhaul of seminaries (already taking place in many countries) is necessary but not sufficient. A radically new approach is also required to obtaining university-trained specialists on the one hand and an adequate number of priests for the simpler tasks of the rural apostolate upon the other. The possibility of the part-time ministry must also be seriously faced.

[6] One might refer to the following recent articles as an opening in this subject: Norman Daniel, "Some Recent Developments in the Attitude of Christians towards Islam", pp. 154–66 of *Rediscovering Eastern Christendom*, ed. Fry and Armstrong, London; F. Anawati, "Vers un dialogue Islamo--Chrétien", *Revue Thomiste*, April-June 1964, pp. 280–326; J. Allen, "Muslims in East Africa", *AFER*, July 1965, pp. 255–62.

10. Special concern with growth points and focal points. Perhaps there is no really crucial requirement which is so generally neglected. We concentrate on country districts and schools, and quite fail to cater adequately for towns, universities and the other real growth points in society. A country with well over 1,000 priests and one university did not find it worth while to make one priest free full time to work in that university from the start. Both personnel and money is involved here. *Propaganda Fide* allocates tens of thousands of pounds for a diocesan minor seminary, but next to nothing for university student centres (unless, of course, a "Catholic" university is in question: vast sums of Church money were poured into the tiny Pius XII University College in Lesotho for many years, but almost nothing is given to places where there may be five times as many Catholic students to look after).

We have in general created hitherto a sort of subsistence Church; this was quite inevitable at the start. What we need now is some concentration on specialized and quality institutions coping with growth points. These are: (*a*) university chaplaincies and student centres; (*b*) town parishes and community centres; (*c*) conference and retreat centres of the Spode House type; (*d*) specialized agencies, such as a Christian literature bureau, a national pastoral institute, a centre for Islamic studies; (*e*) monasteries, bringing different spiritual traditions to the young Churches, and again providing retreat centres or a school with a richer spiritual and cultural formation. Evidently much of this specialized work cannot be done by the existing missionary societies. It is vitally necessary for other societies, which have tended to specialize in one or another kind of work, to enter the young Churches and offer their characteristic service: one of diversification, of enrichment and of catering for the needs of the new élite. But they will not succeed in doing this unless they take their own adaptation to the African milieu very seriously.

11. Far more thought needs to be given to the best ways of relating the mission of the world Church and the needs of the individual young Church. The general call to mission activity, enshrined in the Council's missionary decree, is not in itself enough, especially when we think how little effect the appeal of *Fidei Donum* had. We need to create the right sort of structures, many of which do not at present exist, and also to be aware of the in-

herent dangers in this matter. A regular pairing of dioceses, and even of parishes and schools within dioceses, is a valuable pattern of inter-Church aid which can be encouraged, while the vast anonymous collection should on the whole be discouraged. In the matter of money a sense of stewardship needs to be inculcated at both ends; it is at present sadly lacking, and the anonymous collection does not help that: those giving for the missions have generally no idea at all how their money is actually spent, while those receiving often singularly lack the sense that they have a duty to account for what they are given.

The question of raising money in Europe and America for the poorer Churches is more complex, however, than that. At present it is taken for granted in most quarters that the more money raised the better, and that it can rightly be used for any need in the young Church. This is very gravely mistaken. There is no doubt at all that the rich have a duty to help the poor and that this is true also at an inter-Church level. But external help needs to strengthen, not to pauperize; it should follow and be dependent upon self-help. If it becomes a substitute for the latter, far from building up the Church in Africa external financial assistance merely renders her ever more flabby and ineffective. The recent suggestions (even, alas, approved by the Council's missionary decree, n. 17) that not only the building of training centres for catechists but actually their subsequent monthly salary should be provided for out of foreign funds, appear as an example of the sort of thinking which fails to see that financial self-support is an inseparable attribute of a true Church. The place for external financial assistance is that of non-recurrent expenses establishing an institution which will afterwards be viable within the local context. To accustom the Church to expect external help for her recurrent pastoral needs is to do her the greatest disservice imaginable.

As suggested in Chapter III, the true function of the missionary society and the training of its members also require a great deal of re-thinking. This is true as well, as the Council's missionary decree stressed, for the central congregation of *Propaganda Fide*. No one can doubt the importance of a central agency but it needs far more expert knowledge of the true priorities of mission today, if its efforts and funds are not to be frequently misdirected.

12. Efficiency. This is not a necessary characteristic of the

Church, and no one fears more than I do a tendency to make of her some sort of streamlined business organization. Nevertheless efficiency at its best implies the rational use of men and materials for the glory of God; inefficiency is often a mark of slovenliness, non-co-operation or downright stupidity.

To be brief: (*a*) Use of money. Vast sums are collected for the missions and distributed in various ways; their use is very seldom accounted for effectively. We may be short of money in the young Churches; we have certainly wasted tens of thousands of pounds on misguided projects, often of a showy triumphalistic type.

(*b*) Inter-diocesan co-operation. Certainly there has been a very considerable improvement in this matter, but there is still an enormous amount of unnecessary duplication (e.g. in minor seminary work); lack of effective co-operation also frequently prevents national projects from going ahead quickly and effectively.

(*c*) Use of experts. The need for advance preparation of a topic by experts before its consideration by bishops has been fully recognized by the Council, but it is still often ignored in Africa. Besides the preparation of *ad hoc* reports, the development of religious sociology should be encouraged if we are to find out how to make the best use of our very limited resources.

(*d*) Anticipation. This, of course, is impossible without studies of the type just mentioned. But in a rapidly developing world it is disastrous to be always working on the data of the year before last, instead of on what can be fairly anticipated for five, ten or twenty years ahead.

When faced with uncomfortable facts which really indicate that something is wrong with our Church system or way of working, priests have a habit of shrugging their shoulders and saying with a pious air, *"Deus providebit"*, suggesting that too much concern with such things shows a lack of faith. The Holy Spirit works indeed beyond all our projects and fumblings. He is not limited by the visible Church and its mechanisms. Nevertheless the visible Church is our responsibility while the Holy Spirit is not, and within the holy Church God helps those who help themselves wisely and spiritually. *"Deus providebit"* did not save the great Churches of Syria and Asia Minor and North Africa from virtual extinction; it did not prevent the rending schism of East from West nor the complete breaking apart of the Western Church herself in the sixteenth century; it did not prevent the loss of the continental working class in the nineteenth century, nor the frustration of the Chinese mission time after time, nor the conversion to Protestantism during the last few years of millions of nominal Catholics in South America. Doubtless the providence of God has worked through all these things, but they surely reveal too a massive failure of the visible Church in particular circumstances to respond adequately to the world around her. She proved a broken reed, and the march of history and the providence of God have had to go forward across her broken body; such surely happens not according to the central intention of God's plan for men but as a new accommodation to human failure—Church failure.

Faced with the evident faith and enthusiasm of the missionary Church in Africa today and the enormous efforts being made, it may seem out of place to refer to these things at all. I cannot think so. I hope that it is in no spirit of carping criticism that I have tried to assess both the strength and the weaknesses of the Catholic Church in modern Africa. At least my own heart is in the business. I am sure that in the ways of God, both more twisted and more straight than human brain can hope to unravel, this Church of ours has a great part to play, but I pray also that we who have been called in this generation of such stupendous growth and unexpected challenges to live and minister in it will not fall beneath the judgment of God and of coming generations as unworthy stewards. Threatened, both by those who question the point of all we do, and by those who would identify that point with ways of thought and behaviour belonging to ages that are past, we must not falter in our old faith nor in the painful effort to maintain its relevance to a new world.

May we today continue to communicate and enrich the Catholic Church, the Church of Paul and Augustine and Francis Xavier and Charles Lwanga and the millions of the unremembered, not because of the wealth of its human experience and the thrill of being within it, but because it is the sign lifted up upon earth of the care and love of God, of the mission of his Son, of the renewal of all things—those without as much as those within—in the Omega who is Alpha, the master whose catholicity will only be revealed in the ultimate fullness of the eternal Jerusalem.

Appendix

Some Statistics of Eastern Africa

	1949 (*Catholic Directory of East Africa, 1950*)	1963 *Catholic Directory of East Africa, 1965*)
KENYA		
Catholics	323,772	1,027,614
Priests	248	501
Senior Seminarists	13	56
UGANDA		
Catholics	984,191	2,143,404
Priests	417	706
Senior Seminarists	132	166
TANZANIA		
Catholics	709,384	1,781,914
Priests	558	1,222
Senior Seminarists	175	214
ZAMBIA		
Catholics	263,702	535,059
Priests	180	347
Senior Seminarists	35	23
MALAWI		
Catholics	267,081	560,687
Priests	139	264
Senior Seminarists	46	14
TOTAL		
Catholics	2,548,130	6,048,678
Priests	1,542	3,040
Senior Seminarists	401	473

Note. (1) The figures for priests include Africans and foreign missionaries; (2) the seminarists are spread across a course of either six or seven years; (3) the figures for Catholics do not include catechumens; (4) the chief point in reproducing these figures here is to illustrate the way the number of seminarists —always inadequate—has not been increasing in proportion to that of the Catholic population.

Index